TOP FEDERAL TAX ISSUES FOR 2006 CPE COURSE

CCH Editorial Staff Publication

CCH INCORPORATED
Chicago

A WoltersKluwer Company

Contributors

Editor.. George G. Jones, J.D., LL.M
Contributing Editors...................................... George L. Yaksick, Jr., J.D.
Brant Goldwyn, J.D.
Angela Johnson, J.D.
John Flanagan, J.D., MBA
Production Coordinator.. Gabriel Santana
Layout.. Heather Jonas
Laila Gaidulis
Production .... Lynn J. Brown

ISBN 0-8080-1359-9

© 2005, **CCH** INCORPORATED
4025 W. Peterson Ave.
Chicago, IL 60646-6085
1 800 248 3248
http://tax.cchgroup.com

TOP FEDERAL TAX ISSUES FOR 2006 CPE COURSE

Introduction

Each year, a handful of tax issues typically requires special attention by tax practitioners. The reasons vary, from a particularly complicated new provision in the Internal Revenue Code, to a planning technique opened up by a new regulation or ruling, or the availability of a significant tax benefit with a short window of opportunity. Sometimes a developing business need creates a new set of tax problems, or pressure exerted by Congress or the Administration puts more heat on some taxpayers while giving others more slack. All these share in creating a unique mix that in turn creates special opportunities and pitfalls in the coming year. The past year has seen more than its share of these developments.

CCH's Top Federal Tax Issues for 2006 CPE Course identifies the events of the past year that have developed into "hot" issues. These tax issues have been selected as particularly relevant to tax practice in 2006. They have been selected not only because of their impact on return preparation during the 2005 tax season but also because of the important role they play in developing effective tax strategies for 2006. Some issues are outgrowths of several years of developments; others have burst onto the tax scene unexpectedly. Some have been emphasized in IRS publications and notices; others are too new or too controversial to be noted by the IRS either in depth or at all.

This course is designed to help reassure the tax practitioner that he or she is not missing out on advising clients about a hot, new tax opportunity or is not susceptible to being caught unawares by a brewing controversy. In short, it is designed to give the tax practitioner a closer look into the opportunities and pitfalls presented by the changes. Among the topics examined in the *Top Federal Tax Issues for 2006 CPE Course* are:

- The New Manufacturing Deduction
- Deduction for Foreign Dividends Repatriated to the United States
- The Alternative Minimum Tax: Understanding the Problem, Anticipating Solutions
- Deferred Compensation Developments
- New Tax Breaks from Congress: Energy Incentives, Hurricane Relief, and Phased-In Benefits
- Compliance with Circular 230
- IRS Ramps Up Enforcement to Crack Down on Abuses

Throughout the Course you will find Study Questions to help you test your knowledge, and comments that are vital to understanding a particular strategy or idea. Answers to the Study Questions with feedback on both correct and incorrect responses are provided in a special section beginning on page 191.

To assist you in your later reference and research, a detailed topical index has been included for this Course beginning on page 211.

This Course is divided into three Modules. Take your time and review all Course Modules. When you feel confident that you thoroughly understand the material, turn to the CPE Quizzer. Complete one, or all, Module Quizzers for continuing professional education credit. Further information is provided in the CPE Quizzer instructions on page 221.

October 2005

COURSE OBJECTIVES

This course was prepared to provide the participant with an overview of specific tax issues that impact 2005 tax return preparation and tax planning in 2006. These are the issues that "everyone is talking about;" each impacts a significant number of taxpayers in significant ways.

Upon course completion, you will be able to:

- Understand the workings of the new manufacturing deduction, both its computational details and how it impacts some industries and business models more than others;
- Advise businesses with ties to the global marketplace what it will take to make maximum use of a generous but extremely deadline-sensitive new deduction for repatriated foreign dividends—a major benefit for those who qualify;
- Guard against the alternative minimum tax (the AMT), also known as the "stealth tax" because of how the benefits of deductions and other tax breaks have been turned against the wage earner and investor in ways never intended by Congress;
- Help clients deal with a multitude of new developments in deferred compensation, including a new form of qualified retirement plan, new rules and interpretations for retirement plan distributions and health care accounts, and protection of retirement account assets in bankruptcy;
- Position your clients to take better advantage of new tax laws for installing energy-saving equipment, using "green" vehicles, or recovering from Hurricane Katrina, while protecting them from some older tax laws that are only now being phased in or phased out to create traps for the unsuspecting;
- Help protect yourself and your tax practice from the heavy hand of the IRS Office of Professional Responsibility by knowing your obligations under newly revised regulations governing tax professionals, especially with respect to client disclaimers; and
- Know what IRS audit initiatives are now in high gear and how the recent use of tax shelters and abusive transactions has created an IRS more focused on enforcement and developing even more sophisticated audit techniques in which innocent as well as fraudulent taxpayers will pay a price.

CCH'S PLEDGE TO QUALITY

Thank you for choosing this CCH Continuing Education product. We will continue to produce high quality products that challenge your intellect and give you the best option for your Continuing Education requirements. Should you have a concern about this or any other CCH CPE product, please call our Customer Service Department at 1-800-248-3248.

NEW ONLINE GRADING gives you immediate 24/7 grading with instant results and no Express Grading Fee.

The **CCH Testing Center** website gives you and others in your firm easy, free access to CCH print courses and allows you to complete your CPE exams online for immediate results. Plus, the **My Courses** feature provides convenient storage for your CPE course certificates and completed exams.

Go to **www.cchtestingcenter.com** to complete your exam online.

One **complimentary copy** of this course is provided with certain CCH Federal Taxation publications. Additional copies of this course may be ordered for $25.00 each by calling 1-800-248-3248 (ask for product 0-0905-200).

TOP FEDERAL TAX ISSUES FOR 2006 CPE COURSE

Contents

MODULE 1 — CHAPTER 1

The New Manufacturing Deduction

This chapter explains the important new Code Sec. 199 manufacturing deduction. Understanding the mechanics of the manufacturing deduction is crucial because it is arguably on the most beneficial code sections created in the past few years. However, an enormous amount of complexity has been written into Code Sec. 199. The provision contains a number of new terms that are considered by many to be quite vague, yet critical in determining those businesses entitled to this important deduction. Indeed, the Treasury Department and the IRS have had to work diligently to interpret and capture Congress' intent in enacting Code Sec. 199. This chapter not only provides an overview of the manufacturing deduction but also explains the steps required to calculate the amount allowed.

LEARNING OBJECTIVES

Upon completion of this chapter, you will be able to:
- Determine qualified production activities income;
- Calculate domestic production gross receipts;
- Recognize the applicable wage limitation on the manufacturing deduction;
- Define qualified production property and qualified film; and
- Understand how pass-through entities and expanded affiliated groups take into account the deduction.

¶101 INTRODUCTION

The American Jobs Creation Act of 2004 (2004 Jobs Act) ushered in many new tax incentives for businesses and individuals. Although the 2004 Jobs Act contains several highly publicized tax cuts for individuals, the law also gives American businesses a much needed boost to remain competitive against foreign manufacturers.

The 2004 Jobs Act adds 34 new sections to the Tax Code. One of the most important is Code Sec. 199. This new section provides a deduction for U.S corporations engaging in "manufacturing" activities. Congress intended for a large number of businesses to be eligible for the manufacturing deduction. Thus, the definition of **manufacturing** is quite broad. For example, it includes construction and engineering activities, as well as the production of certain natural resources—clearly not what most people would think of as "manufacturing."

However, Congress' intent has caused some confusion. The bare language of Code Sec. 199 leaves many unanswered questions, not only for taxpayers and practitioners but for the Treasury Department and the IRS, which have to write rules and regs, as well. The 2004 Jobs Act was enacted in October 2004 and became effective for tax years beginning after December 31, 2004. Treasury and the IRS scrambled to issue guidance.

The principal guidance provided by the Treasury and IRS—Notice 2005-14 and a related fact sheet—was issued on January 19, 2005. The goal of the Treasury Department and the IRS in issuing Notice 2005-14 was to capture the intent and purpose of Code Sec. 199 while providing clear and administrable rules for taxpayers and the IRS. Although this guidance is lengthy, the Treasury and IRS has promised still more as additional questions are raised and experience tests the practical application of Notice 2005-14.

¶105   PRELIMINARIES FOR CALCULATING THE MANUFACTURING DEDUCTION

To begin to understand how the manufacturing deduction operates, it helps to look at some new terms introduced by Code Sec. 199. Calculating the manufacturing deduction begins with determining both the taxpayer's taxable income and *qualified production activities income (QPAI)*. Only QPAI attributable to the actual conduct of a trade or business is eligible for the deduction. Although taxable income of a trade or business is a familiar term, QPAI is probably not.

.01   Basic Formula for Calculating DPGR

Code Sec. 199 defines QPAI as the taxpayer's domestic production gross receipts (DPGR) for the tax year minus the sum of the cost of goods sold (COGS) allocable to those receipts, deductions, expenses, or losses directly allocable to those receipts, and a ratable portion of deductions, expenses, or losses not directly allocable to those receipts or to another class of income.

Thus, QPAI equals DPGR *minus* the following:

- COGS allocable to DPGR
- Deductions, expenses, losses directly allocable to DPGR
- Ratable portion of other deductions, expenses, and losses that are not directly allocable to DPGR or to another class of income.

.02   Defining Domestic Production Gross Receipts

The definition of QPAI contains another new term that one must understand before tackling the manufacturing deduction itself: *domestic production gross receipts* (DPGR). DPGR are gross receipts derived from a limited number of activities including:

- Any lease, rental, license, sale, exchange, or other disposition of:
  - Qualifying production property manufactured, produced, grown, or extracted by the taxpayer in whole or in part within the United States;
  - Qualified film; and
  - Electricity, natural gas, or potable water produced in the United States
- Construction performed in the United States; and
- Engineering or architectural services performed in the United States for construction projects in the United States.

Again, Code Sec. 199 creates two more new terms in the process of defining DPGR: **qualifying production property (QPP)** and **qualified film.** Under Code Sec. 199, QPP refers to:
- Tangible personal property;
- Any computer software; and
- Any property described in Code Sec. 168(f)(4) (certain sound recordings).

The definition of **qualified film,** *a "specialty" area carved out for the film industry,* will be explained in detail later in this chapter.

STUDY QUESTIONS

---

1. Qualified production activities income consists of domestic production gross receipts minus COGS related to the DPGR, a ratable portion of deductions, expenses, and losses not directly allocable to DPGR, and:

   a. Net receipts not allocable to DPGR
   b. COGS not related to DPGR
   c. Deductions, expenses, and losses directly allocable to DPGR
   d. None of the above

2. All of the following are activities from which DPGR are derived **except:**

   a. Domestic engineering or architectural services for domestic construction projects
   b. Construction inside the United States
   c. Disposition of QPP; qualified film; and U.S.-produced electricity, natural gas, or potable water
   d. All of the above are activities from which DPGR are derived

---

NOTE

Answers to Study Questions, with feedback to both the correct and incorrect responses, are proved in a special section beginning on page 191.

.03   Calculating QPAI

A contentious issue that has developed based on the first wave of guidance is how QPAI **(qualifying production activities income)** is calculated. Taxpayers and practitioners were hoping that QPAI could be determined by division, production line, or transactional basis. Instead, Treasury and the IRS insist that QPAI must be determined on an item-by-item basis. As a result, QPAI derived from an item can be either positive or negative.

Many practitioners and industry groups have voiced their concern about the difficulty and burden associated with calculating QPAI in this manner. Moreover, confusion exists about what exactly an "item" is because the term has not been defined by either Congress or IRS guidance.

COMMENT

Treasury and IRS expect to issue a second round of guidance. Proposed regs will incorporate the rules of Notice 2005-14 and cover additional issues that need clarification. Despite Treasury and IRS's insistence on their initial positions, the proposed rules are not set in stone. They are subject to adjustments in the continuing regulations process, and practitioners are hoping that some accommodation of their complaints that an item-by-item determination does not make more sense will be recognized, at least in part.

After one identifies and calculates the components of QPAI, he or she can determine the amount of the deduction. The manufacturing deduction is equal to a percentage of the lesser of either the taxpayer's QPAI or taxable income during a tax year (without regard to Code Sec. 199).

Table 1.1 shows the maximum deduction by year according to the applicable percent of QPAI or taxable income.

Table 1.1. Manufacturing Deduction Percentage by Year

Year	Maximum Deduction (%)
2005	3
2006	3
2007	6
2008	6
2009	6
2010 and beyond	9

> **EXAMPLE**
>
> Suppose Company X, located in Paradise City, U.S.A, manufactures lawn chairs. Company X derives $10,000,000 in QPAI from the sale of lawn chairs in tax year 2005. During tax year 2005, Company X has $15,000,000 in taxable income. Thus, the maximum amount Company X can take for purposes of the manufacturing deduction for tax year 2005 is $300,000. That is, $10,000,000 (the lesser of either QPAI or taxable income), multiplied by the maximum deduction percentage for 2005 (3 percent).

STUDY QUESTION

> **3.** The maximum manufacturing deduction is equal to a percentage of the lesser of either the taxpayer's _____ or _____ during a tax year.
>
> **a.** Gross receipts; DPGR
> **b.** QPAI; taxable income
> **c.** QPP income; Code Sec. 199 property proceeds
> **d.** None of the above equals the deduction

.04 Wage Limitation

Even after multiplying the appropriate percentage by either QPAI or taxable income, the calculation is not over. The amount of deduction is limited to 50 percent of the W-2 wages actually paid to employees and reported by the taxpayer during the tax year. For purposes of the wage limitation, **taxpayer** refers to an "employer." Employees are limited to officers of a corporate taxpayer and common law employees as defined by Code Sec. 3121(d). Thus, the more labor-intensive the manufacturing process, the more likely that a deduction will remain at either QPAI or taxable income and not be reduced further by the W-2 wage limitation.

Code Sec. 199 defines **W-2 wages** as the sum of the aggregate amount of W-2 wages reported on Forms W-2, "Wage and Tax Statement," for the calendar year ending during the employer's taxable year. W-2 wages are defined as wages and elective deferrals that must be included on Form W-2 under Code Sec. 6051(a)(3) and (8). This amount includes the total amount of elective deferrals under Code Sec. 402(g)(3), deferred compensation under Code Sec. 457k and designated Roth IRA contributions under Code Sec. 402A for tax years after December 31, 2005.

CAUTION

All of these items cannot be grouped together into one single box on Form W-2. Thus, there is not one single box on Form W-2 that meets the definition of W-2 wages. As a result, Treasury and the IRS provide three alternative methods for calculating W-2 wages for purposes of Code Sec. 199.

Under the first option, a taxpayer's W-2 wages equals the lesser of either:

- The total entries in Box 1 of all the Forms W-2 filed by an employer; or
- The total entries in Box 5 of all Forms W-2 filed by an employer.

Under the second option, W-2 wages are calculated by subtracting the total amounts reported in Box 1 of Form W-2 minus wages reported in Box 1 that are not wages under Code Sec. 3401(a) and items treated as wages under Code Sec. 3402(o) such as supplemental unemployment compensation benefits. Elective deferrals reported in Box 12 of Forms W-2 with Codes D, E, F, G, and S are then added to the total wages.

Under the third option, a taxpayer tracks the actual amount of wages subject to federal income tax withholding, subtracts supplemental unemployment compensation benefits included in this amount, and then adds specific elective deferrals reported in Box 12 of Forms W-2 with Codes D, E, F, G, and S.

The W-2 limitation rules are liberalized for employers who hire agents to handle payroll. An employer can take into account wages paid by an employer's agent to employees of the employer for services rendered. In addition, a taxpayer can take into account wages paid by an employer having control of the payment of such wages under Code Sec. 3401(d)(1) to employees of the taxpayer if the wages are included on Forms W-2 by the Code Sec. 3401(d)(1) employer.

However, the W-2 wage limitation is more restrictive for taxpayers that acquire other taxpayers. For example, if a taxpayer (the successor) acquires a major portion of a trade or business or a major portion of a separate unit of a trade or business from another taxpayer (the predecessor), the successor cannot take into account wages paid to common law employees of the predecessor. This restriction applies even if the wages are reported on a Form W-2 issued by the successor.

Another restriction on W-2 wages is that amounts treated as W-2 wages for one tax year may not be treated as W-2 wages in another year. For example, an amount of nonqualified deferred compensation treated as W-2 wages under an Unmodified Box Method for a tax year may not then be counted again as W-2 wages in another tax year.

EXAMPLE

Assume the facts for Company X in section .03. The maximum amount of the manufacturing deduction Company X could take in tax year 2005 was $300,000. Let us suppose that Company X paid employees $400,000 in wages and reported the same amount on Forms W-2 in tax year 2005. Since the amount of deduction is limited to 50 percent of wages actually paid and reported in a tax year, Company X's deduction for tax year 2005 is limited to $200,000 (50 percent of $400,000 in wages).

Note that this W-2 wage cap of half the otherwise allowable deduction does not get any easier to meet in future years when the 3 percent deduction increases to 6 percent and then 9 percent. In this example, even if the maximum deduction otherwise allowable was $900,000 (the amount that would be allowed in Company X's situation starting in 2010), it still would be limited to $200,000 (50 percent of $400,000 in wages). Consequently, the more automated the manufacturing process, the more likely it is that the manufacturer will find itself restricted by the wage limitation and not able to fully maximize the manufacturing deduction. The manufacturing deduction is that sense is more about retaining jobs in the United States than about subsidizing American manufacturers for shareholder benefit.

STUDY QUESTION

4. The manufacturing deduction is limited to no more than _____ percent of the actual W-2 wages paid to employees and reported for the tax year by the taxpayer.

   a. 10
   b. 25
   c. 30
   d. 50

¶110 WHAT ARE DOMESTIC PRODUCTION GROSS RECEIPTS (DPGR)?

As mentioned above, domestic production gross receipts (DPGRs) are defined under Code Sec. 199(c)(4)(A) as gross receipts of the taxpayer that are derived from:

- Any lease, rental, license, sale, exchange, or other disposition of:
  - Qualified production property (QPP) that was manufactured, produced, grown, or extracted by the taxpayer in whole or in significant part within the United States

- Any qualified film produced by the taxpayer or
- Electricity, natural gas, or potable water produced by the taxpayer in the United States
- Construction performed in the U.S.
- Engineering or architectural services performed in the U.S. for construction projects in the U.S.

On its face, the definition of DPGR seems straightforward. However, many of the terms are cause for confusion because taxpayers subject them to a variety of interpretations. At the heart of the controversy is the difference in interpretation given by Treasury and the IRS and by practitioners on a number of the limitations placed on Code Sec. 199(c)(4)(A). This section explains each element of the definition of DPGR under Code Sec. 199(c)(4)(A) in detail.

.01 "Derived from"

Gross receipts derived from an activity that qualifies as manufacturing, producing, growing, or extracting (MPGE activity) are limited to the direct proceeds from the lease, rental, license, sale, exchange, or other disposition of QPP. To determine whether a lease, rental, license, sale, exchange, or disposition has occurred, taxpayers should look to existing federal income tax law principles for guidance. For example, Rev. 88-65 states that a short-term rental is treated as a service. Thus, a short-term rental is not a qualifying activity.

Notice 2005-14 provides two guideposts for taxpayers in determining what is "derived from." First, the sale of QPP requirement is met if the taxpayer has direct proceeds from the sale of QPP or self-constructed QPP used in the taxpayer's business, which is manufactured in whole or in significant part within the United States. Additionally, business interruption insurance and payments not to produce to the extent the payments are substitutes for gross receipts are treated as qualifying gross receipts.

.02 Qualified Production Property (QPP)

Tangible personal property. Code Sec. 199 borrows the definition of tangible personal property from Reg. Sec. 1.48-1(c). Thus, for purposes of the manufacturing deduction, **tangible personal property** means any tangible property except land and improvements thereto, such as buildings or other inherently permanent structures. Local law is not controlling for purposes of determining whether property is tangible personal property. Definitions of property under federal tax law control.

In addition, if property is classified as tangible personal property, it is automatically excluded from being deemed computer software, a sound recording, or qualified film.

EXAMPLE

A taxpayer sells a computer video game on a CD-ROM. The CD-ROM disk is tangible personal property, but the computer game on the disk is classified as computer software. If the CD-ROM disk was manufactured outside the United States, but the software was developed domestically, the taxpayer must allocate the gross receipts between those qualifying as DPGR (those attributable to the software development activity) and gross receipts that do not qualify as DPGR (the manufacturing of the disks).

Computer software. Determining what constitutes **computer software** for Code Sec. 199 purposes is important, especially given how loosely the term is used these days. Remember, qualified production property (QPP) does not only include tangible personal property (although that will prove to be the primary property used for the credit on a national basis). QPP also include any computer software and certain sound recordings.

The definition of software under Code Sec. 199 is based on Reg. Sec. 1.197-2(c)(4)(iv). Thus, **computer software** is essentially any program or any sequence of machine-readable code that is designed to cause a computer to perform a desired function or set of functions. However, computer software does not mean that the program must be designed to operate on a computer. For purposes of the manufacturing deduction, computer software also includes machine-reading coding for video games and similar programs.

Changes in the way that customers purchase computer software have muddied the waters when practitioners try to determine whether the purchase is actually a purchase or merely a service. As a result, Treasury and the IRS adopted a facts and circumstances test for making this determination, albeit with some hard and fast rules.

A taxpayer must take into account all the facts and circumstances of a transaction to determine whether a sale, exchange, license, or a lease of computer software has occurred. The form, classification, and delivery medium of the transaction is not controlling.

What is clear is that service provided with a disposition of computer software does not result in qualifying gross receipts. Examples of nonqualifying services are:

- Providing customer support in connection with the sale of computer software;
- Online services; and
- Providing Internet access or telephone services over the Internet.

Using this basic rule as a background, Treasury and the IRS concluded that gross receipts derived from computer software sold to customers who download the software are DPGR. However, DPGR do not include gross receipts derived from software that is offered for use online for a fee.

COMMENT

The industry has questioned the logic of the distinction between down-loadable software and online software. According to the software industry, the distinction fails to take into account the similar development process in both types of software. The only difference between the two, industry representatives argue, is the method in which the consumer takes posses-sion of the software.

STUDY QUESTIONS

---

5. To determine whether a sale, exchange, license, or lease of computer software has occurred, which of the following is a controlling factor?
   a. The delivery medium of the transaction
   b. Whether services are provided with the transaction
   c. The classification of the software
   d. None of the above is controlling for the transaction

6. Gross receipts derived from fees charged to use software online are includable in DPGR. *True or False?*

Sound recordings. QPP also includes *sound recordings,* which are defined as any property described in Code Sec. 168(f)(4). Therefore, for purposes of the manufacturing deduction, a sound recording includes any work that results from the fixation of a series of sounds, regardless of the nature of the material in which those sounds are embodied.

Sound recordings are treated in much the same way as computer software for purposes of allocating gross receipts. If the sound recording is recorded on a compact disk, the production of the sound recording and the compact disk are classified differently.

.03 "Manufactured, Produced, Grown, or Extracted"

Congress intended for the manufacturing deduction to be available to a broad range of taxpayers. Thus, in the determination of the type of qualified production property that gives rise to domestic production gross receipts, Treasury and the IRS took a liberal approach in defining the phrase "manu-factured, produced, grown, or extracted" and made it quite broad. According to Notice 2005-14, MPGE activities include not only the activities listed in Code Sec. 199 but also the activities listed in Code Sec. 263A(g)(1), which include constructing, building, installing, manufacturing, developing, or improving property.

To maintain consistency, a taxpayer that engages in MPGE activities should also treat itself as a producer under Code Sec. 263A with respect to QPP for the tax year. If a taxpayer is not accounting for production activities, the IRS advises the taxpayer to change its method of accounting according to Revenue Procedure 2002-19, 2002-54, or 2002-9.

Food and beverages. Gross receipts from the sale of food and beverages prepared by a taxpayer at a retail establishment do not qualify as DPGR. A retail establishment is real property used in the trade or business of selling food or beverages to the public if retail sales occur at the facility.

What about establishments that produce food and beverages for both retail and wholesale sale? If a taxpayer only uses a facility to prepare food or beverages for wholesale sale, the facility is not a retail establishment. However, even if a taxpayer's business is a retail establishment, taxable income derived from food or beverages prepared at the facility that are sold at wholesale qualify for the manufacturing deduction.

If both retail and wholesale sales occur at a taxpayer's facility, the taxpayer is allowed to allocate gross receipts between retail sales that do not qualify as DPGR and wholesale sales that do qualify as DPGR. A safe harbor is provided for facilities in which less than 5 percent of the total gross receipts is derived from the retail sale of food. In such a case, all gross receipts derived from sales at the facility will qualify as DPGR. Operations outside of the safe harbor 5 percent, however, need to prove a reasonable allocation. The president's own Tax Reform Panel recently admitted the complexity of this rule, offering the example of the donut maker that has a small donut-making "factory" in the back and a retail sales area in front. It concluded that small nuances in operations should not, but do in fact, make a difference under the tax law.

In addition, DPGR do not include any gross receipts derived from property leased, licensed, or rented by the taxpayer for use by any related person. A *related person* is defined as a single employer under Code Sections 52(a) or (b) or 414 (m) or (o).

.04 "By the Taxpayer"

Manufactured, produced, grown, or extracted (MPGE) activities must be performed "by the taxpayer" to qualify as DPGR. Treasury and the IRS have determined that "by the taxpayer" foresees more than one taxpayer claiming the manufacturing deduction with respect to the same function performed with respect to the same property. In that respect, it is an all-or-nothing determination.

In situations involving contract manufacturers, determining only one taxpayer eligible to take the deduction can be problematic. Accordingly, when one taxpayer performs MPGE activities under a contract with a related party, only the taxpayer that has the "benefits and burdens of ownership of the property" during the period that the MPGE activities occur is entitled to the DPGR. Property is not manufactured by a customer if the customer does not have the benefits and burdens of owning the property at the time of MPGE activity. The rule applies even if the customer has direct supervision and control over the contractor or is treated as a producer under Code Sec. 263A.

On the other hand, if the contractor does not have the benefits and burdens of ownership at the time of the MPGE activities, the contractor is merely considered to be performing a service for the customer. Thus, under Notice 2005-14, either the contractor or the customer can qualify for the manufacturing deduction for the same activity, but not both.

STUDY QUESTION

> **7.** For contract manufacturers, to determine the sole taxpayer eligible to claim DPGR of property, the rule stipulates examining:
>
> **a.** Whether the customer has direct supervision and control over a contractor
>
> **b.** Whether the contractor is treated as a producer under Code Sec. 263A
>
> **c.** Whether the claimant has the benefits and burdens of property ownership during MPGE activities
>
> **d.** Nothing, because both a contract manufacturer and another taxpayer such as the customer may claim DPGR for the same property

.05 "In Whole or in Significant Part"

To qualify for the manufacturing deduction, MPGE activities must be performed in whole or in part by the taxpayer in the United States. This requirement may be satisfied even if the taxpayer:

- Purchases partially manufactured QPP from another taxpayer that satisfies the "in whole or in significant part" requirement;
- Imports QPP that is partially manufactured outside the United States; and
- Manufactures QPP in significant part in the United States and exports the goods for further manufacturing outside the United States.

For the MPGE activity to be performed in whole or in part by the taxpayer within the United States, the MPGE in the United States must be "substantial in nature." The test for substantiality depends on all of the facts and circumstances surrounding the MPGE activity, including the:

- Relative value added by the MPGE activity in the United States;
- Relative cost of the MPGE activity in the United States;
- Nature of the property; and
- Nature of the MPGE activity performed in the United States.

CAUTION

All of the factors should be considered when applying the substantial-in-nature test.

EXAMPLE

A taxpayer purchases gold abroad. The taxpayer melts and shapes this gold into jewelry at his shop in New York. Although the relative value added by the taxpayer's MPGE activity in the U.S. may be relatively low, the nature of the MPGE activity in the United States is substantial in nature. Thus, the taxpayer has produced the QPP in significant part domestically.

A safe harbor rule exists if the conversion costs, direct labor, and related factory burden to MPGE property incurred by the taxpayer in the United States are 20 percent or more of the total cost of goods sold attributable to the property.

Not every activity performed by a taxpayer in connection with bringing a product to market counts toward the substantial-in-nature test. Activities such as packaging, repackaging, labeling, and minor assembly operations are disregarded activities and should not be considered in applying the safe harbor.

EXAMPLE

ABC Co. grows grape leaves completely outside the United States for export to the United States for labeling and sale. This activity does not meet the substantial in nature test.

Design and development activities may or may not be disregarded for purposes of the substantial-in-nature test. In general, if the design and development of certain tangible property occurs entirely in the United States, but the tangible property is manufactured entirely outside of the United States, the design and development activities are disregarded for both the substantial in nature test and the safe harbor rule.

In the case of intangible property such as computer software and sound recordings, design and development compose a significant portion of the production process. Thus, the design and development activities relating to computer software and sound recordings are not disregarded for purposes of the substantial in nature test or the safe harbor rule.

STUDY QUESTION

---

8. The substantial in nature test considers all of the following facts and circumstances surrounding the MPGE activity *except:*

   a. Useful life of the manufactured product

   b. Relative cost of the MPGE activity inside the United States

   c. Nature of the property

   d. All of the above are considered in the substantiality test

---

.06 "Within the U.S."

The definition of United States is limited. It includes only the 50 states and the District of Columbia; it does not include U.S. possessions and territories.

> **EXAMPLE**
>
> A taxpayer living in the Miami has a rum distillery in the U.S. Virgin Islands. The taxpayer exports the rum to the United States. Gross receipts from the sale of the rum cannot be considered to be DPGR.

.07 Film

Film includes motion pictures, videotapes, and live or delayed television programming if at least 50 percent of the total compensation for services is performed in the United States by actors, production personnel, directors, and producers. However, film is limited to either the master copy of the film or another copy from which a taxpayer makes and produces copies.

Several related items are not considered qualified film, including:

- Tangible property such as DVDs and videocassettes used to hold the film;
- Films, videotape and other materials that depict "actual sexually explicit conduct";
- Ticket sales for viewing qualified film;

- Screenplays or other writings even if developed into a qualified film;
- Revenue from the sale of tangible personal property that is film-themed merchandise; and
- A license of the right to use the film characters.

Compensation paid for services by production personnel must be allocated according to those who are directly involved and those who are ancillary to the production of the film. Only compensation paid to personnel directly involved in the production of the film qualifies toward the 50 percent test.

Examples of production personnel include writers, choreographers, composers, casting agents, camera operators, set designers, lighting technicians, and make-up artists. Persons that do not qualify as production personnel include advertisers, promoters, distributors, studio administrators and managers, studio security personnel, and personal assistants to actors.

.08   Electricity, Natural Gas, and Potable (Drinking) Water

Although production of electricity, natural gas, and potable water in the United States may qualify for the manufacturing deduction, transmission or distribution of these items alone does not. Taxpayers that both produce and transmit or distribute electricity, natural gas, and potable water in the United States can still qualify for the deduction. An "integrated producer" of these items must allocate its gross receipts between qualifying production and nonqualifying distribution or transmission. A safe harbor rule is provided if less than 5 percent of total gross receipts is attributable to the transmission or distribution activities.

Now that the allocation method for electricity, natural gas, and potable water has been laid out, it is time to turn to the definition of these items. **Natural gas** generally means only natural gas extracted from a natural deposit. Natural gas production involves extracting natural gas from the ground and processing the gas into pipeline quality gas.

With respects to potable water, the production of bottled water in the United States is classified as tangible personal property rather than the production of potable water. Fortunately, no allocation of gross receipts between tangible personal property and potable water production is needed.

For actual production of potable water, only gross receipts derived from the acquisition, collection, and storage of raw or untreated water, transportation, and treatment of raw water to a water treatment facility are included in DPGR.

.09   Construction

Gross receipts derived from the construction of real property may qualify as DPGR. Compensation received for construction services performed in the United States is "derived from construction," and thus includable in DPGR. The taxpayer must be actively engaged in the construction trade or business. To be considered "actively engaged" in construction, the taxpayer's trade or business must be considered construction for purposes of the North American Industry Classification System (NAICS) codes.

DPGR may include the proceeds of a sale, exchange, or other disposition of real property constructed in the United States if all the requirements for the manufacturing deduction are met.

Real property includes:

- Residential and commercial buildings;
- Structural components of residential and commercial buildings;
- Inherently permanent structures other than tangible property such as machinery;
- Inherently permanent land improvements; and
- Infrastructure.

Construction includes activities typically performed in connection with the erection or substantial renovation of real property. **Substantial renovation real property** is defined as the renovation of a major component or substantial structural part of real property that materially increases the value of the property, substantially prolongs the useful life of the property, or adapts the property to a new or different use. The improvement of land and painting can also be classified as construction, but only if they are performed in connection with the erection or substantial renovation of real property.

Gross receipts derived from the construction of infrastructure in the United States also may qualify as DPGR. The definition of **infrastructure** includes roads, power lines, water systems, railroad spurs, communication facilities, sewers, sidewalks, cable, wiring, and permanent oil and gas platforms.

Unlike the rule for QPP, in certain situations more than one taxpayer may be regarded as deriving gross receipts from the same construction activity and the same construction project.

EXAMPLE

A taxpayer hires G, a general contractor, to perform a substantial renovation of a building, and G hires S, a subcontractor, to install electrical wiring as part of the substantial renovation. The amounts that both G and S receive qualify as DPGR. However, proceeds from the sale of the building received by the taxpayer do not qualify as DPGR because the taxpayer did not perform any construction activity.

Gross receipts from the lease or rental of real property or sale of tangible personal property constructed by the taxpayer do not qualify as DPGR. Tangible personal property includes items such as appliances or furniture sold as part of a construction project and is not considered real property. A safe harbor rule is allowed if more than 95 percent of the total gross receipts derived from a construction project is attributable to real property, then all of the total gross receipts qualify as DPGR.

> **COMMENT**
>
> **Tangential services,** such as delivering materials to the site, even if necessary for construction, are not considered as construction. However, a taxpayer that both performs the construction and provides tangential services may include gross receipts from these tangential services in its DPGR calculation.

.10 Engineering and Architectural Services

Engineering and architectural services must be performed in the United States for a construction project in the United States Notice 2005-14 imposes a three-prong test for what constitutes engineering and architectural services:

- The engineering or architectural services must relate to real property;
- The services must be performed in the United States; and
- The taxpayer must be able to substantiate that the services relate to a construction project in the United States.

In addition, to claim the deduction, the taxpayer must be in the "active conduct of an engineering or architectural services trade or business. "

A safe harbor is allowed if less than 5 percent of total gross receipts is derived from architectural services performed outside the United States or related to property other than real property. In such a case, all the gross receipts will be treated as qualified DPGR.

In addition, the fact that a construction project for the United States falls through does not disqualify gross receipts derived from engineering or architectural services rendered for the failed construction project.

¶115   CALCULATING DOMESTIC PRODUCTION GROSS RECEIPTS (DPGR)

No single method of determining DPGR works for every taxpayer. Any "reasonable method that accurately identifies gross receipts … based on all of the information available to the taxpayer to substantiate the allocation" is acceptable. As of yet, there is no definition of a reasonable method for accurately identifying gross receipts. However, the Treasury Department and the IRS have come up with a list of factors that will be considered in determining whether the allocation method is reasonable.

The factors, listed in Notice 2005-14, are:

- Whether the taxpayer is using the most accurate information available to the taxpayer;
- The relationship between the gross receipts and the base chosen;
- The accuracy of the method chosen as compared with other possible methods;
- Whether the method is used by the taxpayer for internal management or other business purposes;
- Whether the method is used for other federal, state, or foreign income tax purposes;
- The time, burden, and cost of using various methods; and
- Whether the taxpayer applies the method consistently from year to year.

In addition, Notice 2005-14 sets out some guidelines for choosing a reasonable method to determine DPGR. If a taxpayer already has a system in place to determine where an item was manufactured, produced, grown, or extracted for another purpose or has information available to use a specific identification method for another purpose, ,the taxpayer must use that method. Use of a different, less accurate system than one already in place would not be considered reasonable. However, if a taxpayer does not already have a system in place or available information for a specific identification method, the IRS would probably grant more leeway in determined the reasonableness of the taxpayer's selection of a method.

.01   Apportioning Cost of Goods Sold to DPGR

COGS must be traced to DPGR using the taxpayer's books and records and be determined using the taxpayer's accounting method for federal income tax purposes. If the taxpayer's books and records do not allow the taxpayer to match up COGS and DPGR, any reasonable method may be employed by the taxpayer to do so. The taxpayer must use the same method for allocating COGS as the taxpayer uses for allocating gross receipts between DPGR and non-DPGR.

.02 Apportioning Deductions

Deductions may or may not reduce DPGR or gross income attributable to DPGR. A loss generated by the sale of property will reduce DPGR if the proceeds from the property would have been included in DPGR. However, deductions attributable to net operating losses (NOLs) or personal deductions not attributable to a trade or business are not allocated to DPGR or gross income attributable to DPGR.

There are three allowable methods for allocating and apportioning deductions. Under the first method, which is available to all taxpayers, deductions are allocated and apportioned to DPGR by applying the allocation rules under the Code Sec. 861 regs. Special rules exist for apportioning certain charitable deductions, interest expense, and research and experimentation deductions.

Recognizing that the first method may unfairly burden small taxpayers, the IRS created two alternative deduction allocation methods. Taxpayers with average annual gross receipts of $25 million or less may use the simplified deduction method. Under this method, deductions are generally apportioned between DPGR and other receipts based on relative gross receipts.

For a taxpayer with average annual gross receipts of $5 million or less, the small business simplified overall method is available. This simplified method is also available to those taxpayers eligible to use the cash method outlined in Rev. Proc. 2002-28.

For purposes of meeting the gross receipts threshold, the average of annual gross receipts of the taxpayer is based on average annual gross receipts of the taxpayer for the three tax years preceding the current tax year. Special rules apply for calculating the average annuals gross receipts for members of an expanded affiliated group and for short years.

STUDY QUESTION

9. A taxpayer having annual gross receipts of $4.6 million may **not** use which of the following apportionment methods to allocate deductions?

    a. The simplified deduction method
    b. Application of the allocation rules described in Code Sec. 861 regs.
    c. Small business simplified overall method
    d. All of the above are available to the taxpayer

.03 Allocation of DPGR

Taxpayers that manufacture QPP both inside and outside the United States must perform an additional calculation to determine DPGR. They must calculate the portion of gross receipts attributable to the QPP inside the United States that qualifies for the manufacturing deduction and the portion attributable to nonqualifying QPP manufactured outside the United States. Some taxpayers need not allocate gross receipts using this method if certain conditions are met. A safe harbor rule is provided for taxpayers with less than 5 percent of total gross receipts from items other than DPGR: In such a case, the taxpayer may treat all gross receipts as DPGR.

¶115

.04   Embedded Services

In general, most products have an embedded service cost that is included in the total cost of the good. However, for purposes of the manufacturing deduction, gross receipts derived from services do not qualify as DPGR. Thus, to determine DPGR, a taxpayer must allocate the gross receipts between the property and the embedded service.

As a rule of thumb, the amount of gross receipts attributable to the property cannot exceed the selling price of the property minus the cost of service. Two exceptions to this rule exist:

- Taxpayers may include the gross receipts derived from a qualified warranty if the warranty is (1) in the normal course of business and (2) the warranty is neither separately bargained for nor offered by the taxpayer; and
- A de minimis amount of gross receipts from embedded services equal to less than 5 percent of the gross receipts of the property qualifies as DPGR. For purposes of the de minimis rule, gross receipts from a qualified warranty included in the total price of the property are not considered to be gross receipts.

.05   Advertising Income

The sale of advertising space is a major source of revenue for newspapers and magazines. Gross receipts derived from the sale of advertising space qualify as being derived from the sale of the newspapers and magazines themselves. Examples of advertising space include display advertising and classified advertisements.

.06   Application to Pass-Through Entities

Special rules apply if the taxpayer is an S corporation, partnership, estate, trust or other pass-through entity. For pass-through entities, the deduction applies at the shareholder, partner, or similar level. Each owner computes its share of the manufacturing deduction according to its distributive or proportionate share of the pass-through entity's items.

The W-2 wage limitation on the amount of the manufacturing deduction applies to pass-through entities as well. A shareholder or partner is treated as being allocated in an amount equal to the lesser of:

- The shareholder or partner's allocable share of W-2 wages; or
- Two times 9 percent of the QPAI allocated to the shareholder or partner during the tax year (two times 3 percent in tax years beginning in 2005 and 2006, and 6 percent in tax years beginning in 2007, 2008, or 2009).

Code Sec. 199 applies to tax years of pass-through entities beginning on or after January 1, 2005. As a result of requirements for pass-through entities to provide certain information to owners regarding the manufacturing deduction, rules for information reporting by pass-through entities is likely to be included in the next wave of guidance.

.07 Affiliated Groups

For purposes of calculating the manufacturing deduction, Code Sec. 199 treats all members of an expanded affiliated group as a single corporation. An *expanded affiliated group (EAG)* under Code Sec. 199 is essentially the same entity as an affiliated group under Code Sec. 1504(a). However, an EAG includes a 50 percent vote and value test rather than the 80 percent test contained in Code Sec. 1504.

A single manufacturing deduction is computed for the EAG. The deduction is then allocated to the members of the expanded affiliated group in proportion equal to each member's respective amount of QPAI. The allocation is performed regardless of whether the consolidated group member has either separate taxable income or loss for the tax year or whether the member has W-2 wages for tax year.

The COGS is then subtracted from the aggregate amount of the member's QPAI. Additional rules have been promulgated under Notice 2005-14 for attribution of activities, modifying the amount of the deduction, members with negative amounts of QPAI, and identifying members of an EAG.

.08 Alternative Minimum Taxation

The manufacturing deduction is used when one calculates the alternative minimum tax. For purposes of calculating the AMT, the deduction is 9 percent of the lesser of QPAI or alternative minimum taxable income (AMTI). Instead of this AMTI limitation, an individual's limitation for AMT purposes is the individual's adjusted gross income (AGI). The deduction in computing AMTI is determined without regard to the deduction.

STUDY QUESTION

10. The general rule of thumb applicable to gross receipts attributed to property containing embedded services is:

a. The embedded services constitutes half of the property so that 50 percent of the product qualifies as DPGR.

b. Any embedded services equal to 25 percent or less of the gross receipts qualifies as DPGR.

c. The gross receipts attributed cannot exceed the property's selling price minus the cost of services.

d. None of the above applies because there is no rule of thumb as yet.

¶120 CONCLUSION

The important new Code Sec. 199 manufacturing deduction encompasses a vast array of "manufacturing" endeavors. The percentage of QPAI used for this deduction is poised to increase substantially in years following 2006, offering producers of a broad range of products—from electricity to qualified films—attractive incentives to maintain domestic operations and employ American workers.

MODULE 1 — CHAPTER 2

Deduction for Foreign Dividends Repatriated to the United States

This chapter was prepared to give guidance to practitioners about the operation of the special 2004 American Jobs Creation Tax Act's 85 percent deduction for foreign dividends repatriated to a U.S. corporation.

LEARNING OBJECTIVES

Upon completion of this chapter, you will be able to:

- Calculate the amount of qualifying dividends;
- Describe what amounts are treated as cash dividend payments;
- Understand how to determine the amount of permanently reinvested earnings;
- Make an election to claim the deduction and comply with the reporting requirements;
- Account for increases in related-party debt;
- Determine the effect of the foreign tax credit on the deductible amount;
- Identify the requirements for a domestic reinvestment plan;
- Distinguish between permitted and nonpermitted investments;
- Discuss the requirements for the timing of domestic investments;
- Compare the effects of transferring either a U.S. shareholder or a controlled foreign corporation;
- Analyze the effects of mergers, acquisitions and spin-offs; and
- Describe the treatment of an affiliated group of corporations.

¶201 INTRODUCTION

Congress created a special, temporary reduced tax rate in the American Jobs Creation Act of 2004 (2004 Jobs Act) to encourage repatriation of foreign earnings and investment of the repatriated funds in domestic job-producing activities. Under new Code Sec. 965, U.S. corporations receive an 85 percent dividends-received deduction for qualifying dividends, resulting in an effective tax rate of 5.25 percent for a corporation taxed at the top rate of 35 percent. Corporations have a one-year window to take the deduction.

> **COMMENT**
>
> Congressional conferees emphasized the temporary nature of the provision and stated explicitly that there was no intention to extend the benefit or make it permanent (see the conference report, H.R. Rept. No. 108-755).

Qualifying dividends are payments that exceed the **base period amount** of dividends paid by a controlled foreign corporation (CFC) to a U.S. corporation that owns at least 10 percent of the total combined voting power of the CFC. To qualify for the special tax rate, dividends must be reinvested in the United States pursuant to a domestic reinvestment plan. Estimates are that as much as $400 billion in repatriated dividends could qualify for the special tax rate under provisions of the 2004 Jobs Act known as the Homeland Investment Act.

> **COMMENT**
>
> The term **United States** includes drilling rigs in the territorial waters of the United States but does not include U.S. possessions and territories.

Domestic corporations are generally taxed on all income, whether earned from a U.S. or a foreign source. Income earned by a domestic corporation from a foreign corporate subsidiary is subject to U.S. tax when the income is repatriated as a dividend to the U.S. corporation. Until repatriation, U.S. taxes on the foreign income are deferred. Under certain antideferral regimes, the U.S. parent will be taxed on income earned by its foreign subsidiary that is passive or liquid, even if the income is not repatriated. The antideferral regimes include the CFC rules of Subpart F, Code Sections 951 to 964. A foreign tax credit can offset, in whole or in part, the U.S. taxes owed on foreign-source income, whether earned directly by the U.S. corporation, repatriated as a dividend, or taxable under the antideferral regime.

The U.S. tax on foreign income was a disincentive to repatriating the earnings. As a result, U.S. companies have invested billions of dollars overseas. Congress decided that a temporary reduced rate for repatriated dividends would stimulate the U.S. economy by encouraging corporations to invest dividends from foreign income in the United States.

¶205   GUIDANCE

.01   Notice 2005-10

Issued in January 2005, the notice covered the definition of cash dividends, the requirements for domestic reinvestment plans, permitted and nonpermitted investments, and election and reporting requirements.

.02   Notice 2005-38

The key issue addressed in Notice 2005-38 is the impact of mergers, acquisitions, and other corporate transactions on the calculation of the base period amount and the ceiling on amounts that qualify for the deduction. The notice also addresses the effect of intercompany debt between related parties, the foreign tax credit "gross-up," and the disallowance of certain expenses.

A Treasury official stated that Notice 2005-38 provides fundamental guidance that will give companies the information required to decide on their dividend payments.

.03   Notice 2005-64

Notice 2005-64 provides guidance on key issues that affect a corporation's computation of its tax liability. These issues include the disallowance of deductions for certain expenses; the identification of cash dividends and qualifying dividends; and the disallowance of the foreign tax credit with respect to the deduction, and related issues under Code Sec. 78. The notice also addresses increases in bank debt and the treatment of dividends paid to intermediary pass-through entities.

> **COMMENT**
>
> Notices 2005-10 and 2005-38 provided the essential guidance that taxpayers need to claim the 85 percent deduction. Notice 2005-64 addresses some secondary issues and fills in some details.

The government will issue additional notices, if needed, "until all the questions are answered," a Treasury official has said.

STUDY QUESTIONS

1. Which IRS notice describes permitted and nonpermitted investments for the 85 percent deduction?
   a. Notice 2005-10
   b. Notice 2005-23
   c. Notice 2005-38
   d. Notice 2005-64

2. Which IRS notice provides guidance on how corporations compute their tax liability and treat dividends paid to pass-through entities?
   a. Notice 2005-10
   b. Notice 2005-23
   c. Notice 2005-38
   d. Notice 2005-64

3. Which IRS notice clarifies how companies calculate the base period amount for the dividends-received deduction and the effect of inter-company debt between related parties?
   a. Notice 2005-10
   b. Notice 2005-23
   c. Notice 2005-38
   d. Notice 2005-64

NOTE

Answers to Study Questions, with feedback to both the correct and incorrect responses, are proved in a special section beginning on page 191.

¶210   QUALIFYING PAYMENTS

.01   Election Year

The temporary dividends-received deduction can be claimed for one of two tax years:

- The first tax year during the one-year period that begins on or after the October 22, 2004, enactment date of the 2004 Jobs Act (e.g., 2005 for calendar-year taxpayers); or
- The last tax year that begins before October 22, 2004 (e.g. 2004 for calendar-year taxpayers).

The election year can be a short taxable year. The 85 percent deduction applies only for the year elected, known as the **election year,** and cannot be used for dividends paid in a later year.

> **COMMENT**
>
> Because of the temporary nature of the provision, taxpayers will have to act quickly to take advantage of this provision, paying particular attention to effective dates and when to make the election.

The common parent of a consolidated group can elect the group's eligible year on behalf of the group. The election applies to each corporation that is included in the group's income tax return for the election year. A group member can receive an eligible dividend during any period the recipient is a member of the group. The examples in Section 5 of Notice 2005-38 illustrate how the consolidated return rules interact with the tax year election under Code Sec. 965(f).

STUDY QUESTIONS

> **4.** Calendar-year taxpayers can elect to claim the temporary dividends-received deduction in either 2004 or 2005. *True or False?*

.02 Cash Dividend Payments

The special rate applies to cash dividends paid by a CFC to its U.S. corporate shareholder. Dividends include:

- Code Sec. 302 redemptions of stock;
- Code Sec. 304 redemptions of stock in a related corporation;
- Code Sec. 316 dividends; and
- Cash received in an inbound liquidation described in Code Sec. 332 and treated as a dividend under Code Sec. 367(b).

Amounts treated as dividends under Code Secs. 367 or 1248 (gain on sale of stock in foreign corporation treated as dividend) would not qualify.

> **COMMENT**
>
> Because the law requires the payment of cash dividends, it is important to minimize foreign withholding taxes. The deduction cannot be claimed for 85 percent of the withholding taxes. Treaties that exempt foreign dividends from withholding, e.g., the U.K. treaty, would avoid this problem.

Distributions from earnings and profits (E&P) included in income under Code Sec. 951 **(Subpart F income)** and described in Code Secs. 959(c)(1) and (2) **(previously taxed income (PTI))** do not qualify as dividends.

¶210

Distributions described in 959(c)(3) do qualify. However, an ordering rule requires that amounts first be allocated to nonqualifying dividends described in 959(c)(1) and (2). Corporations may designate which cash amounts are attributable to cash dividends and subpart F inclusions. The identification is made on Form 8895, Part V (see "Election and Reporting Requirements"). If the CFC distributes more PTI than the qualifying dividend amount, the U.S. corporation can identify which cash PTI distributions are treated as being attributable to underlying subpart F inclusions that do not qualify for the deduction.

Qualifying cash dividends include cash amounts treated as dividends under Code Sec. 965(a)(2) (boot treated as a dividend). The dividend can be paid in U.S. or foreign currency. Transfers of cash equivalents from the CFC to the U.S. shareholder, or temporary reinvestments in cash equivalents, will be treated as distributions of cash, rather than cash equivalents.

Cash dividends paid by the CFC directly to the U.S. shareholder are translated into dollars at the spot rate on the date of distribution. If the dividend is paid through a pass-through entity, the dividend is translated from the foreign currency when the U.S. shareholder receives cash, not when the partnership or disregarded entity received the dividend. The U.S. shareholder's receipt of cash does not give rise to currency gain or loss.

Cash distributions paid indirectly from the CFC and excluded from current income because of the PTI rules of Code Sec 959 qualify as dividends if paid to the CFC from another CFC in the chain of ownership under Code Sec. 958(a), or if paid to any other CFC in the chain of ownership, to the extent of cash distributions to the CFC which paid a distribution to the U.S. shareholder (see Code Sec. 965(a)(2)). This exception enables multinational corporations to qualify for the deduction for earnings repatriated from lower-tier CFCs.

STUDY QUESTIONS

> **5.** All of the following are dividends that qualify for the special tax rate ***except***:
>
> **a.** Code Sec. 316 dividends
> **b.** Code Sec. 332 dividends
> **c.** Code Sec. 367 dividends
> **d.** All of the above qualify for the reduced rate

---

6. Cash dividends paid by a CFC directly to shareholders are converted into dollars:

a. When the shareholder receives the dividends

b. When the CFC ends its accounting period

c. At the spot rate on the date of distribution

d. None of the above is the date of conversion

.03   Other Entities

The deduction is not available for dividend payments made by a foreign partnership or other noncorporate entity. The U.S. shareholder cannot be a partnership or other passthrough entity. However, dividends paid by the CFC to a partnership or disregarded entity can qualify if the U.S. shareholder receives cash in the amount of the CFC dividend during the election year.

A **disregarded entity (DE)** does not have to actually distribute a cash dividend to the U.S. shareholder if the shareholder receives other cash from the entity that does not have to be repaid. For example, if the DE pays cash to the U.S. shareholder to repay a loan to the DE, these funds qualify as a payment from the DE. A loan of cash from the disregarded entity to the U.S. shareholder would not qualify.

Amounts paid by a partnership qualify only if the dividend amount is allocated to the U.S. shareholder/partner under the partnership rules and is separately stated under Sec. 702 regulations.

If the U.S. shareholder receives a cash payment from a disregarded entity that is less than the dividend paid by the CFC to the disregarded entity, the entire payment to the U.S. shareholder is an eligible dividend. Similarly, if the U.S. shareholder receives a smaller distribution from a partnership than the partner's distributive share of the dividend received by the partnership, the entire distribution is an eligible dividend. However, the requirement that a partnership make a cash distribution to the U.S. shareholder is not satisfied by a guaranteed payment or a payment that was made to the shareholder as a partner.

If the partnership or disregarded entity pays the U.S. shareholder a greater amount than it received from the CFC, the shareholder may identify which payments are eligible dividends. Generally, a dividend payment must be either an eligible dividend or an ineligible dividend in its entirety.

.04   Extraordinary Dividends and Base Period

The dividend repatriation rules apply to "extraordinary" dividends that exceed average dividends paid during the base period (**base period dividends**). **Extraordinary dividends** are the excess of the dividends received from the CFC over the average annual dividends received during the base period, including amounts includible in gross income under Code Sec. 951(a)(1)(B), and amounts that would have been included except for Code Sec. 959(a), concerning previously taxed income. Amounts included in base period dividends include dividends of property, deemed repatriations under Code Sec. 956, and distributions of PTI under Subpart F.

Dividends paid by a CFC to a partnership or disregarded entity owned by a U.S. shareholder in a base period year are treated as received by the shareholder, to the extent the dividends are included in the U.S. shareholder's income, even if the U.S. shareholder did not receive a distribution of cash or property.

The base period is the five-year period ending on or before June 30, 2003. The base period years are the three years left after throwing out the highest and lowest years in the five-year period. If a taxpayer had fewer than five years before June 30, 2003, all tax years ending on or before that date are considered.

The amount invested does not have to exceed U.S. investments in prior years or exclude investments planned before Code Sec. 965 was enacted.

A corporation that is spun off from another corporation is treated as having been in existence for the same period that the transferor corporation was in existence. The pre-spin-off dividend history must be allocated among the two corporations, based on their interests in the CFC immediately after the spin-off.

A consolidated group is treated as a single U.S. shareholder. The group will determine its base period dividends by aggregating the base period amounts of each member and then determining the average inclusions. Short tax years during the base period must be taken into account; the base period amount for a short tax year is not adjusted or annualized.

The base period amount attributable to previously taxed income is determined by multiplying the foreign currency amount of PTI by the spot rate.

STUDY QUESTION

7. Which of the following amounts is **not** included in base period dividends?

   a. Dividends of property
   b. Code Sec. 956 deemed repatriations
   c. Distributions of PTI under Subpart F
   d. All of the above are included

.05 Ceiling

Under Code Sec. 965(b), the ceiling on repatriated dividends is the greater of $500 million or the amount shown on the U.S. corporation's balance

Corporations can elect an alternative initial measurement date of September 30, 2004. If the taxpayer uses a 52-53 week taxable year, the corporation can use the end of the month ending nearest to October 3, 2004.

If the CFC pays off a portion of the debt principal before the final measurement date, the U.S. shareholder's final date RPI will be less than the initial date RPI. The U.S. shareholder must reduce the initial RPI that is attributable to a CFC that severs its relationship with the U.S. shareholder before the final measurement date. This reduction is not required if the CFC pays all or a portion of the principal on the debt. A U.S. corporation that acquires a CFC during the measurement period and is a U.S. shareholder on the final measurement date can increase its initial date RPI by the amount of related-party debt of the CFC immediately after the acquisition.

Exception: Intercompany trade payables are not treated as debt. This exclusion applies to debt arising in the ordinary course of business from sales, leases, or the performance of services, provided the debt is paid off within 183 days.

The related-party debt rule created a problem for financial institutions that have a steady flow of funds in the ordinary course of business. Notice 2005-64 rectified this with an exception for banks and dealers in securities. Any increase in debt that arises in the ordinary course of business will not be treated as debt. The notice also excludes debt from licenses that arises in the ordinary course of business, provided the debt is paid off within six months.

COMMENT

Notices 2005-38 and 2005-64 are favorable, practitioners say, because they scale back the items, such as trade payables, that are treated as related-party debt.

.07   Foreign Tax Credit

An important issue was the interaction of the 85 percent deduction and the foreign tax credit. Under Code Sec. 965(d), U.S. corporations cannot claim the foreign tax credit for taxes paid on a dividend that is eligible for the 85 percent deduction. Thus, the disallowance applies to the 15 percent of the dividend that is not eligible for the deduction. Notice 2005-64 reiterates that distributions of PTI treated as cash dividends are subject to the disallowance rule. The disallowance also applies to a U.S. shareholder's distributive share of foreign taxes paid or accrued by a partnership and allocated to the shareholder, and 85 percent of foreign taxes paid by a disregarded entity, if the DE paid the dividend to the U.S. shareholder.

Taxpayers may specifically identify which dividends are treated as carrying the deduction and which do not. This allows the taxpayer to target dividends that are included in its base amount and thus carry foreign tax credits. The deduction reduces the taxpayer's foreign tax credit limitation. Therefore, it will be advantageous to take the deduction (and therefore lose the credit) for dividends from low-tax countries.

Both the Code Sec. 78 gross-up and the expense allocation rules had statutory defects that the IRS addressed in the notice. The IRS relied on a statement of Congressional intent from Congress's tax leaders.

COMMENT

Senate Finance Committee Chairman Charles Grassley, R-Iowa, Ranking Finance Member Max Baucus, D-Mont, and House Ways and Means Committee Chairman Bill Thomas, R-Calif, wrote to the IRS and Treasury that the statute did not reflect Congressional intent and that they would introduce a technical corrections bill in the 109th Congress. Associate Chief Counsel (International) Hal Hicks said the letter from the Hill was extremely helpful on these issues.

Under Code Sec. 78, U.S. corporations claiming the foreign tax credit must "gross up" dividends received from foreign corporations, increasing U.S. taxes owed on the dividends. Notice 2005-38 clarifies that the gross-up rules do not apply to dividend payments qualifying for the 85 percent deduction. This was important because Code Sec. 965 does not allow a foreign tax credit for the deductible portion of the dividend. The notice's approach prevents U.S. corporations from having to pay taxes on phantom income that would increase the rate for repatriated dividends above the 5.25 percent intended rate. Code Sec. 965 does not modify the amount of foreign taxes deemed paid under Code Sections 902 and 960.

COMMENT

One practitioner stated that the gross-up rules and the M&A rules were needed so that U.S. corporations knew how much to include in their base period.

STUDY QUESTIONS

9. Because taxpayers may specify which dividends are treated as carrying the dividends-received deduction, taxpayers will find it advantageous to:

  a. Lose the credit (take the deduction) for dividends from low-tax countries

  b. Claim the deduction for dividends from high-tax countries

  c. Forego the deduction to take the credit on dividends from low-tax countries

  d. None of the above is advantageous

10. Which pronouncement clarifies the exemption from the gross-up rules of dividend payments qualifying for the 85 percent deduction?

  a. Code Sec. 78

  b. Notice 2005-38

  c. Code Sec. 965

  d. Notice 2005-64

.08   Alternative Minimum Tax

Code Sec. 965 provides that the tax on nondeductible dividends is not treated as a tax in applying the AMT, but this exclusion does not apply to a credit for the previous year's minimum tax or the credit for foreign taxes attributable to nondeductible dividends. Notice 2005-64 said that credits for prior year minimum tax may be allowed in an election year to reduce the regular tax on nondeductible dividends.

Qualifying Code Sec. 965 dividends do not create or increase any AMT liability in the election year.

Expenses. Code Sec. 965 disallows the 85 percent deduction for expenses allocated to qualifying dividends. Notice 2005-38 clarifies that only directly related expenses, such as legal fees, must be taken into account. The disallowance rule applies regardless of whether the expenses are paid or accrued in the election year or in a different tax year. Taxpayers do not have to take into account large items such as interest expense that could have been allocated to the deductible payments. Foreign withholding and U.S. taxes imposed on the dividend also do not reduce the amount.

COMMENT

A broader approach that disallowed expenses such as interest payments or R&D costs would have been more complex.

The list of directly allocable expenses is exclusive. Notice 2005-64 treats the following expenses as directly allocable to deductible dividends:

- Stewardship expenses (incurred for the U.S. shareholder's oversight of its investment in the CFC) that are definitely related and allocable to qualifying dividends;
- Legal, tax, accounting, consulting, and similar fees and other expenses, including employee compensation, paid for advice and document preparation concerning plans to repatriate earnings in the election year, the adoption and approval of the DRP, and the declaration and payment of qualifying CFC cash dividends;
- Fees and expenses for tax accounting and reporting of qualifying dividends; and
- Wire transfer, currency exchange, and similar fees for paying qualified dividends.

COMMENT

Expenses that are directly allocable reduce the amount of the qualifying dividend eligible for the 85 percent deduction (i.e., the "disallowance of the deduction").

In-house expenses that would have been incurred regardless of the dividend payment may also be treated as directly allocable. Practitioners say that Notice 2005-64 appears to look at what employees do, and treats time spent on Code. Sec. 965 activities as directly allocable. Corporations will have to keep records of direct time spent on Code Sec. 965.

The notice also applies a pro-rata rule, for administrative simplicity, to determine the amount of stewardship expenses treated as directly related. This figure may be disproportionately high because taxpayers will have a large Code Sec. 965 dividend and a less than normal non-965 dividend. The pro-rata rule only applies to stewardship expenses.

Expenses that are related but not directly allocable to the repatriated dividends do not give rise to disallowance of the 965 deduction. These include:

- Interest expense;
- R&D expenses;
- Depreciation and amortization;

- General and administrative expenses;
- Sales and marketing expenses; and
- State and local taxes.

The notice allows legal, tax, accounting, consulting, and similar fees related to the investments contemplated by the domestic reinvestment plan. Expenses incurred by CFCs that are deductible in computing subpart F income also are disallowed.

.09   Taxable Income Limitation

The U.S. corporation's taxable income for the year cannot be less than the amount of nondeductible dividends received from abroad. Furthermore, the deductible dividends cannot be taken into account when the U.S. corporation determines whether it has a net operating loss for the year. However, the corporation's expenses and deductions can reduce U.S. income that exceeds the amount of nondeductible dividends, including income attributable to the Code Sec. 78 gross-up for foreign taxes paid on nondeductible dividends from the CFC.

¶215   REINVESTMENT OF REPATRIATED DIVIDENDS

.01   Domestic Reinvestment Plans

The repatriated funds must be invested by the company in the United States pursuant to a formal domestic reinvestment plan (DRP). Notice 2005-10 provides the essential guidance needed to establish a plan. Notice 2005-38 also has some guidance on DRPs. A DRP approved before May 10, 2005, the date of the latter notice, could be amended by July 11 to reflect Notice 2005-38, even if the dividend had already been paid.

If the U.S. shareholder approved its domestic reinvestment plan before Notice 2005-64 was issued, the taxpayer may modify the plan by October 19, 2005, even if the dividend has already been paid. Any plan that is modified must be reapproved by the head of the company and its board of directors. If the shareholder already filed its tax return for the year it elected to apply Code Sec. 965, the taxpayer may file an amended return by December 31, 2005, to reflect the notice.

A modified plan must be subsequently approved by the corporation's chief executive officer and board of directors.

Before repatriating the earnings, the company must have a plan, approved by the company's CEO, president, or comparable official. The plan must subsequently be approved by the company's board of directors, management committee, executive committee, or similar body. Subsequent approval can occur after the dividend is paid, and no special meeting is required.

The plan must be in writing and must describe specific anticipated investments in the United States. The plan may apply to cash dividends from one or more CFCs, or the taxpayer may adopt separate plans for different cash dividends. There is no required form or template for the plan.

A U.S. shareholder may adopt separate DRPs for dividends paid by different CFCs during the year. If this is done, dividends paid by other CFCs will not qualify for the 85 percent deduction, even if the amount of cash dividends from the specified CFCs is less than the total dollar amount of investments proposed in the DRP. Furthermore, a U.S. shareholder may not decline to take the deduction if amounts are properly reinvested in accordance with the DRP.

> **COMMENT**
>
> Separate DRPs may be useful if one CFC is in a low-tax country and another CFC is in a high-tax country. The latter would give rise to a higher foreign tax credit and would not be a good candidate for qualified dividend treatment.

.02   Description of Investments

The plan must describe the anticipated U.S. investments in reasonable detail and specificity, and must state the total dollar amount for each principal investment. The plan does not have to specify an amount for components of an investment (e.g. advertising for product brands A and B). The plan must provide sufficient detail for an IRS examiner to determine that actual investments were contemplated by the plan. The components of the plan can vary for the type of anticipated investment (e.g., R&D or capital improvements), the investment period, and factors that would affect the corporation's ability to make the investments. Plans that merely cite the statutory language will be rejected. Taxpayers are allowed to shift amounts invested among investments cited in the plan.

Businesses have some flexibility to adjust their plans to economic changes. The government recommends that businesses include alternative investments in their plan in case the original investments are not made. The plan does not have to specify the conditions for making an alternative investment. Once the dividend is paid, however, the plan cannot be modified or amended. Transition rules provide an exception for dividends paid before January 13, 2005. If a DRP approved before January 13, 2005, did not comply with Notice 2005-10, taxpayers could modify their DRP by March 14, 2005, even if dividends had already been paid. The approval process is the same for the modified DRP.

.03 Consolidated Groups

If the U.S. shareholder is a member of a consolidated group, officials and directors from the common parent must approve the plan, but the plan does not have to be approved by other members of the group, even if they make investments under the plan. A consolidated group may rely on the domestic reinvestment plan of any corporation in the group that is a member of the group at any time on or after the first day of the group's election.

Any U.S. member of a consolidated group can make permitted investments, regardless of whether the member owns a CFC, as long as the corporation was a member of the group at any time during the election year. Investments by the member during or after the election year count against the group's investment ceiling, even if the member leaves the group during the election year. Similarly, if a U.S. corporation joins the group during the election year, the group may count the member's investments after it joined the group against the group's investment ceiling.

Furthermore, a U.S. corporation may use the permitted investments of any other domestic corporation, as long as both corporations are members of the same consolidated group at the time of the investment. The corporations need not have been members of the same group during the election year. Thus, if a corporation with a DRP joins a consolidated group after its election year, the corporation can count the subsequent investments of any group member against its investment ceiling. This treatment applies if a consolidated group adopts a DRP and the entire group is acquired by another group after the first group's election year.

.04 Asset Acquisitions

If a corporation buys the assets of another corporation, the acquiring corporation does not succeed to the investment obligations of the corporation selling its assets. However, if a corporation acquires the assets of another corporation in a tax-free liquidation or Code Sec. 368(a) reorganization, subsequent investments of the acquiring corporation can be used to satisfy the acquired corporation's DRP. This successor rule does not apply to assets acquired in a stock-for-stock reorganization or in a recapitalization.

EXAMPLE

United States Corp 1 acquires the assets of U.S. Corp 2. Corp 1 is not treated as a successor to Corp 2. Investments by Corp 1 cannot be used to satisfy the investment obligations of Corp 2. However, Corp 1 will be treated as a successor to Corp 2 if it acquired Corp 2's assets in a tax-free reorganization or liquidation. In that case, Corp 1's investments can be used to satisfy Corp 2's investment obligations. Corp 2 can continue to make investments itself to satisfy its own DRP.

If U.S. Corporation 1 acquires the assets of U.S. Corporation 2, Corp 1 is not treated as a successor to Corp 2. Therefore, Corp 1 does not have to satisfy the investment obligations of Corp 2. However, Corp 1 can be a successor to Corp 2 if the acquisition was a tax-free reorganization or liquidation of Corp 2 (other than a stock for stock reorganization described in Code Sec. 368(a)(1)(B)). Corp 1 must then satisfy its obligations under its own DRP, as well as Corp 2's DRP.

.05   Timing and Designation of Investments

The plan must state a reasonable time period during which the company anticipates completing the investments. Companies are not required to trace or segregate the repatriated funds. Companies simply must demonstrate that an amount equal to the amount of repatriated funds is invested under the domestic reinvestment plan. Using funds for nonpermitted investments does not affect the eligibility of the dividends. If the corporation already had plans in place to spend money on a qualified use, such as domestic advertising, it can prepare a DRP that covers the previous plan, freeing up actual dividends to be spent elsewhere.

COMMENT

Practitioners breathed a sigh of relief that the Treasury Department rejected a tracing or segregation approach.

The investments do not have to be completed in the election year. Investments may be completed in a tax year after the year the funds are repatriated. There is no specific time limit for making the investments. Investments made at any time during the election year will be treated as made pursuant to the plan, even if made prior to receipt of the cash dividend or the adoption of the DRP. However, investments made in a prior year will not qualify as permitted investments.

In Notice 2005-10, the IRS said that if an investment is planned over several years, spending during that period on nonpermitted investments may be subject to greater scrutiny. The IRS recommends using a segregated account for the dividend proceeds.

An investment cannot be counted twice. For example, a $100 investment by an acquired corporation cannot be counted against the DRPs of both the selling consolidated group and the acquiring group. The investing corporation can designate which plan will receive credit for the investment.

If no designation is made, there is an ordering rule: first against the acquired corporation's own election year if that year is the earliest; second, against any plan adopted for the corporation's own subsequent election year; and third, against any other corporation, in the order that the acquired corporation is required or permitted to make investments that satisfy the acquired corporation's DRP.

STUDY QUESTION

11. To reinvest repatriated dividends under a DRP, a corporation must:

    a. Complete the investments in the election year

    b. Segregate the repatriated funds

    c. Use the funds for permitted investments only

    d. None of the above is required

.06 Types of Permissible Investments

A corporation must invest the amount of dividends that qualifies for the 85 percent deduction. This dividend amount must be invested in domestic job-producing activities, pursuant to the corporation's domestic reinvestment plan (DRP).

Investments that contribute to job production are known as **permitted investments.** Investments that do not contribute to job production are known as nonpermitted investments.

Notice 2005-10 lists permitted and nonpermitted investments. Investments must be made in cash and paid to unrelated persons, except for pension payments. Stock may not be used to make investments. Thus, acquiring a corporation in exchange for stock is not a permitted investment.

Described here are common investments that are considered job-producing investments. Investment in these items satisfies the U.S. corporation's requirement to reinvest the foreign dividends domestically to be eligible for the 85 percent deduction. There is no tracing of cash dividend amounts received by the U.S. corporation. There are no restrictions on the use of specific funds to make investments that do not satisfy the DRP. Any cash held by the U.S. corporation can be used to make permitted or nonpermitted investments.

Hiring and training workers. Job creation was on Congress members' minds when they enacted the 2004 Jobs Act. Amounts can be used to hire new workers and train current employees. Employees must work in the U.S. Amounts also can be used to enhance compensation and benefits of rank-and-file employees, but not executives. In funding a qualified plan, amounts must be allocated to executive and nonexecutive compensation. An amount also must be allocated to permitted investments if services are performed both within and outside the United States.

Infrastructure, capital investments, and intangible property. This covers property, and plant and equipment that support the corporation's business, as well as other assets that are integral to the conduct of the corporation's business. This category includes communication and distribution systems, patents, computer hardware and software, databases, and supporting equipment. The corporation can use the funds to construct, develop, purchase, improve, rent, or license the asset.

This category also includes services performed in the U.S. that are related to or provided with the qualifying investment. Infrastructure and capital investments must be located in the United States. An allocation is required if the property or services are partly within and partly outside the United States.

Research and Development. This covers the funding of R&D projects conducted in the United States. R&D funded by the taxpayer will qualify, even if nonemployees are providing the R&D services.

Financial stabilization for the purposes of U.S. job retention or creation. Such a use of funding would include debt repayment if the payments keep current workers on the job, create more jobs, or improve cash flow. The corporation cannot pay a debt and then replace it with a loan on substantially similar terms. However, there does not have to be a net "global" reduction in debt. Thus, the CFC could borrow funds to pay the dividend, and the U.S. shareholder could use the funds to repay a debt to an unrelated party.

Debt repayment includes the funding of qualified benefit plans. A payment to a qualified plan that satisfies the U.S. shareholder's funding obligation is a permissible investment. Contributions under a fixed formula satisfy this rule; discretionary contributions to a profit-sharing or stock bonus plan do not qualify.

Notice 2005-10 does not specifically address expenditures for tort liabilities, but these conceivably are permitted investments.

The IRS will consider other financial stabilization payments on a case-by-case basis. The IRS will look at whether the taxpayer exercised reasonable business judgment to determine that the investment contributed to financial stabilization.

Acquisitions of business entities, such as corporations or partnerships with U.S. assets, even if the entity itself is foreign. Taxpayers must own 10 percent of the acquired business, directly or indirectly. An acquisition of a foreign company qualifies to the extent the company owns assets that, if acquired directly, would be a qualifying investment. If more than 95 percent of the investment would be permitted or nonpermitted, the entire investment shall be treated as permitted or nonpermitted.

Advertising and marketing in the United States. This type includes investments in trademarks, trade names, brand names, and similar intangible property.

.07   Types of Nonpermissible Investments

To be entitled to the 85 percent dividends received deduction, the corporation must invest the dividend amount in permitted investments. If the DRP provides for investing the full dividend amount in permitted investments, but the U.S. corporation invests less than the full amount of the dividend in permitted investments, the deduction can only be claimed on the amount invested. There is no penalty for amounts invested in a nonpermitted investment.

> **EXAMPLE**
>
> A U.S. corporation receives a cash dividend of $100 from its CFC. The U.S. corp's DRP specifies $100 of permitted investments, but the corporation only invests $90 in permitted investments described in the DRP. Ten dollars of the dividend received does not qualify for the 85 percent deduction and will be taxed at the normal corporate rate. The remaining $90 qualifies for the 85 percent deduction.

Described here are examples of disallowed investments. These examples are representative but not exhaustive.

Executive compensation. This treatment is mandated by the statute. In some circumstances, the taxpayer may treat the 10 highest paid employees as the proscribed individuals.

Intercompany transactions. Nonpermissible transactions include sales, leases, distributions, and obligations between affiliated members of a consolidated group.

Dividends and other shareholder distributions. This disallowance applies regardless of the treatment of the distribution under Code Sec. 301 (which defines a dividend).

Stock redemptions and buybacks. This exclusion was a major disappointment to practitioners. Treasury said it gave the issue a hard look.

Portfolio investments in business entities. Portfolio investments refer to investments in stock of other companies, partnerships, real estate investment trusts, and S corporations.

Purchase of Debt Instruments. This exclusion applies to purchases of corporate bonds, Treasury bills, and municipal bonds.

Tax Payments. Tax payments comprise federal, state, and local taxes on the U.S. company's trade or business, including income, property, and excise taxes.

¶220   ELECTION AND REPORTING REQUIREMENTS

A corporation elects to apply the Code Sec. 965 repatriation provision by Filing Form 8895, "One-Time Dividends-received Deduction for Certain Cash Dividends from Controlled Foreign Corporations," with a timely filed return (including extensions) for the election year. If the taxpayer filed its return before Form 8895 was released, the election should be made on a statement attached to the return. The IRS issued a draft of Form 8895 on May 11, 2005, and a final draft of Form 8895 on August 19, 2005, when it released Notice 2005-64. For returns filed before January 13, 2005, taxpayers may file an amended return by the due date (including extensions) of the tax return for the election year.

U.S. shareholders receiving dividends from a CFC, partnership, or disregarded entity can identify on Form 8895 which dividend will be treated as meeting the base-period amount and which dividend is eligible for the 85 percent deduction.

COMMENT

This identification is important because, in addition to the 85 percent deduction, it determines which dividends are subject to the foreign tax credit disallowance and the expense disallowance.

In general, Notice 2005-64 does not permit taxpayers to treat one dividend payment as carrying the 85 percent deduction and another dividend as carrying the 15 percent nondeductible amount. However, if no identification is made, a pro-rata portion of each dividend received will be treated as an eligible dividend. It is permissible to designate a portion of a dividend as qualified to avoid exceeding the ceiling on qualified dividends that generate the 85 percent deduction.

If the U.S. corporation takes the 85 percent deduction and has a net operating loss (NOL) that exceeds its taxable income, the corporation still must pay income tax on the 15 percent of the dividend that is taxable. The U.S. corporation's taxable income must at least equal the amount of nondeductible CFC dividends. The corporation cannot increase its NOL for the election year by the amount of income it had to recognize. However, if deductible expenses and losses for the election year exceeds the U.S. shareholder's gross income (excluding the nondeductible CFC dividends), the excess deductions can be treated as an NOL.

Notice 2005-38 reduces each eligible dividend by a pro rata amount if there is increase in the CFC's related-party debt. Notice 2005-64 permits the U.S. shareholder to identify which dividend payment will be reduced and which will be a qualifying dividend.

Information must be reported to the IRS annually regarding investments made under a domestic reinvestment plan, until the full amount has been reinvested. Taxpayers must file a statement with their return describing the investment in general, the amount of the investment, the percentage of total investments completed under the DRP, and whether the investment is an alternative investment.

STUDY QUESTION

---

12. If a taxpayer does **not** identify which dividend carries the 85 percent deduction, under Notice 2005-64:

   a. The deductible and nondeductible percentages must be taken from the same total dividend.

   b. A pro-rata portion of each dividend received will be treated as an eligible dividend.

   c. A portion of the dividend may not be designated as qualified to avoid exceeding the ceiling on qualified dividends generating the 85 percent deduction.

   d. None of the above occurs.

.01   Maintenance of Record

The taxpayer must maintain a record of its investments and provide the records within 30 days of an IRS request. The taxpayer should keep records of its investments for three years after the year in which it reinvests the full amount of its qualifying dividends. Records should also be retained for any period that the taxpayer extended the statute of limitations. The documentation should include, if relevant, an allocation between permitted and nonpermitted investments. Records must be retained and provided on request for: any dividend paid through an intermediary partnership; adjustments to base period inclusions or APB 23 amounts because of a merger or acquisition; an adjustment to the initial measurement date related-party debt; a permitted investment by a U.S. shareholder that is not the member of the consolidated group that adopted the DRP that applies to the investment; investments that satisfy more than one

DRP, and the DRP that the investment applies to; and domestic corporations that participate in more than one election year.

The records must provide the name, address, and tax identification number of all relevant parties, plus relevant dates and the amount of the adjustment resulting from the transactions.

If the investments of a former member of a consolidated group will satisfy the group's DRP, the reporting obligation remains with the group, as long as the group or common parent continues to exist.

.02   Facts and Circumstances

Taxpayers must be able to establish, based on the facts and circumstances, that they have satisfied or will satisfy the requirement to invest the dividend amount pursuant to the DRP. Relevant facts and circumstances include:

- The time period in the plan for making particular investments;
- The plan's specificity in describing anticipated investments;
- The extent to which the taxpayer has invested the dividend amount;
- Compliance with reporting requirements;
- The taxpayer's willingness to extend the statute of limitations for the election year;
- The taxpayer's willingness to enter into a multiyear agreement regarding its completion of the DRP; and
- The taxpayer's willingness to satisfy reporting and documentation requirements.

Audits. Practitioners say that Code Sec. 965 will raise a lot of audit issues. On the other hand, IRS officials have said that they do not expect international examiners to spend a lot of time auditing compliance with a temporary two-year provision.

Nevertheless, practitioners have indicated that corporations will not want to violate the Code Sec. 965 requirements, because the consequences—full taxation of the repatriated dividends—would be drastic. Practitioners say that it is better that the IRS brings clarity to Code Sec. 965 through published guidance, rather than in an audit. "We don't need an issue," one practitioner declared. "We need to be right."

Safe harbor. A safe harbor, based on a showing of progress toward completion of the planned U.S. investments, may be used to establish conclusively that the domestic reinvestment plan requirement has been satisfied. The requirements are that:

- At least 60 percent of the required investments have been made or are subject to a binding contract or commitment with an unrelated person; and
- The investments are specifically enumerated in Notice 2005-10.

The taxpayer must report by the second year following the election year that the safe harbor requirements have been met and that the taxpayer will make the remaining investments by the end of the fourth year following the election year. The taxpayer may cease annual reporting after submitting this statement.

Additional representations are required if the taxpayer's investments include the repayment of debt or the funding of a qualified pension plan.

STUDY QUESTIONS

---

13. All of the following are relevant facts and circumstances *except:*

a. The extent to which the taxpayer has invested the dividend amount

b. Compliance with reporting requirements

c. The plan's specificity in describing anticipated investments

d. All of the above are relevant facts and circumstances

14. The safe harbor for completing planned U.S. investments under Notice 2005-10 requires that at least _____ percent of investments have been made or committed to.

a. 51

b. 60

c. 75

d. 90

¶225   MERGERS, ACQUISITIONS, AND DISPOSALS

Sections 6 and 8 of Notice 2005-38 discuss the effect of acquisitions and disposals of corporations that occurred from 1998 until the beginning of a company's election year. In determining the base period amount, the rules in Notice 2005-38 focus on mergers, acquisitions, and disposals of the U.S. group of corporations.

COMMENT

The IRS said that this section of the law is modeled on Code Sec. 41(f), which allows a research credit for payments exceeding a base amount.

.01   Base Period Inclusions

Base period inclusions, i.e., the history of a CFC's dividend payments to a U.S. corporation (parent or subsidiary) as calculated under Code Section

965(b)(2), are attributes of the U.S. corporation that remain with the domestic company if it is sold or acquired. The APB 23 limit—i.e., the amount of earnings reported as permanently invested overseas and attributed to the foreign subsidiaries of a domestic company (as calculated under Code Sec. 965(b)(1)—also is an attribute of the U.S. company.

If a U.S. corporation joins a consolidated group, the acquiring group must increase its base period inclusions and APB 23 limit by the amounts allocated to the corporation joining the group. If a U.S. corporation leaves the group, the selling group must reduce these items by the amounts allocated to the departing corporation.

If a U.S. parent disposes of a U.S. subsidiary with a history of receiving a high amount of foreign dividends, the corporation acquiring the U.S. subsidiary must apply that history to determine its base period amount. These rules also apply when a U.S. subsidiary is liquidated or when a U.S. corporation is part of a tax-free reorganization involving another U.S. corporation.

If a U.S. corporation is acquired after the end of the acquiring group's base period, the acquiring group must include in its base period all five years of the acquired corporation ending on or before June 30, 2003. The acquired group's amount is added to the acquiring group's amounts on a year-by-year basis for the five years.

If the acquisition occurs before the end of the acquiring group's base period, the acquired corporation's tax year that ends when it is acquired shall correspond to the acquiring group's year that ends on or before the acquisition. The acquiring group takes into account the base period inclusions from the corresponding years of the acquired group. The acquiring group may take into account all five years of the acquired corporation, even if the acquiring group did not exist in its full five-year base period.

.02   Transactions Involving CFCs

In contrast, the sale or acquisition of a CFC does not affect the base period amount of the U.S. parent or the APB 23 limit. Thus, a U.S. corporation cannot benefit from acquiring a foreign subsidiary with a history of paying a low amount of dividends, or selling a foreign corporation with a history of paying all its earnings to the U.S. parent.

EXAMPLE

A foreign subsidiary of a U.S. corporation pays a $100 dividend each year to a U.S. subsidiary. Prior to the election year, the CFC is sold to an unrelated corporation. The U.S. corporation's base period amount is $100; this is unchanged by the sale of the CFC. However, if the U.S. parent had sold its U.S. subsidiary, the sale would clear out the $100 base period amount.

.03   Exception

Corporations do not have to make adjustments in certain cases. If a group sells a U.S. shareholder during its election year, the group does not have to reduce its base period inclusions or APB 23 limit. The acquiring group may still increase these amounts when it acquires the U.S. shareholder. The movement of a U.S. corporation before the APB 23 determination date will naturally show up in the calculations of this amount by the selling and acquiring groups, so no adjustment is required at the time of the sale.

.04   Spin-offs

A corporation that is spun off is treated as having existed for the same period that its shareholder was in existence. The Tax Code calls for an allocation of the dividend history in the event of a spin-off, based on the corporations' respective interests in the CFC after the spin-off. These rules apply only if the distributing corporation and the corporation that was spun off both continue to be U.S. shareholders of the CFC.

The spin-off of a controlled corporation during the base period is treated in the same manner as a disposition of the corporation. If, because of a base period spin-off, the controlled corporation leaves a consolidated group, then the base period inclusions are allocated between the old-group and the spun-off corporation (and other corporations that left the old group and are affiliated with that corporation), in proportion to their respective interests in each CFC owned by both the old group and the spun-off corporation immediately after the spin-off. The inclusions are further allocated among the members of each group in proportion to their interests in each CFC immediately after the spin-off.

Dividend ceiling. With regard to the dividend limitation, if the spin-off occurs after the determination date of the APB 23 limitation, the U.S. parent is not a member of a consolidated group, and the stock of a CFC is transferred between the parent and a spunoff subsidiary, the limitation is allocated in proportion to the interests of each corporation in the CFC immediately after the spin-off.

If a member of a consolidated group is spun off and leaves the group, the APB 23 limitation is allocated based on the parties' interests in each CFC owned by both parties immediately after the spin-off. The limitation is then allocated among the members of the parent's group and if applicable, the subsidiary's new group.

STUDY QUESTION

15. A spun-off corporation that continues to be a U.S. shareholder of a CFC is treated as:

   a. A newly formed entity with no dividend history
   b. Having an existence separate from its parent
   c. Having existed for the same period that its shareholder existed
   d. None of the above is its treatment

¶230   CONCLUSION

The 85 percent deduction for repatriated dividends is a generous benefit available to the U.S. corporation that owns a controlled foreign corporation. U.S. corporations must be prepared to act quickly. The election to claim the deduction must be made on a timely-filed income tax return (including extensions) for the election year, which can be no later than the corporation's first tax year beginning on or after October 22, 2004.

Treasury and the IRS issued three notices in 2005 that provide the guidance needed to claim the deduction. Practitioners should look carefully at this guidance and become familiar with the extensive requirements for claiming the deduction. U.S. corporations must be careful to retain records demonstrating that the dividends were reinvested in permissible investments within a reasonable period.

CPE NOTE

When you have completed your study and review of chapters 1 and 2 which comprise this Module, you may wish to take the Final Exam for this Module. CPE instructions can be found on page 221.

The Module 1 Final Exam Questions begin on page 223. The Module 1 Answer Sheet can be found on pages 243 and 245.

For you convenience, you can also take this Final Exam online at www.cchtestingcenter.com.

MODULE 2 — CHAPTER 3

The Alternative Minimum Tax: Understanding the Problem, Anticipating Solutions

This chapter helps practitioners to understand the basic structure and current rules governing the alternative minimum tax (AMT), the impact that the AMT has on a rapidly growing number of taxpayers across an increasingly broad spectrum, and last but not least, the future of the AMT.

LEARNING OBJECTIVES

Upon completion of this chapter, you will be able to:

- Understand the underpinnings of the AMT and why it came about;
- Discuss the AMT's current state and which taxpayers are impacted most;
- Calculate basic AMT liability;
- Identify the triggers that generate AMT liability;
- Understand the basic planning techniques for minimizing AMT liability; and
- Discuss options for reforming the AMT and how to anticipate future changes.

¶301 INTRODUCTION

The AMT is a system of taxation parallel to the regular income tax regime. Congress designed it in the 1960s to ensure that high-income taxpayers—both corporate and noncorporate (including estates and trusts)—would pay at least a minimum tax. Without the AMT Congress feared that some well-off tax-payers would take too many tax deductions, exemptions, credits, and losses, and end up escaping the bulk of their tax liability, and in some cases, escaping taxation entirely.

Since the AMT's creation in 1969, it has been tweaked and has endured three official revisions. The first AMT, which lasted until 1976, imposed a 10 percent add-on tax when the sum of eight main tax preference items (TPIs, as discussed in their current state later), exceeded $30,000.

The eight TPIs summed were excess investment interest income; accelerated depreciation on personal property; accelerated depreciation on real property; amortization of certified pollution control facilities; amortization of railroad rolling stock; tax benefits from stock options; bad debt deductions of financial institutions; and capital gains deductions.

In 1976, Congress made two changes. The add-on tax increased from 10 percent to 15 percent and the threshold for triggering the add-on was reduced from $30,000 to $10,000. Two years later, Congress removed the add-on for capital gains deductions and created a complicated progressive rate structure. In 1982, Congress repealed the 15 percent add-on entirely. Finally, in 1986, AMT underwent another makeover in the *Taxpayer Relief Act of 1986*. Now, when AMT applies, it is no longer an add-on, but replaces regular tax entirely. Nevertheless, many people continue to refer to their AMT liability as the "extra amount of tax" they need to pay over and above what would be due under the regular tax system.

AMT applicable rates are 26 percent on amounts not exceeding $175,000 ($87,500 for married taxpayers filing separately) and 28 percent on amounts exceeding that level. The rates are applied to an amount that is reduced by a substantial exemption amount that varies depending on the taxpayers filing status as married filing jointly, unmarried single, etc... Lower rates apply to capital gains that are subject to the same lower rates as are applied for regular tax purposes.

AMT, therefore, runs parallel to the regular federal income taxation system. It serves as a recapture mechanism, reclaiming some of the tax breaks otherwise available to taxpayers who are considered to have too many tax breaks. Favorable tax treatments under the regular tax, when viewed under AMT, are curbed by adjustments and preferences. Adjustments may increase or decrease a taxpayer's income for AMT relative to regular taxable income, while preferences only increase it.

A taxpayer's AMT liability is the excess of tentative AMT liability over the taxpayer's regular tax liability. That excess must be paid in addition to the regular tax liability. AMT liability is calculated on Form 6251, "Alternative Minimum Tax—Individuals," for individuals, Form 4626, "Alternative Minimum Tax—Corporations," for corporations, or Schedule I of Form 1041, "U.S. Income Tax Return For Estates and Trusts," for Estates and Trusts.

¶305   THE GROWING GRASP OF THE AMT

.01   Impact of Nonindexing

In theory *all* taxpayers are potentially subject to the AMT (except small corporations, which are exempt by statute). There are no automatic exclusions for people within certain income levels, filing status, or other economic circumstances. Everyone hypothetically must go through the AMT computation before filing a return to test for possible AMT liability. Of course, some taxpayers fit the profile of the "typical" AMT candidate more than others.

Congress's original intent in implementing the alternative minimum tax was to target only the highest income taxpayers. These days, however, AMT is not just a concern for the ultra-rich; it is a growing "trap" for hundreds of thousands of middle-income taxpayers.

A major reason so many Americans are finding themselves ensnared by the AMT is that the income requirements under AMT are not indexed for inflation. According to the National Taxpayer Advocate, if the original 1969 exemption of $30,000 had been indexed for inflation, today it would be greater than $150,000. Instead, it hovers around $40,000 for single individuals and $58,000 for joint filers). The projections by the Congressional Budget Office estimate that by 2010, one-fifth of all taxpayers (approximately 30 million) will be liable for AMT.

> **COMMENT**
>
> Corporate AMT is another, separate battle being waged by opponents who believe it is the ultimate double tax, once on the corporate level and again for shareholders thrown into the AMT in part because of dividends passed through to them.

The complexity of the AMT baffles many taxpayers. The AMT calculations and rules are far more complex than those used to compute regular tax.

> **COMMENT**
>
> The Joint Committee on Taxation has estimated that less than 1 percent of all taxpayers with AMT liability prepare their own returns. The rest rely on the expertise of tax professionals to assist in the multistep calculations and complex rules. As more taxpayers find themselves liable for the AMT, they too likely will turn to tax professionals for help.

.02 Pluses and Minuses of the Tax

The AMT is not all bad. It is a huge revenue raiser for the federal government. Between 2005 and 2015, the Tax Policy Center estimates that the AMT will bring in $1.2 trillion in revenues. If the federal government were to abolish the AMT, it would lose approximately $600 billion in revenues over the next decade. Given its high rate of return, repeal of the AMT is unlikely, although politicians may tweak it and eventually call it something else to claim success. What is bad about the AMT, however, is that revenue may be extracted from taxpayers whom Congress originally never dreamed would be subject to the AMT. Planning for that group of taxpayers is especially urgent.

.03 Calculating AMT for Individuals

The first step in planning to reduce AMT liability is to understand the basic calculations.

An individual taxpayer's AMT liability is best determined by following Form 6251, "Alternative Minimum Tax—Individuals." If the tax calculated on Form 6521 is greater than the tax on a taxpayer's regular return, the taxpayer must pay the difference as AMT in addition to whatever regular tax he or she owes.

> **CAUTION**
>
> Taxpayers who may claim any general business credit, the qualified electric vehicle credit, the nonconventional source fuel credit, or the credit for prior year minimum tax must file a Form 6251.

Form 6521 sets out the following steps for determining AMT liability:

1. Calculate the taxpayer's regular taxable income.
2. Add back any personal exemption amounts claimed on the taxpayer's regular return into the taxable income.
3. Add back all AMT disallowed itemized deductions claimed on the taxpayer's regular return. Disallowed itemized deductions include home equity interest not used for actual improvement of the home, state and local taxes, employee business deductions, and medical and dental expenses. Taxpayers who took the standard deduction in computing regular tax instead of itemizing must add back the standard deduction because it is not allowed for the AMT.
4. Subtract any itemized deductions that cannot be claimed on Schedule A due to phaseout (income limits).
5. Subtract any refunds of state and local taxes.
6. Adjust taxable income for specific business-related tax preferences and adjustment items such as AMT net operating losses (NOLs) that are different than the disallowed regular net operating losses. The result is the adjusted minimum taxable income, or AMTI.
7. Subtract the AMT exemption amount from AMTI. The result will be the net AMTI.
8. Multiply the net AMTI from Step 7 by the AMT rate. This rate will be 26 percent up to $175,000, and 28 percent for any excess of $175,000 (adjusted for any net capital gains).
9. Subtract from the product of Step 8 any AMT-allowed credits.
10. Examine the AMT tax liability as well as the regular tax liability, and pay any excess AMT liability over the regular tax.

EXAMPLE

A family of five, including three minor aged children, has income of $300,000 annually, and no capital gain or dividend income. The family claims itemized deductions of approximately $50,000, including $22,000 in state income and real estate taxes, $5,000 in personal property taxes, $13,000 in unreimbursed health care costs, and $5,000 in mortgage interest used to repay credit card debt. None of these deductions is permitted under AMT, as will be discussed later. Assuming in 2005 this family has approximately $250,000 in taxable income, this family would owe approximately $63,000 in regular tax, and $65,000 under AMT. In 2006, however, the same family with the same income ($245,000 of which is taxable), and the same deductions would owe only $61,000 in regular tax, but would owe $69,000 in AMT, because none of the deductions qualify and AMT is not indexed for inflation.

Form 6251 is reproduced on the following two pages. If you would prefer to view and download this form electronically, please go to:

http://www.irs.gov/pub/irs-pdf/f6251.pdf.

Form **6251**	**Alternative Minimum Tax—Individuals**	OMB No. 1545-0227
	▶ See separate instructions.	2004
Department of the Treasury Internal Revenue Service (99)	▶ Attach to Form 1040 or Form 1040NR.	Attachment Sequence No. **32**
Name(s) shown on Form 1040		Your social security number

Part I Alternative Minimum Taxable Income (See instructions for how to complete each line.)

1	If filing Schedule A (Form 1040), enter the amount from Form 1040, line 40, and go to line 2. Otherwise, enter the amount from Form 1040, line 37, and go to line 7. (If less than zero, enter as a negative amount.)	**1**	
2	Medical and dental. Enter the **smaller** of Schedule A (Form 1040), line 4, **or** 2½ % of Form 1040, line 37	**2**	
3	Taxes from Schedule A (Form 1040), line 9	**3**	
4	Enter the home mortgage interest adjustment, if any, from line 6 of the worksheet on page 2 of the instructions	**4**	
5	Miscellaneous deductions from Schedule A (Form 1040), line 26	**5**	
6	If Form 1040, line 37, is over $142,700 (over $71,350 if married filing separately), enter the amount from line 9 of the **Itemized Deductions Worksheet** on page B-1 of the Instructions for Schedules A & B (Form 1040)	**6** (	)
7	Tax refund from Form 1040, line 10 or line 21	**7** (	)
8	Investment interest expense (difference between regular tax and AMT)	**8**	
9	Depletion (difference between regular tax and AMT)	**9**	
10	Net operating loss deduction from Form 1040, line 21. Enter as a positive amount	**10**	
11	Interest from specified private activity bonds exempt from the regular tax	**11**	
12	Qualified small business stock (7% of gain excluded under section 1202)	**12**	
13	Exercise of incentive stock options (excess of AMT income over regular tax income)	**13**	
14	Estates and trusts (amount from Schedule K-1 (Form 1041), line 9)	**14**	
15	Electing large partnerships (amount from Schedule K-1 (Form 1065-B), box 6)	**15**	
16	Disposition of property (difference between AMT and regular tax gain or loss)	**16**	
17	Depreciation on assets placed in service after 1986 (difference between regular tax and AMT)	**17**	
18	Passive activities (difference between AMT and regular tax income or loss)	**18**	
19	Loss limitations (difference between AMT and regular tax income or loss)	**19**	
20	Circulation costs (difference between regular tax and AMT)	**20**	
21	Long-term contracts (difference between AMT and regular tax income)	**21**	
22	Mining costs (difference between regular tax and AMT)	**22**	
23	Research and experimental costs (difference between regular tax and AMT)	**23**	
24	Income from certain installment sales before January 1, 1987	**24** (	)
25	Intangible drilling costs preference	**25**	
26	Other adjustments, including income-based related adjustments	**26**	
27	Alternative tax net operating loss deduction	**27** (	)
28	**Alternative minimum taxable income.** Combine lines 1 through 27. (If married filing separately and line 28 is more than $191,000, see page 6 of the instructions.)	**28**	

Part II Alternative Minimum Tax

29 Exemption. (If this form is for a child under age 14, see page 6 of the instructions.)

IF your filing status is . . .	AND line 28 is not over . . .	THEN enter on line 29 . . .		
Single or head of household	$112,500	$40,250	}	**29**
Married filing jointly or qualifying widow(er)	150,000	58,000		
Married filing separately	75,000	29,000		

If line 28 is **over** the amount shown above for your filing status, see page 6 of the instructions.

30	Subtract line 29 from line 28. If zero or less, enter -0- here and on lines 33 and 35 and stop here	**30**	
31	• If you reported capital gain distributions directly on Form 1040, line 13; you reported qualified dividends on Form 1040, line 9b; **or** you had a gain on both lines 15 and 16 of Schedule D (Form 1040) (as refigured for the AMT, if necessary), complete Part III on the back and enter the amount from line 55 here. • **All others:** If line 30 is $175,000 or less ($87,500 or less if married filing separately), multiply line 30 by 26% (.26). Otherwise, multiply line 30 by 28% (.28) and subtract $3,500 ($1,750 if married filing separately) from the result. }	**31**	
32	Alternative minimum tax foreign tax credit (see page 7 of the instructions)	**32**	
33	Tentative minimum tax. Subtract line 32 from line 31	**33**	
34	Tax from Form 1040, line 43 (minus any tax from Form 4972 and any foreign tax credit from Form 1040, line 46). If you used Schedule J to figure your tax, the amounts for lines 43 and 46 of Form 1040 must be refigured without using Schedule J (see page 8 of the instructions)	**34**	
35	**Alternative minimum tax.** Subtract line 34 from line 33. If zero or less, enter -0-. Enter here and on Form 1040, line 44	**35**	

For Paperwork Reduction Act Notice, see page 8 of the instructions.   Cat. No. 13600G   Form **6251** (2004)

Form 6251 (2004)   Page **2**

Part III   **Tax Computation Using Maximum Capital Gains Rates**

36 Enter the amount from Form 6251, line 30 . . . .   **36**

37 Enter the amount from line 6 of the Qualified Dividends and Capital Gain Tax
Worksheet in the instructions for Form 1040, line 43, or the amount from line
13 of the Schedule D Tax Worksheet on page D-9 of the instructions for
Schedule D (Form 1040), whichever applies (as refigured for the AMT, if
necessary) (see page 8 of the instructions) **37**

38 Enter the amount from Schedule D (Form 1040), line 19 (as refigured for the
AMT, if necessary) (see page 8 of the instructions) **38**

39 If you did not complete a Schedule D Tax Worksheet for the regular tax or
the AMT, enter the amount from line 37. Otherwise, add lines 37 and 38, and
enter the **smaller** of that result or the amount from line 10 of the Schedule
D Tax Worksheet (as refigured for the AMT, if necessary) **39**

40 Enter the **smaller** of line 36 or line 39 . . . .   **40**

41 Subtract line 40 from line 36 . . . .   **41**

42 If line 41 is $175,000 or less ($87,500 or less if married filing separately), multiply line 41 by 26% (.26).
Otherwise, multiply line 41 by 28% (.28) and subtract $3,500 ($1,750 if married filing separately) from the
result . . . . ▶   **42**

43 Enter:
• $58,100 if married filing jointly or qualifying widow(er),
• $29,050 if single or married filing separately, or **43**
• $38,900 if head of household.

44 Enter the amount from line 7 of the Qualified Dividends and Capital Gain Tax
Worksheet in the instructions for Form 1040, line 43, or the amount from line
14 of the Schedule D Tax Worksheet on page D-9 of the instructions for
Schedule D (Form 1040), whichever applies (as figured for the regular tax). If
you did not complete either worksheet for the regular tax, enter -0- . . .   **44**

45 Subtract line 44 from line 43. If zero or less, enter -0- **45**

46 Enter the **smaller** of line 36 or line 37 . . . .   **46**

47 Enter the **smaller** of line 45 or line 46 . . . .   **47**

48 Multiply line 47 by 5% (.05) . . . . ▶   **48**

49 Subtract line 47 from line 46 . . . .   **49**

50 Multiply line 49 by 15% (.15) . . . . ▶   **50**

If line 38 is zero or blank, skip lines 51 and 52 and go to line 53. Otherwise, go to line 51.

51 Subtract line 46 from line 40 . . . .   **51**

52 Multiply line 51 by 25% (.25) . . . . ▶   **52**

53 Add lines 42, 48, 50, and 52 . . . .   **53**

54 If line 36 is $175,000 or less ($87,500 or less if married filing separately), multiply line 36 by 26% (.26).
Otherwise, multiply line 36 by 28% (.28) and subtract $3,500 ($1,750 if married filing separately) from the
result **54**

55 Enter the **smaller** of line 53 or line 54 here and on line 31 . . . .   **55**

Form **6251** (2004)

STUDY QUESTIONS

1. A taxpayer's AMT liability is essentially the excess of tentative AMT liability over:
   a. The taxpayer's adjusted gross income
   b. The taxpayer's income minus the standard deduction(s)
   c. The taxpayer's regular tax liability
   d. None of the above

2. In determining AMT liability, the practitioner starts with the taxpayer's regular taxable income, adds back personal exemption amounts to the taxable income, then:
   a. Subtracts state and local tax refund amounts
   b. Subtracts the AMT exemption amount from AMTI
   c. Adjusts taxable income for any adjustment items different from the disallowed regular losses
   d. Adds back all disallowed itemized deductions that are claimed on the taxpayer's Form 1040 for regular tax

NOTE

Answers to Study Questions, with feedback to both the correct and incorrect responses, are proved in a special section beginning on page 191.

¶310 CALCULATING AMTI

.01 Tax Preference Items

The crux of the AMT is a taxpayer's **alternative minimum taxable income (AMTI).** A taxpayer's AMTI is the key figure for determining how much of a taxpayer's excess deductions, credits, exemptions, and other tax benefits and preferences will be recaptured. For the unincorporated business taxpayer or those receiving tax benefits from pass-through entities such as partnerships and S corporations, AMTI includes add-backs (additions to regular taxable income) for **tax preference items (TPIs).**

COMMENT

Individuals with or without business-related TPIs must still make adjustments to account for personal exemptions, the portion of itemized deductions disallowed under the AMT, the portion of any itemized deduction, if any, disallowed under regular tax because of phaseout income limits, and state and local income tax refunds.

TPIs are used for recapturing business-related tax benefits in two ways:

- A straightforward, dollar-for-dollar add-back of all or a predetermined portion of certain business-related deductions and exclusions that were claimed in arriving at taxable income under the regular tax system. Remember that taxable income under the regular tax is the starting point for determining AMTI; or
- A change from the regular tax in the method used to determine a particular business-related deduction. This change usually, although not always, reduces the amount of the deduction or increases the amount of income otherwise subject to regular tax. This in turn increases the starting-point amount for AMTI.

COMMENT

In the regular tax system, TPIs lower a taxpayer's taxable income. Because the AMT adds back TPIs into taxable income, the tax breaks represented by TPIs are recaptured.

STUDY QUESTION

> **3.** Once TPIs and NOLs that differ in the AMT system from regular income taxation are figured into taxable income, the result is the taxpayer's AMTI. *True or False?*

.02 Form 6251 "Adjustments"—Primary Guide to AMT Computations

A careful examination of Form 6251, "Alternative Minimum Tax—Individuals," helps to customize tax planning for clients. By seeing what itemized deductions and tax preferences must be added back into taxable income for AMT purposes, an individual can determine whether avoiding certain situations that generate those "excessive" deductions or preferences might make sense (see also ¶325, Planning to Avoid (or Minimize) AMT Liability for further AMT-reduction strategies).

Form 6251 contains 22 line items for "give-back" adjustments for deductions and other tax preferences. Four additional lines items are devoted to items that will lower the amount of income potentially subject to AMT.

> **COMMENT**
>
> It is important that the taxpayer's Form 1040 be completed before the practitioner begins to complete Form 6251, because entries for many of the lines are dependent on amounts entered on the 1040.

STUDY QUESTION

> **4.** A useful approach for practitioners to employ as they plan for taxpayers to minimize or avoid the AMT is to:
>
> **a.** Examine Form 6251 to determine which add-backs apply to the taxpayers who might be subject to the AMT.
>
> **b.** Review last year's return for omitted itemized deductions to claim when the AMT form is completed next year.
>
> **c.** Maximize the number and amount of itemized deductions claimed on the Form 1040.
>
> **d.** None of the above proves useful.

Medical and dental expense deductions. For AMT purposes, deductible medical expenses are only those in excess of 10 percent of adjusted gross income, not in excess of the 7.5 percent amount allowed for regular income tax purposes. As a result, an individual must add back any itemized medical deductions taken for regular tax purposes up to a maximum 2.5 percent of adjusted gross income.

Tax add-backs. Taxes deducted on a regular tax return are added back for AMT. These include personal property taxes, foreign income taxes, state or local taxes, or foreign real property taxes. The only taxes that can reduce a noncorporate taxpayer's AMTI are the itemized deductions for federal estate tax paid in respect of the decedent and the federal generation-skipping tax paid on income distributions.

> **COMMENT**
>
> Residents of "high-tax" states and municipalities are clearly at a disadvantage because of this state and local tax add-back.

The add-back is sweeping. All taxes, except for generation-skipping transfer taxes on income distributions, are entered on Form 6251. This includes all state and local general sales taxes entered on Form 1040, line

9, in lieu of deducting property taxes. Business-related taxes, however, are not part of this add-back because they are taken as a deduction on Form 1040, Schedule C, rather than as a personal itemized deduction on Form 1040, Schedule A.

> **PLANNING TIP**
>
> A taxpayer with AMT liability in only one tax year may be able to save by paying state, local, and foreign taxes that are not deductible in another year. This is possible because taxpayers often have the choice of paying a tax at the end of one year or the beginning of the next.

Home mortgage interest adjustment. The deduction for home mortgage interest is also treated differently under the AMT from treatment under regular taxes.

The only eligible mortgage for AMT purposes is one whose proceeds were actually used to build, buy, or substantially improve an individual taxpayer's main or second home. For a main home to qualify, it must be the taxpayer's main dwelling (a house, apartment, condo, or stationary mobile home) for family use. **Family** is defined as any of the taxpayer's brothers, sisters, spouses, ancestors, and lineal descendants.

> **COMMENT**
>
> Especially affected are those individuals taking out home equity loans or refinancing first mortgages to buy consumer items such as a new car or to pay for a vacation. Interest allocated to mortgage money used for those purposes must be added back.

Like the regular tax deduction, the AMT mortgage interest deduction can arise from a first mortgage, second mortgage, or home equity loan. However, unlike the $100,000 mortgage amount for which interest is allowed for regular tax regardless of whether it is used for home improvements, there is no cushion in computing AMT for money used for purposes other than mortgaged property improvements.

> **CAUTION**
>
> Because not all home mortgage interest is eligible, planners should make note of what will qualify and what will add to the taxpayer's income, encouraging the taxpayer to make the necessary adjustments.

STUDY QUESTIONS

5. All of the following are add-backs of deductions allowed on the Form 1040 when the AMT liability is calculated *except:*
   a. State sales taxes deduction on federal Form 1040, line 9
   b. Interest deduction on home equity loans used to pay off credit card balances
   c. Medical expenses of between 7.5 percent and 10 percent
   d. All of the above are add-backs

6. The deduction for taxes that may be claimed on the Form 1040 but that must be added back in calculation of the AMT include all of the following *except:*
   a. Federal income tax due
   b. Foreign income tax paid
   c. Personal property tax paid
   d. All of the above must be added back

Miscellaneous itemized deductions. Miscellaneous itemized deductions from Form 1040, line 26, are added back in their entirety for determining AMT liability. For AMT purposes, therefore, investment expenses, unreimbursed employee expenses, union dues and tax preparation fees all completely lose their ability to reduce taxable income.

PLANNING TIP

Taxpayers who do not have a reimbursement arrangement with their employers for business expenses may find that losing their miscellaneous employee business expense deduction because of AMT will provide sufficient reason to press the employer to change its policy.

Investment interest. Investment interest is interest from debt incurred or continued to buy or carry property held for investment purposes. It is reported on Form 4952 "Investment Interest Expense Deduction." Taxpayers who completed Form 4952, for a regular tax return must fill out an additional Form 4952 according to specialized AMT instructions provided with the Form 6251.

Tax-exempt interest earned by the taxpayer from **specified private activity bonds,** also called **private activity municipal bonds,** must be added back into income to determine AMTI. Private activity bonds are state and local bonds issued to provide financing for private, nongovernmental activities, such as industrial development, student loans, and low-income housing.

PLANNING TIP

If the bonds were issued before September 1, 1986, and meet certain other qualifications, they will not be subject to the preference.

The interest on private activity municipal bonds can be reduced (but not below zero) by any deduction that would have been allowable if the interest were includible in gross income for regular tax.

CAUTION

Exempt interest dividends paid by regulated investment companies (mutual funds) may be treated as income, so be sure to check the instructions carefully to see if the taxpayer's dividends will qualify.

The AMT can take a significant bite out of bond returns. In one case, because of the private activity bond add-back, 40 percent of a bond return was subject to AMT, scaring away many investors. To counter this, investment banks now offer AMT-free bonds. Like all investments, though, these bonds should be selected carefully, as some taxpayers find that bonds subject to AMT actually suit their investment objectives better, given the greater yields. Note, too, that the names investment companies are giving to their bonds are not always indicative of the true AMT liability for that particular fund.

EXAMPLE

Alicia purchased private activity bonds and received $100,000 in interest that was not included under regular tax. Alicia had expenses of $8,000 in connection with her investment activities, $2,000 of which would have been otherwise deductible, but were disallowed as they were allocable to the tax-exempt interest. Therefore, on her AMT return, Alicia must increase her AMTI to include the $100,000 from the private activity bond, less the $2,000, for a total addition of $98,000.

Depletion. Depletion must be refigured for AMT. To determine depletion limit for AMT, use only the taxpayer's income and deductions allowed for the AMT. This will account for AMT limitations on taxable income from property. The proper amount on the Form 6251 will be the difference between the regular tax and the AMT deduction.

Qualified small business stock. If, for regular tax purposes, the 50 percent exclusion was taken under Code Sec. 1202 for gain on qualified small business stock held for more than five years (see Schedule D of Form 1040), 42 percent of that excluded amount must be added back for AMT purposes.

Exercise of incentive stock options. In determining AMTI, a taxpayer generally must include in income an exercise of an incentive stock option (ISO) under Code Sec. 422(b). This differs from computing regular tax, which does not recognize income on the exercise of an ISO as long as the stock is not sold in the year of exercise. For AMT purposes, the taxpayer must include any excess of the fair market value of the stock when the rights in that stock first become transferable over the amount paid for the ISO to acquire the stock.

COMMENT

Especially during the late 1990s and early 2000s, ISO forced many high-tech employees into AMT territory on the high-bargain element they received on exercise of the options, only to find that the value of the stock suddenly dropped the following year and couldn't even be sold for enough to cover the AMT tax that they discovered was due in the previous year. This "twilight zone" situation continues to haunt taxpayers, especially in the high-tech zones, and may be one of the "straws" that break the proverbial camel's back in connection with AMT liability and force some legislative solution.

STUDY QUESTION

7. All of the following are subject to the AMT calculation of AMTI *except:*

   a. All of the miscellaneous itemized deductions claimed on line 26 of Form 1040
   b. All tax-exempt interest earned from private activity municipal bonds
   c. The entire 50 percent excluded amount of gain on the sale of qualified small business stock
   d. All of the above are subject to the AMTI calculation

Disposition of property. Refiguring is necessary to determine any AMT due from property disposition in four areas. This calculation is one of the primary reasons AMT deviates so dramatically from the computation of regular tax for many taxpayers and is one of the more confusing calculations for many taxpayers. The refiguring is necessary if there is:

- Gain or loss from sales, exchanges, or involuntary conversions of business property as reported on Form 4797, "Sales of Business Property";
- Casualty gain or loss to business or other income-producing property as reported on Form 4684, "Casualties and Thefts";
- Ordinary income not accounted for as Form 4797 or casualty gain or loss property, or any other line in Form 6251 from disposition of property; and
- Capital gain or loss, including any carryover, which is different under AMT, reported on Schedule D of Form 1040, "Capital Gains and Losses." The $3,000 capital loss limitation for regular tax applies separately under AMT, and the instructions for Form 6251 include in-depth instructions, as well as examples for guidance.

Depreciation. A taxpayer generally will have to recalculate depreciation for AMT, because AMT generally requires a slower write-off. The instructions to Form 6251 outline dozens of specific instances in which depreciation must or must not be refigured as part of determining AMTI. If depreciation must be refigured, it is calculated by using the Alternative Depreciation System (ADS), with the same convention used for regular tax. It is figured by subtracting the AMT deduction for depreciation from the regular tax deduction and entering the result. If the AMT deduction is more than the regular tax deduction, it must be entered as a negative amount.

CAUTION

Class life for AMT may not necessarily be the same as under regular tax. Generally, adjustments and preferences for depreciation, as well as the applicable depreciation system, differ between Code Sec. 1250 and Code Sec. 1245 property. The year in which the property was put in service has significant impact as well.

Passive activities. Generally, deduction of passive, nonfarm activities must follow the rules limiting deductibility for regular tax. This is true for individuals, estates and trusts, closely held C corporations, and personal service corporations. Deductions for passive losses may only be deducted against passive income. However, under AMT, a taxpayer must reduce the amount of denied losses by the amount of any insolvency for that tax year. Passive activities do not account for qualified housing interest and must be adjusted to eliminate tax preferences, as is necessary under other AMT rules.

PLANNING TIP

Reporting passive activities is one of the special cases in which keeping extensive records for both AMT and regular tax is crucial because the amount of any AMT passive activity loss that is not deductible and is carried forward will probably differ from the amount of regular tax. To determine the difference, enter the amount that would be reported on that taxpayer's Schedule C, C-EZ, E, F, or Form 4835 for AMT, and subtract the amount that would be reported for regular tax. If the AMT loss is greater than the loss claimed for regular tax, the AMT gain is less than the regular tax gain, or the calculations show an AMT loss and a regular tax gain, enter the adjustment as a negative amount.

EXAMPLE

Calculating regular tax liability, Ted has a passive loss deduction of $15,000 for net losses. The losses are partially based on a tax preference. Ted's AMT liability is determined by calculating depreciation deductions under the alternative depreciation system (ADS). That means Ted has a passive loss deduction of only $5000 to lessen AMTI. Because depreciation deductions have already been adjusted from the passive loss preference determination, Ted need not include them in any adjustment for tax preferences.

Passive farm shelter losses. Noncorporate taxpayers who do not materially participate in farming but use a farming tax shelter to avoid tax liability under regular tax may not deduct passive farming losses when calculating AMTI. Taxpayers may not net gains and losses from one activity disallowed as deductions in one year and may be claimed as a deduction from income on that activity the following year.

COMMENT

A farm tax shelter is a farm syndicate or a passive farming activity in which the taxpayer (or the taxpayer's spouse) does not materially participate in the farming activity or business.

Loss limitations. AMT also accounts for loss limitations not related to passive activities or tax shelter farms. Again, it is important that the taxpayer maintain sufficient records for both AMT and regular tax. Why? Because the gain or loss the taxpayer has for which they are not at risk will likely differ after taking into account all AMT adjustments and preferences than under regular tax. This is true also of the taxpayer's basis in partnerships and S corps.

Circulation costs. Circulation costs, the expenditures to establish, maintain, or increase the circulation of a newspaper, magazine, or other periodical, are deducted in full for the year they are incurred or paid under the regular tax. Under AMT, however, circulation costs must be capitalized and amortized over three years.

Mining costs. If a taxpayer expensed mining, exploration, and development costs expenditures in their regular tax computation, the taxpayer must, under AMT, capitalize and amortize those expenses over 10 years, as opposed to deducting them in full for the year they are paid or incurred under regular tax. However, if the taxpayer chose to use the 10 year write-off for the regular tax, the adjustment need not be made. Also, if a mine incurs a loss, any expenditures that have been capitalized but not yet amortized may be deducted from the taxpayer's AMTI. When mining property that generated mining exploration and development is sold, its adjusted basis must be computed under AMT guidelines to determine any gain or loss under AMT. The disparity between a gain or loss for AMT purposes is considered a tax preference adjustment in the year of the sale of the property.

Research and experimental costs. Research and experimental costs that can be deducted in full during the year that they are paid or incurred for regular tax must be capitalized and amortized over 10 years for AMT calculations. For AMT, the amount that matters is the difference between regular tax and AMT deduction. If the AMT deduction is greater, enter the amount on the return as a negative value. Losses for property are also handled like mining and explorations costs, and likewise if the taxpayer elected the optional 10-year write-off for regular tax the adjustment for AMT need not be made. However, with research and experimental costs, the taxpayer should not make the AMT adjustment for costs paid or incurred in connection with activities in which the taxpayer materially participated under the passive activity rules.

Foreign tax credit. Deserving special mention is how the AMT handles the foreign tax credit (FTC). The FTC is the only credit that directly offsets liability under AMT. It may offset up to 90 percent of AMT liability. It is called the Alternative Minimum Foreign Tax Credit, AMT-FTC, thanks to the American Jobs Creation Act of 2004.

Any excess AMT-FTC for a tax year may be carried back or forward the same way they are allowed to be carried back and forward under regular tax schemes. This means they may be carried back through the second preceding tax year, then the first, and then through the first through fifth succeeding tax years. It is calculated by taking the amount of foreign taxes on foreign source AMTI and then finding the limit on the size of an FTC that may be claimed during the tax year.

¶310

To find that limit, the taxpayer has two options. One method is to multiply the tentative minimum tax by the ratio of the taxpayer's foreign source regular taxable income to worldwide AMTI. The other method is to multiply the tentative minimum tax by the ratio of the taxpayer's foreign source AMTI to worldwide AMTI.

Net capital gain and qualified dividends. Like regular tax, AMT allows a lower maximum rate of net capital gains. For adjusted net capital gain of an individual, the maximum rate shared by both regular tax and AMT is 15 percent, and for adjusted net capital gains that would normally be taxed at a rate below 25 percent, the maximum rate is 5 percent. In 2008, that maximum will shrink to zero percent. If tax basis in property for AMT purposes is different from basis for regular tax (for example, because of depreciation adjustments), however, a further computational adjustment is required.

ATNOLD. Additional calculations must be made for any alternative tax net operating loss deduction (ATNOLD). A business taxpayer's alternative tax net operating loss is determined for a loss year by taking the excess of all other allowed deductions for AMTI over the income included in AMTI. ATNOLD, once determined, may be limited. The ATNOLD limitation will be 90 percent of that tentative amount. Any unused ATNOLD generally may be carried back two years or carried forward up to 20 years. If the taxpayer chooses to forego the carryback period for regular tax, that election applies to AMT.

STUDY QUESTION

8. The only tax credit that is fully allowed for AMT purposes is the:
   a. Research credit
   b. New markets tax credit
   c. Mining exploration credit
   d. Foreign tax credit

¶315 AMTI AND AMTI EXEMPTIONS

AMTI is generally tallied by computing the aggregate of Lines 1–27 on Form 6251. However, additions may be necessary for taxpayers who use the filing status of married, filing separately:

- If the taxpayer is married, filing separately, and the AMTI calculated from Form 6251 lines 1–27 (the above-the-line AMTI deductions) is more than $191,000, add 25 percent of the excess of the Lines 1–27 combination exceeding $191,000 to the entire amount.

EXAMPLE

A taxpayer with $201,000 would have to add an extra $2,500 because $2,500 is 25 percent of the $10,000 that exceeds $191,000.

- If the combination of Lines 1–27 is $307,000 or greater, and the taxpayer is married filing separately, he or she must add a blanket $29,000 to the entire amount.

COMMENT

The $29,000 adds back into the AMTI the exemption amount that to which the taxpayer would otherwise be entitled, functioning as a method to eliminate the exemption. This is explained further below under Exemption Phaseout.

.01 Dollar Exemption Amounts

Filing-status exemption amounts. Once AMTI has been established, exemptions specific to AMT must be examined to determine if the taxpayer is eligible to utilize one, and if so, to what extent.

CAUTION

An AMT exemption amount has no counterpart in the regular tax system. It should not be confused with the regular tax personal exemptions. The closest analogy to the regular tax system for the AMT exemption is that it serves as a "standard deduction" to make certain that taxpayer with AMTI below a certain minimum threshold will not be subject to AMT.

For the 2005 filing seasons, the following AMT exemption amounts apply:
- Single individuals or heads of household whose total AMTI does not exceed $112,500 are allowed an exemption of $40,250;
- Married taxpayers filing jointly and qualifying widowers are allowed $58,000, provided their AMTI does not exceed $150,000;
- Married taxpayers filing separately with less than $75,000 in AMTI can take a $29,000 exemption;
- Trusts are treated to the same exemption amounts as married taxpayers filing separately; and
- Corporations may take an exemption of $40,000.

The exemptions may not seem generous, but they have a significant impact. According to the White House, the higher exemptions prevent 9 million additional individual taxpayers from paying AMT. After 2005, however, the individual exemptions on this list are scheduled to fall to $33,750, $45,000, and $22,500, respectively. It is likely, however, that before the end of 2005 (but after the initial publication of this course), Congress may extend the higher exemption amounts for at least another year.

.02   Exemption Phaseout

Taxpayers with income above the exemption amount designated for their filing status will find that they may be "phased out" from being able to take an AMT exemption. This means that if the taxpayer's income for AMT purposes (AMTI) is too high, no exemption is available.

CAUTION

The phaseout amounts are not adjusted for inflation.

Exemption amounts are reduced by 25 cents for every dollar that AMTI exceeds $150,000 for married joint filers and surviving spouses, $112,500 for single filers, and $75,000 for married individuals filing separately and estates and trusts.

Table 1. Phaseout of AMTI Exemption for Taxpayers by Filing Status

Filing Status	Maximum AMTI	2005 Exemption	2006 or Later Exemption
Single	$112,500	$40,250	$33,750
Head of household	112,500	40,250	33,750
Married filing jointly	150,000	58,000	45,000
Surviving spouses	150,000	58,000	45,000
Married filing separately	75,000	29,000	22,500
Trust or estate	75,000	22,500	22,500
Corporation		40,000	40,000

For the 2005 tax year, the phaseout listings generally mean:
- For married taxpayers filing joint returns, their exemption is completely phased out when their AMTI is $382,000;
- For single taxpayers, the exemption is totally phased out at $273,500;
- For married taxpayers filing separately, the exemption ceases at $191,000;

- The exemption for corporate taxpayers is not totally phased out until AMTI reaches $310,000; and
- For children under 14, a special exemption of their earned income plus an additional $5,750 is available.

> **CAUTION**
>
> The phaseout amounts are not adjusted for inflation.

Nonrefundable tax credits. In 2006 and in subsequent years, nonrefundable tax credits will reduce an individual's regular tax liability only to the extent that the regular tax exceeds the taxpayer's tentative minimum tax liability—without regard for the foreign tax credit. There are, of course, exceptions. They are the child tax credit, the adoption credit, nonrefundable personal tax credits, and the credit for qualified retirement savings contributions.

STUDY QUESTION

> **9.** For every dollar that AMTI exceeds the amounts listed for single and married taxpayers, exemption amounts are reduced:
>
>   **a.** By 25 cents
>   **b.** By 50 cents
>   **c.** By 75 cents
>   **d.** Dollar for dollar

.03   Special Maximum Capital Gains Rate Computation

For AMT purposes, an individual's capital gains are computed in the same manner as for the regular income tax, including netting of gains and losses in separate tax-rate groups. For tax years beginning after December 31, 2002, qualified dividend income is treated as part of net capital gain.

> **CAUTION**
>
> Although the rates for long-term net capital gains are the same of for regular tax purposes, the gain or loss amounts may differ from the regular tax amounts because of AMT adjustments and preferences affecting the bases of the capital assets.

> **COMMENT**
>
> Because of the exclusion of net capital gains from the AMT rates of 26 or 28 percent, investors in AMT territory should especially value long-term capital gains and avoid short-term gains. Net long-term capital gains are taxed at a maximum 15 percent rate.

¶320 Impact of 2005 Energy Acts

One of Congress' big 2005 additions to tax legislation, the Energy Tax Incentives Act of 2005, provides a number of tax credits that positively impact individual taxpayers and encourage environmentally friendly purchases and uses. The credits, like credits in general, produce a greater income tax benefit than do deductions, so this is a welcome change. But, like many incentives and credits available to individual taxpayers, not all of the provisions will impact every taxpayer. Those taxpayers subject to AMT will not be able to enjoy the benefits to the extent their "regularly taxed" counterparts will, and in some cases, not at all.

.01   Incentives Added

Alternative motor vehicle credit. The 2005 Energy Act provides for a new tax credit for "green" vehicles. However, the credit may not be applied against the AMT.

Residential energy property credit. The new residential energy property credit rewards homeowners who invest in energy conservation.

Residential alternative energy expenditures. The residential alternative energy credit is equal to 30 percent of the cost of eligible solar water heaters, solar electricity equipment, and fuel cell plants.

In an interesting twist of the 2005 Energy Act, Code Sec. 26(a) currently allows offset against **both** regular **and** AMT liability. However, this provision sunsets on December 31, 2005. Because credits like the residential energy property credit and residential alternative energy expenditures credit are only available for property placed in service during 2006 and 2007 (after the sunset), they are not eligible under this provision.

¶325   PLANNING TO AVOID (OR MINIMIZE) AMT LIABILITY

Many experts worry that the AMT will have a chilling effect on the U.S. economy, by changing how taxpayers/consumers behave. AMT can subject taxpayers to higher marginal tax rates, which in turn may impact decisions about how to work and save.

.01 To Itemize or Not

AMT significantly complicates the decision about whether to itemize deductions. If there were only the regular tax to contend with, the decision would be fairly simple: total the deductions that may be itemized, adjust for phaseout (if necessary), compare that aggregate with the standard deduction, and claim the larger of the two.

EXAMPLE

Under regular tax, a married couple filing jointly with significant unreimbursed medical expenses totaling 8.5 percent of their adjusted gross income, considerable state and property tax liability, mortgage interest from a loan not used to improve a home may find, after totaling their deductions, that their itemizations produce a greater deduction than the standard deduction. Also, under the regular tax scenario, they are allowed to take personal exemptions for themselves and any qualifying dependents they may have. However, each of those deductions must be added back to taxable income for AMT purposes, and so these hypothetical taxpayers would find they would have no deduction available, because none qualify under AMT. Likewise, they may not take any personal exemptions. If the taxpayers instead chose to take the standard deduction, that too would have to be added back for AMT purposes, as it is not available. Each taxpayer will have to determine individually whether itemizing will produce a greater tax benefit to determine how beneficial itemizing deductions will be.

For AMT, the same choice is available: itemize or take the standard deduction, except that taxpayers who claim the standard deduction on the regular tax are foreclosed from itemizing deductions under AMT. Because some deductions are allowed under AMT, however, taxpayers subject to AMT may in fact have lower total tax liability if they choose to itemize deductions, even though those deductions total less than their standard deduction. The result is that the taxpayer has to calculate his or her liability four different times: to determine whether the taxpayer is subject to AMT, and if so, how to pay the least amount of tax necessary; and then, finally, to determine whether that means they are better off itemizing or taking the standard deduction in the first place.

PLANNING TIP

Knowing what deductions are allowed for AMT and which are not can help construct a plan that offsets AMT liability most effectively. Tax planning focused on this information, therefore, can be productive. In some cases, AMT planning requires action opposite to that called for under regular tax planning.

.02 Special Business Consideration

Different mitigation methods exist for businesses and individuals. For businesses, considerations such as leasing rather than owning building space, making accounting changes to recognize income and defer deductions, and creating accountable reimbursement plans for employee business expenses may help lessen AMT liability.

.03 Special Considerations for Individuals

For individuals, encouraging payoff of home equity loans where the proceeds were not used to improve the home, making IRA or pension distributions, using intrafamily transactions, and recognizing capital losses when capital gains are raising income above the AMT exemption phaseout amount may be helpful. Shifting deductions from one year to another might also help those individuals who may find themselves just inside of AMT territory to straddle between paying regular tax and AMT every other year.

¶330 THE FACE OF THE AMT TAXPAYER

.01 Families

A serious problem with the current AMT is that no one taxpayer group is subject to it. Families—and particularly larger families—are feeling the pain. Ninety-four percent of married couples with two or more children and AGI between $75,000 and $100,000 pay AMT, according to the Tax Policy Center. According to the Congressional Budget Office (CBO), married couples filing jointly are more likely to have AMT liability than unmarried taxpayers with similar incomes. The Tax Policy Center estimates that 48 percent of married couples are subject to AMT, versus 3 percent of singles.

> **COMMENT**
>
> Married couples face the same AMT tax brackets as other taxpayers, but their exemption is only one-third larger, which is a stark contrast to the regular tax scheme, under which married taxpayers get an exemption twice as large as that granted to single and high-income taxpayers.

.02 High-State-Tax Residents

Taxpayers living in places with high local and state taxes are also more likely to pay AMT. This is because the AMT denies the deduction for state and local taxes. This has the effect of giving a tax preference to taxpayers who live in low tax states.

> **COMMENT**
>
> The CBO points out the irony that many of the wealthiest taxpayers, for whom AMT was originally intended, are not subject to AMT because they are taxed at regular rates exceeding AMT rates, and thus have a higher regular tax liability.

.03   Other Taxpayer Profiles

Other taxpayers at risk for AMT liability are those with significant long-term capital gains and dividend income that is subject to preferential low income tax rates, tax preference, or other adjustments. Often these taxpayers are retirees or business owners with large depreciation deductions or NOLs.

STUDY QUESTION

> **10.** Why are married couples and families more likely to be subject to the AMT than single taxpayers who earn the same amount?
>
> **a.** Married couples have more tax breaks under the regular tax system, so the AMT "balances the books" in lower tax liability for singles.
>
> **b.** Single taxpayers tend to have more applicable tax credits than do married filers.
>
> **c.** Although the tax brackets are the same for singles and married taxpayers, the exemption for married filers is only one-third larger under AMT than that for single taxpayers.
>
> **d.** Married couples and families are not subject to the AMT in greater numbers than taxpayers having another filing status.

¶335   AMT SOLUTIONS, SHORT AND LONG TERM

.01   Call for Repeal

The AMT was almost repealed in 2000, under the Financial Freedom Act, which would have gradually phased out AMT over 10 years. Congress voted to abolish the AMT, but President Clinton vetoed the bill. Since then, no other measure has come close.

Now, lawmakers in Washington have introduced a host of new legislation in 2005 calling for the modification or repeal of the AMT. Senator Charles Grassley, R-Iowa, Chairman of the Senate Finance Committee has called AMT "a mess," and has recognized that absent Congressional intervention, "the situation will get worse."

Outright repeal of the AMT, however, is unlikely. A more likely option is "fixing," the AMT. Congress could do this by indexing the AMT for inflation, extending increased exemptions, and allowing for additional deductions.

Another "fix" would be to allow dependent exemptions under AMT, as is the case under regular tax. This would curb the rapidly growing reach AMT has on large families. Likewise, allowing deductions for state and local taxes under AMT would alleviate the AMT burden for many taxpayers.

.02 President Bush's Tax Reform Panel

The AMT is one of the biggest considerations of the President's Advisory Panel for Tax Reform. The president assembled this group of experts and charged them with developing a report before the end of 2005 on ways to make the Tax Code simpler, fairer, and more oriented toward economic growth. The panel reported in April 2005 that the AMT violates those three principles: It is not fair, it is not simple, and it is not efficient. Reform of the entire AMT scheme is expected to be recommended by the panel.

¶340 CORPORATE AMT

Although not garnering as much political and media attention, corporations are subject to AMT, too, but under a different mechanism. The cost recovery and adjustments that apply to individuals apply also to corporations, with narrow exceptions. For both individuals and corporations, under AMTI, the generous treatment available under regular tax for capital expenditures is eliminated entirely, because the deductions normally available are treated as tax preferences and adjustments.

> **COMMENT**
>
> S corps., partnerships, LLCs, LLPs, and other pass-throughs are not subject to AMT because their shareholders and partners must determine their tax liability on the individual shareholder level.

.01 Small Corporation Exemption

Corporations that meet certain gross receipts tests are considered "small corporations," the only classification completely exempt from AMT. To qualify, the corporation's average gross receipts must not exceed $7.5 million for all three-year tax periods prior to the year for which the corporation seeks AMT exemption. For the first three-year period after 1993 that the corporation seeks to use for AMT exemption averaging, the gross receipts may not exceed $5 million. A new corporation is considered to have zero minimum tax liability for the first year the corporation exists, regardless of gross receipts.

Once a corporation is liable, it must fill out Form 4626, which is akin to Form 6251 but applicable to business entities. Many of the adjustments for AMTI that noncorporate taxpayers must make must also be made by corporations: depreciation, mining exploration and development costs, long-term contracts, ATNOLD, and pollution control facilities. In addition, however, corporations must make adjustments for adjusted current earnings, merchant marine capital construction funds, Blue Cross and Blue Shield organizations, and property and casualty insurance companies. Of these corporation-specific adjustments, the most noteworthy—and the most prevalent—is the adjusted current earnings.

.02   Adjusted Current Earnings (ACE) Adjustment

Under AMT, the ACE adjustment is complex. Because part of the difference between AMTI and ACE for certain corporations (excluding S corps, RICs, real estate investment trusts, and real estate mortgage investment conduits) is not recaptured, but treated as a tax preference, recapture must be achieved by increasing by 75 percent the amount that a corporation's ACE exceeds its AMTI (as calculated without the adjustments for either ACE or ATNOLs). In some years AMTI may be decreased, rather than increased, by ACE preference. If a corporation's ACE is less than its AMTI, it may reduce AMT by 75 percent of the amount which AMTI exceeds ACE. In mathematical terms:

$$0.75 \times (AMTI - ACE)$$

There are ceilings to this amount, however.

COMMENT

The key, then, is in the determination of what composes a corporation's adjusted current earnings. ACE is an odd amalgam of adjusted earnings and profits, beginning with AMTI as a base.

Additionally, not unlike tax preference items, certain corporate tax benefits are reduced or eliminated under AMT with the intent of preventing excessive tax benefits. In most cases, the reduction is 20 percent. The benefits are reduced before they offset the income, instead of subjecting them to AMT after claiming them against regular income. Note however, that some of the benefits are also TPIs subject to AMT and may still be levied if the tax benefit, once reduced, remains too large. Those that are subject to AMT must be reduced before the minimum tax is imposed to prevent a double-cutback.

¶340

¶345   DECEDENTS' ESTATES

Generally, estates and trusts are subject to AMT. In most cases, estates and trusts are subject to the same taxes as individuals, and are allowed the same credits, although the credits traditionally must be apportioned between the estate or trust and the beneficiaries. However, some important distinctions deserve mention. Estates and trusts, unlike other taxpayers, are not liable for federal employment or self-employment taxes. Also, AGI plays a lesser role for estates than for individuals, and estates may not take dependent exemptions. Otherwise, estates and trusts are generally treated like individuals to calculate AMT.

Under the regular tax, after adjustments and distributions, the result is more or less the estate's taxable income. If special deductions like the federal generation-skipping tax also apply, then the estate or trust's taxable income may be further reduced. Similar rules apply to AMT.

COMMENT

Few estates are subject to AMT liability because they are already taxed at a very high tax rate under the regular tax system. The top regular tax rate, 35 percent, applies to almost all estates.

¶350   CONCLUSION

AMT is on many people's minds, including lawmakers, the IRS, and especially taxpayers. The consensus is that something needs to be done to return the system to function as originally intended. In light of these concerns, changes seem likely for AMT, but only time will tell which changes will actually transpire.

In the interim, the best a taxpayer can do is prepare for AMT by learning how it is calculated, what triggers it, who is most at risk, and planning carefully to avoid it. Practitioners can help by understanding which elections should and should not be taken, and encouraging clients to take those steps.

MODULE 2 — CHAPTER 4

Deferred Compensation Developments

This chapter provides an overview of new developments in deferred compensation, including a new form of qualified retirement plan, new rules and interpretations for retirement plan distributions and health care accounts, and protection of retirement account assets in bankruptcy.

LEARNING OBJECTIVES

Upon completion of this chapter, you will be able to:

- Understand the provisions for the formation and maintenance of designated Roth accounts and the rules for contributing to and taking distributions from them;
- Weigh the factors in making the decision to contribute to a designated Roth account;
- Identify and understand types of distributions from qualified retirement plans and IRAs;
- Understand the rules regarding the taxation of distributions from retirement accounts, including when a distribution may be subject to additional taxes and how to avoid those situations;
- Differentiate among the types of tax-favored health care plans;
- Determine whether a retirement account is protected in bankruptcy under the Bankruptcy Abuse Prevention and Consumer Protection Act of 2005 and what other protection may be available; and
- Understand new rules regarding making changes to deferred compensation plans.

¶401 INTRODUCTION

Deferred compensation includes not only retirement savings plans but also plans that help employees to pay for health care. The number of types of deferred compensation plans is growing, and it can be difficult for employees and employers to understand the distinctions among the many options. Remembering the rules for contributions, distributions, and plan administration can be even more daunting, but in some cases even small missteps can prove costly. The knowledgeable tax professional can guide clients through this maze of options, and in doing so, help them feel more secure in planning for their future.

¶405 DESIGNATED ROTH ACCOUNTS: A NEW WRINKLE IN RETIREMENT PLANNING

One of the latest developments in deferred compensation has been on the books nearly five years. The Economic Growth and Tax Relief Reconciliation Act of 2001 (EGTRRA) created Code Sec. 402A, which authorized the creation of nontax-deferred qualified retirement accounts. Like the Roth IRA, contributions will be made with after-tax dollars that allow the participant to receive tax-free income upon distribution. In other respects, these accounts, called **designated Roth accounts** in the Code and **Roth 401(k)s** and **Roth 403(b)s** popularly, match the 401(k) and 403(b) accounts that employees of businesses and tax-exempt organizations now have.

Participants in these retirement plans will be able to contribute by means of payroll deductions, just as employees do with current 401(k) and 403(b) plans, except that the amount deducted from their paychecks will be taxed. Designated Roth accounts have two distinct advantages over Roth IRAs: annual contribution limits are higher, and employees who earn more than the phaseout limit for Roth IRAs will still be able to make designated Roth contributions.

There are also two significant drawbacks to the new accounts:

- Roth 401(k) and 403(b) plans will not be universally available, and their government-employer analog, the 457(b) plan, is not permitted to accept designated Roth contributions at all. Employers will have the final decision as to whether to offer them to employees; and
- The provision authorizing them currently has a sunset clause terminating availability for tax years beginning after December 31, 2010, unless Congress acts to extend it. Those employers who usually wait to see if a benefit arrangement will catch on may decide not to offer them given the limited window.

.01 Formation and Requirements

The Roth 401(k) and 403(b) plans follow the same general rules as their tax-deferred counterparts, except for rules regarding contributions and distributions. This means that establishing a designated Roth account involves the same procedures as do traditional qualified retirement plans.

Separate accounting requirement. Employers are not required to make designated Roth accounts available to employees. However, because the employee must make an election to designate contributions as Roth contributions, it follows that for an employee to make that choice, designated Roth accounts can only be made available if both options are offered.

The employer plan must maintain designated Roth contributions in a separate account from untaxed employee contributions. Such contributions must be credited and debited to a designated account maintained for the employee, and the separate accounting requirement is in force until all Roth contributions have been distributed. This means that even if the provision is not extended beyond the December 31, 2010, sunset date, employers may have to maintain the separate accounts for 50 years or more, with all of the attendant compliance activities and expenses.

.02 Contributions

Code Sec. 401(k) permits employees to elect whether to receive a portion of their compensation in cash or to have it deferred instead to a qualified trust under one of several plans. Designated Roth contributions are also elective contributions under cash or deferred arrangements (CODAs). An employee must make an irrevocable designation of a Roth contribution at the time he or she makes the cash or deferred election.

> **PLANNING TIP**
>
> Employees will not be able to shift contributions from a designated Roth account to a traditional plan or vice versa after the contributions have been made if their tax priorities change. Employees who participate in both types of plans but have been making contributions to only one will be able to designate that future contributions go to the alternate account, and the employees will be able to make both excluded and Roth contributions simultaneously.

Employers must treat designated Roth contributions as included in the employee's gross income for the purpose of all taxes, just as if the employee had received cash.

Matching contributions. Employer-paid matching contributions cannot be designated as Roth contributions but must be treated as traditional contributions. Because these contributions are not included in the employee's income, they must be taxed upon distribution. In effect, any employee who receives matching contributions will have both Roth and non-Roth contributions even if all of the deferred contributions go to a Roth account.

Contribution and income limits. One of the significant advantages that designated Roth accounts offer employees is that they do not have the significant income thresholds and contribution limits that Roth IRAs have. Although contributions to Roth IRAs are limited to $4,000 for 2006 ($4,500 for taxpayers older than age 50) and taxpayers must have adjusted gross income not exceeding $110,000 ($160,000 for married taxpayers filing jointly), 401(k) and 403(b) contributions may be made of up to the lesser of 100 percent of compensation or $15,000 ($20,000 for employees over 50). There are no income restrictions on who can contribute, but the rules for highly compensated employees apply to both traditional and Roth 401(k) plans. The contribution limits apply to both types of qualified retirement plans, however, so any amount that is contributed to a traditional 401(k) or 403(b) plan must be subtracted from these limits to determine the amount available for designated Roth contributions.

STUDY QUESTIONS

---

1. Which of the following is an *advantage* of designated Roth accounts compared with Roth IRAs?

   a. Employees who earn more than the phaseout maximum for Roth IRAS may still contribute to a designated Roth account.

   b. There is no income tax on contributions to a designated Roth account.

   c. Contributions are made with pretax, not after-tax, earnings with designated Roth accounts.

   d. Employers are required to make designated accounts available to employees, unlike Roth IRAs.

2. Which of the following is a *disadvantage* of funding Roth 401(k) and 403(b) plans?

   a. The maximum allowable contribution is lower than for traditional 401(k) and 403(b) plans.

   b. Employer-paid matching contributions cannot be designated as Roth contributions and are treated as part of gross income for tax purposes.

   c. Funds may be switched from a designated Roth account to a traditional plan, but not vice versa.

   d. None of the above is a disadvantage.

NOTE

Answers to Study Questions, with feedback to both the correct and incorrect responses, are proved in a special section beginning on page 191.

¶410 DISTRIBUTIONS AND ROLLOVERS

To qualify for the exclusion from gross income, a distribution from a Roth account must not occur before at least five years after the end of the tax year in which the contributions were first made, regardless of the participant's age when this was done. In addition, qualified distributions may be made:

- No sooner than on or after the recipient reaches age 59½;
- To pay qualifying first-time home purchase expenses;
- At or after the death of the contributor; or
- On account of disability.

These terms are defined in Code Sec. 72(t), which provides exemptions from the 10 percent additional tax on early distributions from qualified retirement plans.

> **EXAMPLE**
>
> Greta Schmidt makes her initial contribution to a Roth 401(k) plan in 2006 when she is age 56. Although she reaches age 59½ in 2009, she cannot take a tax-free distribution until January 1, 2012.

Designated Roth accounts differ from Roth IRAs when it comes time to take distributions. Although Roth IRAs have no age at which distributions become mandatory and no required minimum distributions (RMDs), designated Roth accounts do. As with traditional qualified retirement plans, designated Roth accounts require minimum distributions starting at age 70½ or upon retirement, whichever is later.

The minimum distribution amount is based on the participant's life expectancy and the account balance as of the beginning of each tax year. As with other plans requiring minimum distributions, a 50 percent excise tax is imposed on the amount by which the RMD exceeds the distributions actually taken. Unlike with Roth IRAs, a participant cannot plan on passing the funds on to beneficiaries after his or her death by choosing not to take distributions from the account.

> **PLANNING TIP**
>
> For participants in designated Roth accounts who wish to pass account assets on at death, it is possible to roll them over to a Roth IRA. The designated Roth account's higher contribution limits make saving easier than with just a Roth IRA, and because distributions are not taxed, there will be nothing owed on the rollover. This is also an effective way to avoid the minimum distribution requirements, because all or part of the minimum distribution can be deposited into the Roth IRA.

STUDY QUESTIONS

3. To qualify for exclusion from gross income, a distribution from a designated Roth account must be held for at least _____ years.
   a. Two
   b. Five
   c. Ten
   d. There is not holding period to qualify for the exclusion

---

4. Which of the following is a disadvantage of withdrawals from designated Roth accounts compared with Roth IRAs?

   a. Designated Roth accounts are subject to required minimum distributions, but participants are not required to take distributions at any age from Roth IRAs.

   b. Withdrawals from designated accounts may not be used without penalty in cases of disability or to pay from first-time home purchase expenses, whereas withdrawals from Roth IRAs may.

   c. The excise tax on RMDs not taken is higher than for other plans requiring minimum distributions.

   d. All of the above are disadvantages of designated Roth account withdrawals.

¶415 DECIDING WHETHER TO START A ROTH ACCOUNT

How will employees know whether a designated Roth plan is right for their retirement needs? The first general rule is that the younger the worker is, the greater the potential benefit is from contributing to a designated Roth account. Here is why. Most individuals determine how much after-tax income they need to support their current lifestyles and contribute to their retirement plans from the excess. Although they can contribute larger pretax sums to traditional plans than the after-tax amounts available for Roth plans, taxes will eventually catch up to the traditional plans. When they begin taking distributions, retirees will owe taxes on both the money contributed and the earnings on that money.

Time frame is an important consideration, even if the employee is planning on early retirement. If an individual is more than 15 years from retirement, he or she should definitely consider a Roth plan. However, the more important consideration is when the money will actually be needed. Since Roth distributions are not taxed and not mandatory until age 70½, it may make more sense to take taxable distributions earlier on in retirement, when the income on those contributions is less, and wait until the Roth distributions become mandatory. Anyone who can afford to leave retirement contributions alone for a significant duration should consider this option.

Contributors to Roth IRAs are immediate candidates for designated Roth accounts, particularly if they are already contributing the maximum amount. They have already decided that the tax-free distributions available are the right choice for them, and designated Roth accounts simply allow them to contribute far more.

The last significant issue is tax certainty. Some people assume, rightly or wrongly, that they will be in lower tax brackets when they retire, and that tax deferral is the correct option. In many cases, their retirement income will be lower than what they currently earn, but other tax deductions are also important to consider.

Most retirees will have paid off their home mortgages, if not before retirement, then shortly afterward. This eliminates one of the most significant factors in whether one itemizes deductions. In addition, work-related itemized deductions will also disappear. The loss of itemized deductions is offset to some extent by the increased standard deduction for taxpayers over age 65. The other significant change in retirees' tax situations is the loss of deductions and credits for dependents, even if their children still live with them. The net result is that retirement income may have to be significantly lower before a retiree drops to a lower tax bracket. And of course, it is extremely difficult to predict what tax rates will look like more than five years in the future. Finally, employees should also consider nontax issues such as their expectations for their lifestyle in retirement and what steps they are prepared to take to achieve their goals.

STUDY QUESTION

5. As a general rule, the younger the worker is, the more preferable participating in a designated Roth account as opposed to a traditional 401(k) or 403(b) plan is. *True or False?*

¶420   DISTRIBUTION TRAPS (AND A FEW OPPORTUNITIES)

Few things can be more costly to retirement planning than failure to understand the rules governing distributions from tax-favored accounts. An ill-timed distribution, whether intentional or not, can cost someone as much as half of the money involved. Sudden income tax liability, tax penalties, and lost opportunities to defer tax may all result from what may appear to be a simple mistake. Insurance and financial services companies have been marketing products designed for the purpose of avoiding taxes on distributions or rollovers, forcing the IRS to take a hard look at these products. In some cases, taxpayers can find themselves dealing with the consequences of distributions even when they did not intend to take a distribution or do a rollover.

In the past year, the IRS, Treasury, and the courts have issued a significant number of letter rulings, revenue rulings, decisions, and regulations designed to clarify some of the rules of distributions and rollovers and eliminate abuses. Knowing how to use these new rulings and regulations or avoid their adverse effects can save a substantial amount of money and grief at retirement time, or even earlier.

.01 Review of distributions

There are essentially four types of distributions from retirement plans. Each has some unique and some overlapping areas of concern. These types are:

- Voluntary distributions;
- Required distributions;
- Deemed distributions; and
- Rollovers.

Voluntary distributions. These include normal distributions, which occur usually without problems, and early distributions, which are often subject to additional taxes.

Required distributions. Such distributions occur when a plan participant has reached age 70 ½ or upon retirement after reaching that age. Roth IRAs are the only retirement accounts that do not require distributions.

Deemed distributions. Such distributions are those transactions not intended to be distributions, but which the Tax Code treats as such. The most common form of deemed distribution happens when a participant in a qualified retirement plan such as a 401(k) takes a loan from the plan and defaults on the loan.

Rollovers. Rollovers are also a type of distribution because the plan that originally held the assets distributes them, either to the participant, because a new plan has not yet been chosen, or directly to a new plan in what is known as a trustee-to-trustee transfer.

.02 Early Distribution Penalties and Exemptions

Code Sec. 72(t) imposes a 10 percent surtax on all nonexempt distributions from qualified retirement accounts such as IRAs, 401(k) 403(b) and 457(b) plans, and simplified employee pension (SEP) and savings incentive matching plans for employees (SIMPLE) IRA accounts. Distributions taken in the first two years after a SIMPLE IRA is opened are subject to an even harsher penalty: 25 percent of the amount of the distribution. The penalty is called a **surtax** because it is imposed in addition to the regular income tax that is paid on the distribution, which may itself be at a higher rate than the taxpayer usually pays because the distribution bumps him or her into the next tax bracket. The purpose of the penalty is to deter plan participants from using the retirement plans as tax-favored savings accounts rather than for building a base for retirement income.

Distributions are fully exempt from the surtax if they are received when:

- The plan participant has reached age 59½;
- The plan participant has separated from service after reaching age 55 (not applicable to IRAs);
- The participant is permanently disabled;
- The participant has died;
- The participant elects to receive a series of substantially equal distributions over his or her life expectancy or over the joint lives of that person and his or her designated beneficiary;
- The payment is received by an alternate payee under a qualified domestic relations order (QDRO); or
- There is an IRS levy on the qualified retirement plan.

In addition, distributions from Roth IRAs and designated Roth accounts must be taken no earlier than five years after the end of the tax year in which the first contribution to a Roth account was made. This period does not restart if the account holder rolls the account assets over to another Roth plan during that time.

Distributions may also be exempt from the surtax to the extent that the funds are used for certain purposes. The penalty does not apply if the funds are used for:

- Medical expenses, to the extent that they do not exceed 7½ percent of the distributee's adjusted gross income, or 10 percent if the alternative minimum tax applies (whether or not deductions are itemized);
- Health insurance premiums of the distributee and his or her spouse and dependents, if the distributee has received unemployment compensation for 12 consecutive weeks in the tax year the distribution is made or in the year before it (self-employed individuals qualify if they would have received unemployment but for being self-employed);
- Qualifying higher education expenses (IRAs, SEPs, and SIMPLEs only);
- Expenses of up to $10,000 for the first-time purchase of a home (IRAs, SEPs, SIMPLEs, and designated Roth accounts only).

The IRS will waive the penalty in a few instances. If the distribution has become taxable despite the diligent efforts of the taxpayer or when imposition of the penalty would cause unfair hardship, the taxpayer may petition for abatement.

¶425   AVOIDING THE PENALTY

.01   Waivers

The IRS issued several rulings in 2005 that help explain its position on waivers. Although the preferred method of transferring funds from one retirement plan to another is a trustee-to-trustee rollover, when the funds are sent directly from one institution to another, it is possible for a participant to receive the funds and make the transfer at a later time.

There are two important warnings for taxpayers who do this, however. The first is that the distributing account custodian is required to withhold 20 percent of an eligible rollover distribution, regardless of whether the funds will be deposited into another qualifying account. The recipient will have to deposit the entire amount of the distribution, including an amount equal to the withholding, to avoid taxes.

> **EXAMPLE**
>
> Paul Wilson wishes to do a rollover of $10,000 from his current IRA to an IRA with a new custodian. He requests that the money be sent to him. The IRA custodian issues him a check for $8,000 and withholds the remainder. He must still deposit $10,000 to the new account or pay taxes (and a penalty) on the $2,000.

There is also a time limit on rollovers of this type. An eligible rollover distribution must be deposited within 60 days from the date the original custodian issues the distribution. The time period begins regardless of whether the recipient cashes the check. In some cases, the rollover may not be completed in time, and the recipient will have to pay taxes on the entire distribution.

In one instance, the taxpayer, the father of four college students, took a distribution to pay his daughter's tuition. He intended to replace the funds with proceeds from her student loan, and he was informed that he would not be liable for any penalty if he put the money back within 60 days. However, the processing of the student loan took longer than expected and the money was not available within the time limit. The IRS ruled that because the purpose of the rollover provision was to facilitate transfers and not to permit short-term loans, the penalty would not be waived.

> **CAUTION**
>
> Although the IRS does not intend to facilitate short-term loans, it will not pre-vent a taxpayer from taking a distribution for this purpose. However, regardless of the purpose of the eligible rollover distribution, only one such distribution is permitted during a tax year without penalty. If a second rollover is desired, only a trustee-to-trustee transfer would be allowed without penalty.

Another ruling involved a 79-year-old taxpayer who was receiving monthly distributions from her IRA. She intended to continue withdrawing money until the funds were exhausted, but after numerous problems with the ac-count, withdrew the balance in what was referred to as a "normal closeout." She deposited the balance in her personal savings account and used most of the money to pay for two months of assisted care. No one told her of the consequences of this action until her tax returns were prepared the follow-ing year. Because the funds had been used for personal expenses, the IRS determined that she was not eligible for a waiver of the rollover deadline.

But in a third situation, a permanently disabled taxpayer on a disability pen-sion decided to close out his IRA. He took his savings to another bank, which assured him that he could open a new IRA. A bank employee recommended that part of the money be invested in certificates of deposit and the rest in a money market fund. The taxpayer mistakenly assumed that he was opening an IRA. The following year, he discovered that he owed additional taxes because the money had not been placed in an IRA. The bank informed him that the failure to deposit the money into an IRA was due to the employee's experience and acknowledged the mistake to the IRS in writing. After receiving the bank's acknowledgment, the IRS agreed to waive the 60-day deadline.

STUDY QUESTION

> **6.** Problems that occur when a taxpayer chooses to receive payouts from one retirement plan account, gets a check in the mail, uses the funds as a short-term loan, then transfers the funds to a different account include all of the following **except:**
>
>   **a.** The entire rollover process must be completed within 60 days or it will be taxable.
>   **b.** Withholding of 20 percent on the withdrawal means that the taxpayer receives less money than must be contributed to the new account or the 20 percent will be taxable.
>   **c.** A penalty is imposed if the taxpayer makes more than one such transfer per year.
>   **d.** All of the above are possible problems when taxpayers do not use trustee-to-trustee rollovers.

.02   Exemptions

Although a waiver must be requested from the IRS in writing, an exemption from penalties (but not ordinary income tax) can be claimed when the taxpayer's return is filed for the tax year in which the distribution is taken. Several recent decisions remind taxpayers that to be exempt from penalties, distributions for qualified purposes must be taken in the year that the expenses are incurred. In one of these cases, a taxpayer withdrew funds from her IRA in 2002 to pay for educational expenses. However, she did not enroll in classes until 2003. Because the distribution was not taken in the same year that the expenses were incurred, the distribution was subject to penalty.

Another recent case shows that qualifying expenses are considered paid when the taxpayer has made funds available to the source of the expense, regardless of how payment was made. In this situation, the taxpayer had previously been enrolled in higher education coursework and had used credit cards and student loans to finance the cost of classes taken between 1999 and 2001. She transferred money from an account in the Public Employees Retirement System of her state after waiting for the passage of legislation that increased the value of her retirement account.

The transfer was completed in 2001, and she subsequently withdrew funds to repay the debts incurred in connection with her coursework. Although the taxpayer contended that the exemption to the penalty applied to all funds used for educational purposes, the Tax Court found that the plain meaning of the relevant Tax Code provision was that expenses must be incurred in the year of the distribution. She was permitted an exemption for the cost of the classes taken in 2001, but the remainder of the distribution was disallowed.

In this case, the expenses had been paid when the educational institution received funds from the taxpayer's credit card company and student loan provider, despite the fact that she still had debts related to those expenses. This result is in keeping with the fact that for purposes of the Hope and Lifetime Learning Credits, as well as the tuition and fees deduction, tax benefits are allowed for expenses that are paid with credit cards and student loans.

PLANNING TIP

Many higher educational institutions permit or require students to register in December for classes that begin the following January. Payments for these classes may be made in either calendar year, so a calendar year taxpayer is in effect given a choice of tax year in which to take a distribution. The courts have not ruled, however, on any cases in which a distribution was used to fund a prepaid tuition plan.

In contrast to the rule stating that a distribution used for higher educational expenses must be taken in the year that the expenses are incurred, distributions used to pay nondeductible medical expenses may be taken regardless of when the expenses were actually incurred. The rule on these expenses is simply that the exemption for distributions is granted to the extent that eligible expenses are paid.

.03 Exemption Trap

Although most of the former student's expenses in the case above were disallowed for the reason that they were not incurred in the year that the distribution was taken, she did avoid one of the most common errors committed by retirement plan participants when she rolled the proceeds of her retirement fund into an IRA before taking a distribution. Many taxpayers are not aware that the exemptions from the surtax for higher educational expenses and expenses for first-time home purchases currently apply only to distributions from IRAs, including SEP and SIMPLE IRAs, although distributions from designated Roth accounts will eventually qualify as well.

Another taxpayer withdrew funds from his 401(k) plan and was assessed the penalty tax. He was asked why the penalty should not apply. The taxpayer admitted that the distribution was not covered by any of the exemptions listed in Code Sec. 72(t) but alleged that the funds were used for educational expenses. The Tax Court held that the statute specified that the educational exemption was only for individual retirement accounts and individual retirement annuities (the acronym IRA actually refers to both). It noted the distinction between plans of these types and 401(k) accounts, holding that it was not empowered to make exceptions from the plain meaning of the law.

Because money is fungible, the exemption may be granted for distributions taken after a qualifying expenditure is paid by loan or credit, provided that the distribution is taken that same tax year. In some cases, however, a distribution is said to be taken in a year other than that in which the funds were received. These are the deemed distributions and related traps discussed next.

STUDY QUESTION

7. Distributions from IRAs taken for nondeductible medical expenses follow the same exemption rules as those for higher education expenses. **True or False?**

¶430 DEEMED DISTRIBUTION TRAPS

Some qualified retirement plans permit participants to borrow funds from the balance to their credit. Generally, 401(k) and 403(b) plans are allowed by law to permit loans, but each plan must specifically state whether loans are in fact permitted. IRAs cannot permit account holders to borrow from the funds they hold. When a plan participant **borrows** funds from a qualified retirement plan, as opposed to simply **withdrawing** them, the receipt of those funds is not a distribution. The loan must be repaid according to the terms of the loan agreement.

It is when the borrower fails to repay the loan according to these terms that the loan goes into default and becomes a *deemed distribution*. Another recent case demonstrates that the time when the distribution is deemed to have occurred is when the borrower defaults, not when the funds are made available.

A taxpayer took a plan loan from her 401(k) in 2000. She was terminated from her position at the end of that year and, unable to repay the loan, was charged with the penalty for an early distribution when the grace period for repayment ended in 2001. She contended that the loan should have been deemed a distribution in 2000 and attempted to claim the exemption from the penalty for nondeductible medical expenses incurred in 2000 and 2001. The Tax Court held that the statute indicated that the loan did not become a distribution until 60 days following the due date of the first missed payment. As this date was in 2001, the exemption only applied to those medical expenses incurred that year.

In another unfortunate incident, a taxpayer took a plan loan from his 401(k) to pay for his daughter's college expenses, having the repayments made through payroll deductions. In the third year of his repayment plan, the taxpayer declared bankruptcy. Upon receiving confirmation of the Chapter 13 plan, his employer stopped withholding payments, and the remainder of the loan became a deemed distribution. The taxpayer contended that he should not have to pay the penalty because his bankruptcy plan had forced the discontinuation of the payments. However, the Tax Court held that it could not deviate from the statutorily prescribed exemptions. An exemption under the circumstances of this case was nowhere in the statute and the court could not create one.

.01 Plan Loan Hazards

Qualified retirement plan loans are often attractive to participants who experience financial difficulties because the interest rates are often much lower than available alternatives and because the participant may feel a sense of entitlement to the money. Indeed, the funds are not much more difficult to access from plans than from a credit card company, and accessing assets is significantly easier than entering into a bank loan. However, the risk of a plan loan is that the loan will become a deemed distribution at a time when the borrower is least able to afford the penalty.

In the previous two examples, the taxpayers had qualified expenses that would have exempted them from penalties had they taken voluntary distributions, although the second taxpayer would have needed to roll the funds over to an IRA first. Much of the problem with plan loans is that if they are treated as deemed distributions, they are usually subject to the early distribution penalty. Normal early distributions are more advantageous when there are applicable exemptions at the time the funds are needed and will not apply at a later time.

A plan loan may be better for the participant if an exemption will apply in the event a distribution is deemed in the future. For instance, if a plan participant is 55 or older, he or she would not be assessed the 10 percent penalty in the event the loan could not be immediately repaid because of job loss. Once the participant reaches age 59½, any deemed distribution would become a normal distribution, but a loan would enable him or her to replenish the account in time for later retirement. For the same reason, a participant has less reason to worry about inability to repay plan loans because of permanent disability; the distribution would become a normal one, without penalty.

.02   Pledging Accounts

Another type of deemed distribution problem can arise if a retirement plan is pledged as security for a debt. The Fifth Circuit Court of Appeals has held that a retirement account pledged to secure an alimony obligation could be attached by creditors in bankruptcy. It held that because the funds were validly pledged under state law, the assignment was a deemed distribution under Code Sec. 72(p). This effectively removed those funds from the retirement account and made them nonexempt property.

Under the terms of his divorce agreement, the debtor was required to make monthly deductible alimony payments. He pledged an amount equal to the total alimony payments from his 403(b) plan, which he maintained in lieu of participation in the state teachers' retirement system, as security for the alimony payments. The debtor made the initial alimony payments, but he then stopped and began making sizable withdrawals from the 403(b) plan. His ex-wife sued to recover the funds and he filed Chapter 7 bankruptcy in response.

The bankruptcy court and the circuit court each found that the 403(b) plan was not a "retirement system" that could not be assigned under Texas law, but rather an individualized annuity alternative plan made available to college and university faculty and administration under a law that did not have an antiassignment provision. They agreed that the interest in the 403(b) plan was not only assignable, but validly pledged, and that the security interest was perfected through the divorce decree.

The circuit court agreed with the debtor that the interest would be exempt from bankruptcy if it qualified under applicable provisions of the Tax Code, but disagreed on whether the interest was qualified. Code Sec. 72(p)(1)(B) provides that any portion of a qualified employer plan that is assigned or pledged shall be treated as a loan received by the participant, which under Sec. 72(p)(1)(A) means that it is a deemed distribution. The court held that the debtor had wrongly distinguished between a deemed distribution and an actual one for purposes of the exemption.

Although it was probably never this person's intent that the funds in the 403(b) be used to pay the alimony, doing so could have resulted in better consequences for him. Recall that funds distributed under a qualified domestic relations order (QDRO), as to an ex-spouse, are exempt from the 10 percent penalty that would otherwise apply if the payor has not yet reached age 59½. As alimony, the amount of each distribution would have been excluded from his income (and included in his ex-wife's), so none of the money would have been taxed to him.

STUDY QUESTION

8. Which of the following is **not** a reason why Ann Connally incurs no penalty for failing to repay a loan against her retirement plan benefits after she loses her job?

a. She is 60 years so, so her deemed distribution becomes a regular distribution free of penalty.

b. She is older than age 55, so no 10 percent penalty applies.

c. She becomes permanently disabled.

d. All of the above are reasons why she is not subject to penalty for failing to repay the loan.

¶435   REQUIRED DISTRIBUTIONS

When a participant in a qualified retirement plan or the holder of any type of IRA except a Roth IRA reaches age 70½ or, if he or she is still employed at that time, retires later on, he or she must begin taking distributions. The reason such distributions are required is that, because the participant has had the benefit of tax deferral, the government wishes to ensure that taxes are collected from that person. Doing so also helps to establish a relationship between the amount of the taxes paid at the time of the distribution and the amount of tax avoided at the time the funds were contributed.

The amount of the required distribution is determined on an annual basis, and is based on the value of the assets as of a designated measuring date and the life expectancy of the participant or of the joint life expectancy of the participant and a designated beneficiary. The designated beneficiary is usually a spouse, but the payment period may be extended by naming a younger individual as the beneficiary, particularly if the spouse has other means of support. This would have the effect of reducing the amount of the RMD. Any amount may be distributed at any time during the tax year, but the total of all distributions made for the tax year must at least equal the minimum amount by April 15 of the following year.

Another form of required distribution occurs when the plan participant elects to start receiving distributions before reaching age 59½. Ordinarily, such a distribution would be subject to the 10 percent surtax, but the tax may be avoided by setting up a distribution sequence of substantially equal payments over the life expectancy of the participant or the joint life expectancy of the participant and a designated beneficiary. In effect, the participant sacrifices control over the amount of the distribution for the right to begin receiving payments at an earlier age without paying additional tax.

Both required distribution regimes impose significant penalties for failing to take required distributions. The penalty for failure to take an RMD is 50 percent of the difference between the RMD and the amount actually taken. When a plan participant elects to receive a series of substantially equal payments, and at a later date materially modifies the distributions in even a single payment before (1) five years have elapsed from the date of the first payment but after the participant reaches age 59½ or (2) the participant reaches age 59½, the penalty is 10 percent of the entire amount distributed, back to the first payment, plus interest.

EXAMPLE

At age 52, Inge Torgeson elects to take distributions from her 401(k) plan in the form of substantially equal payments of $5,000 per year. After six years, she materially modifies the distribution schedule. The penalty imposed is $3,000 (6 × $5,000 × 10%) plus interest.

STUDY QUESTION

9. When qualified plan participants take required minimum distributions from plan benefits, the total of all distributions for the tax year must be made by:

   a. December 1 of that year
   b. January 1 of the following year
   c. April 15 of the following year
   d. None of the above is the cutoff date

.01 Make-up Payment Can Correct Bank Error

In 2005, the IRS issued a letter ruling indicating that when an IRA custodian failed to make part of a required annual distribution one year but issued a "make-up" payment the following year, the taxpayer would not be subject to the 10 percent penalty. The IRS waived the penalty because the failure to receive a timely payment was not an attempt to modify the distribution plan and was not the taxpayer's fault.

The taxpayer had established an IRA by rolling over a distribution from a qualified retirement plan. As he wished to begin receiving payments before age 59½, he arranged to receive substantially equal payments from the IRA over his life expectancy through his financial representative at the custodian. At one point, he received only a portion of his required distribution. The taxpayer later met with his financial representative, completing a distribution form for the remainder. He provided all of the necessary information, including the account number and the percentage of federal taxes to be withheld.

Despite the fact that the form was sent to the custodian for processing, the distribution was not issued. The financial representative alerted the custodian, who sent this amount to the taxpayer the following year. As a result, there were two consecutive years for which the amounts listed on the taxpayer's Forms 1099R differed from the calculated amount.

The taxpayer requested a ruling that this was not an attempt to modify the series of substantially equal payments and that the penalty did not apply. Looking to determine the taxpayer's intent, the IRS noted that he had taken all of the necessary steps to receive the payment in a timely fashion and that the failure was not his own. The IRS ruled that the taxpayer had no intent to modify the arrangement, and if the plan otherwise conformed to Tax Code requirements, he would not be subject to the penalty.

.02 Deferring RMDs

For some taxpayers, it is possible to defer the starting date for RMDs. In another letter ruling, the IRS approved a rollover maneuver by a taxpayer who was employed at two companies that maintained separate profit-sharing plans. He was a 5-percent owner of one of the two companies but not the other and participated in both of the profit-sharing plans. The plan of the company where he was a part owner allowed participants to receive in-service distributions upon reaching the "required beginning date" as defined by Code Sec. 401(a)(9).

This date is April 1 of the calendar year **following** the year in which the employee reaches age 70½ or retires, except in the case of employees who are 5-percent owners, when it is April 1 of the year in which the employee reaches age 70½ or retires. This meant that the taxpayer's required beginning dates for distributions differed by a year between the two plans. Because the plan maintained by the company at which the taxpayer was not a part owner was permitted to accept eligible distributions from other plans, the taxpayer requested a ruling from the IRS on the validity of the rollover. The IRS agreed that a rollover was permissible because the different required beginning dates applied, giving the taxpayer an additional year of tax deferral.

¶440 VALUATION ABUSES IN RETIREMENT PLANS

The IRS and Treasury issued two sets of regulations in 2005, one proposed and one final, designed to eliminate abusive valuations of investment vehicles held by some retirement plans. The proposed regulations address the valuation of annuity contracts in conversions from traditional IRAs to Roth IRAs, whereas the final regulations concern the valuation of life insurance policies in distributions from qualified retirement plans such as 401(k)s.

In each case, the distribution is taxable, and the Tax Code states that the amount includable in the taxpayer's gross income is the fair market value of the policy or annuity. Previously issued regulations were unclear on how to determine the fair market value of these contracts, and many taxpayers asserted that this value was equal to the cash value of the contract at the time of the distribution.

This had led to the creation of annuities and insurance policies with "springing cash values." In such vehicles, the purchaser of the contract pays for the full value of the benefit paid out and receives a tax benefit for doing so. In the case of the insurance policies, the employer deducts this payment as compensation paid, and the employee defers taxes on the cost of the annuity contract. Each contract contains significant penalties for the surrender of the contract within the first few years after purchase, which artificially depresses its cash value. When the policy or annuity is distributed to the employee, the employee reports only the depressed value in his or her gross income.

The new regulations establish several methods of determining the fair market value of a contract. If an insurance policy or annuity is issued by a company in the regular business of selling them, the value may be determined through the sale of that contract or similar contracts. When there is a gift of a contract upon which further premium payments are owed, the value may be approximated.

In the case of an annuity, the dollar amount credited to the employee or beneficiary under the contract is added to the actuarial value of any additional benefits, such as survivor benefits in excess of the account balance, that will be provided. The value of a life insurance policy is arrived at by adding the net terminal reserve (the amount the underwriter sets aside to cover its liabilities) to the pro-rata portion of the most recent payment that covers the time period from the date of payment to the valuation date.

¶445   HRAS, HSAS, AND FSAS: SORTING THEM OUT

Deferred compensation has come to mean more than saving for retirement; it has increasingly included saving for health care, the burden of which more employers are shifting onto employees, at least in part. Congress has responded by expanding the number of options available to employers and their employees. At first, the options included only flexible spending accounts (FSAs) and the Archer Medical Savings Accounts (MSAs). This list has grown to include health reimbursement accounts (HRAs) and the new health savings accounts (HSAs). HSAs were so important last year that they required a whole chapter in *Top Tax Issues for 2005 CPE Course* to explain them.

This year's edition lacks the space to recapitulate the details in their entirety (last year's edition is still worth reading – or rereading), but the alphabet soup of acronyms can be difficult to keep straight and confusing even for some who can. A good starting point, then, is a brief explanation of these terms and how the accounts can be used.

Flexible spending accounts are the simplest option available in saving for health expenses. Strictly speaking, contributions to FSAs are not deferred compensation, because they are made and received by the employee in the same tax year (or are deemed to be received within the same tax year). Contributions to FSAs are made through payroll deductions from pretax income to designated accounts for participating employees. Qualified health care expenses may be reimbursed from these accounts, but there are some significant restrictions.

Funds from an FSA cannot be used to reimburse health care expenses if the same expenses can be reimbursed from another source. If an employee has both an FSA and an HRA, the FSA cannot be used to pay for medical expenses that would be covered by the HRA, unless the HRA plan documents state that the HRA covers expenses only to the extent that they exceed the FSA balance. Funds in an FSA also have a "use-it-or-lose-it" provision; unused contributions for the year are forfeited and returned to the employer.

Archer medical savings accounts work like traditional IRAs for health care instead of retirement. A taxpayer could contribute up to 65 percent of the deductible for a self-only, high-deductible health plan (HDHP) or 75 percent of the deductible for a family HDHP and take an above-the-line deduction. The maximum amount of the deduction was subject to adjustments for inflation. Account assets could be invested in the same fashion as IRA assets, providing income in addition to the contributions that could also be used for medical expenses. Unlike FSAs, there is no date by which the funds must be spent, allowing participants to use them when needed.

To be eligible, a taxpayer could not have any other type of health insurance besides an HDHP. Distributions not used for qualified health care expenses are subject to a surtax of 15 percent. Archer MSAs will not accept new participants after December 31, 2005. Current participants may maintain their MSAs or roll the account assets over into an HSA.

Health savings accounts are an updated version of the Archer MSA. One of the more significant differences is that the contribution limits are easier to calculate. Rather than a percentage of the deductible based on the type of plan held, maximum HSA contributions are set at $2,650 and $5,250 for 2005 and will be adjusted for inflation in $50 increments. Also, participants older than age 55 will be permitted to make additional contributions. This additional amount is $700 for 2006 and rises to $1,000 for 2009 and beyond.

HSA distributions are not included in the participant's gross income to the extent that they are used for qualified medical expenses, and there are no mandatory distributions during the participant's lifetime. Excess contributions not removed before the due date of the return and nonqualified expenditures are each subject to tax.

The White House has been promoting HSAs heavily since they were introduced. Although less than one-third of all workers have heard about HSAs, industry analysts report that as many as 36 percent of employers intend to offer them by the end of 2006.

Health reimbursement arrangements are employer-funded accounts that the employer uses to reimburse employees for their medical expenses. They are not funded through salary reductions. Although an employer may purchase insurance to be held in the HRA, an HRA is primarily a vehicle for direct insurance of an employee by the employer. HRAs allow the employers to have greater control over employee health care expenditures. Distributions from an HRA for qualified medical expenses are not included in the employee's gross income, but employers may deduct qualified contributions to the accounts. Although unused HRA funds cannot be distributed to employees as compensation or bonuses, they can be rolled over to succeeding years.

STUDY QUESTIONS

10. Which type of deferred compensation account is an update of the Archer MSA?

   a. Flexible spending accounts

   b. Health savings accounts

   c. Health reimbursement arrangements

   d. None of the above is an updated version of the Archer medical savings account

11. For 2006 the "catch-up contribution" for participants age 55 and older in health savings accounts will be:

   a. $500

   b. $600

   c. $700

   d. $800

12. All of the following are employee-funded plans for medical expenses *except:*

   a. Health savings accounts

   b. Health reimbursement arrangements

   c. Flexible spending accounts

   d. Archer medical savings accounts

¶450   IRS EXTENDS PERIOD FOR USING FSA FUNDS

In 2005, the IRS responded to what was the principal taxpayer complaint about FSAs: the "use-it-or-lose-it" rule. In many cases, contributions to FSAs are made at each payroll period. This meant that the contributions made in December had to be spent almost immediately, at a time when participants were least thinking about scheduled medical care. This rule has been one of the chief reasons for nonparticipation among eligible employees.

The IRS could not eliminate this provision, but it did amend the regulations to provide for a 2½-month grace period into the following tax year when funds could be spent. Now, provided that the employer amends its plan documents to include the grace period, a calendar-year taxpayer has until March 15 to use the remainder of his or her FSA contributions from the previous year.

The IRS noted that in other tax provisions, compensation for services is not considered deferred if it is paid during a short, limited period following the end of the tax year. It cited the example of the Code Sec. 404 regs allowing an employer to deduct compensation in the year it is earned if it is paid within 2½ months of the year that the employee performed the services.

As a result, it established a similar 2½-month period during which an employee may be reimbursed from the unused contributions for expenses incurred during that time as though the expenses were incurred during the tax year. Unused contributions may not be used to pay or reimburse expenses for any other type of benefit.

¶455   NEW GUIDANCE ON HSA CONTRIBUTIONS

Two sets of guidance were issued in the past year regarding employer contributions to HSAs, one on the subject of contributions to employee accounts, the other on those to accounts held by partners and S corp shareholders.

.01   Contributions to Employee HSAs

Employers are not required to make contributions to HSAs, but if they do, "comparable" contributions must be made for every comparable participating employee. If an employer makes contributions that are not comparable, it is subject to a 35 percent excise tax on all contributions. Fortunately for some employers, if their failure to make comparable contributions is due to reasonable cause and not willful neglect, the IRS may waive all or part of the excise tax imposed to the extent that the tax is excessive relative to the failure involved.

The IRS had published two notices in 2004 on the subject of comparable contributions, and the new proposed regulations incorporate and expand on those. **Comparable participating employees** are defined as eligible individuals who have the same category of high-deductible health plan (HDHP) coverage. There are two categories: self-only and family.

The IRS stated in Notice 2004-2 that comparable contributions can fit one of two descriptions. They can be either:

- The same amount; or
- The same percentage of the employee's deductible.

The comparability rules apply separately to each category of HDHP coverage, and because contributions are not mandatory, an employer may make contributions to one category and not the other. For example, an employer may make contributions to employees with family coverage and not to those with self-only coverage.

Separate categories for comparability testing also exist based on the employment status of covered individuals. Current full-time employees (working 30 or more hours per week), current part-time employees, and former employees are addressed separately for the purpose of this rule, which means that there are effectively six separate categories on which contribution comparisons are based.

The rules do not apply separately to collectively bargained employees. Contributions to the HSAs of employees covered under collective bargaining agreements are to be treated the same as those of other employees with the same employment status and HDHP coverage. The rules also do not apply to contributions to HSAs made under a cafeteria plan.

The proposed regs address some contributions to accounts other than employer HSAs. Comparability rules also apply to Archer MSAs. They apply separately to employees who have HSAs, but an employer may not contribute to an HSA and an Archer MSA for the same employee. Employers are not required to contribute to HSAs when the employee is covered by an HDHP not provided by the employer, but if the employer contributes to the HSA of any employee with an HDHP not provided by the employer, the comparability rules apply to all comparable participating employees.

Employers cannot satisfy the comparability rules by making contributions that are dependent on employee elections. For instance, matching contributions based on the amount an employee contributes to an HSA violates this provision, because comparable participating employees might not necessarily contribute identical amounts. An employer may not condition contributions on participation in health assessments or programs that are not a condition of employment. If an employee elects not to participate in one of these programs, employer contributions will not be comparable. Finally, employers may not make additional contributions based on age or time in service.

Employers must take into account all full-time and part-time employees who met all of the eligibility requirements under Code Sec. 223(c) as of the first of any month during the calendar year. They may make comparable contributions one or more times during the year if the contributions are all made at the same time. Employers may also make contributions on either a "look-back" basis, if they make the correct amount of contributions by April 15th of the following year, or "prefund" contributions by making them for all eligible employees at the beginning of the calendar year. However, an employer who opts for the latter method must make comparable contributions for all comparable participating employees who are eligible for any month during the calendar year, including those who were hired after the initial contributions were made.

An employer can only make contributions comparable by adding to those whose contributions were less than other comparable employees, because contributions cannot be forfeited. If "catch-up" contributions are made, the employer must also contribute reasonable interest.

Some employees are not covered by the comparability rules. Contributions to the HSAs of independent contractors, sole proprietors, two-percent shareholder employees of S corps, and partners in partnerships are not factored into comparability calculations. After-tax employee contributions and amounts that are rolled over from Archer MSAs or other HSAs are also excluded under these rules.

STUDY QUESTION

13. Comparability rules applied to HSAs require contributions for all employees to be either:
  a. The same amount or the same maximum lifetime coverage
  b. The same amount to family coverage and to self-only coverage
  c. The same percentage of each employee's deductible or the same amount
  d. None of the above is the requirement

.02 Contributions to Partners and S Corp Shareholders

Not only are partners in partnerships and S corp shareholder employees not covered by the comparability rules, the tax treatment of company contributions to their HSAs also differs greatly from that of other contributions.

In Notice 2005-8, the IRS explained that contributions by a partnership to a partner's HSA are not the equivalent of contributions by an employer to an employee's HSA. Instead, they are distributions to the partner, reportable on Schedule K-1 of Form 1040, and the partnership cannot deduct them. The partner may, however, deduct the amount of the contributions as an adjustment to gross income. For a partnership to be able to deduct such contributions, it would have to treat them as guaranteed payments under Code Sec. 707(c), which are included in the partner's gross income. This method is the treatment used when an S corp contributes to the HSA of a two-percent shareholder employee for services rendered.

Contributions to the HSAs of partners or S corp shareholders also have employment tax consequences. If the partnership does not deduct the contributions, they are not included in net earnings from self-employment. Guaranteed payments do count in self-employment income for partners, but whether S corp shareholders must pay FICA taxes depends on the circumstances.

STUDY QUESTION

14. The IRS stated in Notice 2005-8 that a partnership's contributions to partners' HSAs are:

a. Equivalent to those of an employer to an employee's HSA
b. Distributions reportable on Schedule K-1 and nondeductible by the partnership
c. Subject to the same comparability rules as HSAs for employees
d. None of the above was stated in Notice 2005-8 about HSAs of partners

¶460 OTHER HEALTH CARE ACCOUNT TRAPS

Employers can unwittingly cause significant problems for themselves by improperly structuring reimbursement accounts for employee's health care. Two recent revenue rulings demonstrated the effects of exceeding the boundaries of the rules governing these accounts.

In the first ruling, an employer ran afoul of the nonforfeiture rule for qualified retirement plans. The plan had combined a medical reimbursement account (MRA) with its profit-sharing plan, a defined contribution plan qualified under Code Sec. 401(a). The plan allocated two-thirds of the employer's contributions to the profit-sharing plan and the remainder to the MRA. Contributions to the profit-sharing plan would be distributed after the termination of employment, whereas MRA funds would reimburse employees, their spouses and children for medical expenses incurred. Any MRA funds remaining after the employees' death would be forfeited.

Funds in an employee profit-sharing account must generally be distributed under defined circumstances:

- After a fixed number of years;
- At a specific age; or
- On the occurrence of a specific event (such as termination of employment, retirement, death, or disability).

Funds must also be vested and not subject to forfeiture. If rights to any portion of the funds are conditioned on a subsequent event, then they are forfeitable and the plan is not a qualified retirement plan—it would lose its tax benefits.

Code Sec. 401 also indicates that an incidental amount—generally no more than 25 percent—of a participant's profit-sharing account may be used to provide health insurance. Funds disbursed from an MRA are treated as insurance for such purposes and are not taxable if the disbursements can be made only for medical expenses. If the employee is able to receive the MRA funds without having medical expenses, the funds are taxable even when they are for medical expenses.

The IRS noted that those two provisions were in conflict. Disbursement of the MRA funds could not be conditioned on a subsequent event, namely the incurrence of medical expenses, or the profit-sharing plan would be disqualified. However, to keep the plan qualified, the MRA funds would have to be taxable.

In another ruling that was unusually tough on taxpayers, the IRS determined that if an HRA makes any payments in cash or benefits for unused reimbursement amounts, all payments by the HRA would be taxable to the employees, regardless of whether any were for medical expenses.

The IRS described a situation illustrating a permitted form of HRA, followed by three variations that would be disqualified.

EXAMPLE 1

The employer sponsors a plan that reimburses employees solely for substantiated medical expenses and is available to current and former employees, their spouses and dependents, and the surviving spouses and dependents of deceased employees. Any unused amounts are forfeited upon the death of the last eligible family member of the employee. The plan is entirely employer-paid, involving no salary reductions or cafeteria plans.

Medical reimbursements are provided up to an annual maximum dollar amount per year and only to the extent that eligible persons have not been reimbursed from any other plan. The plan requires a portion of unused funds to be forfeited at the end of each year, with the remaining unused portion carried over to succeeding years.

Upon the retirement of the employee, the employer makes a contribution to the reimbursement plan up to the value of all of the employee's unused vacation and sick leave. No eligible person is entitled to receive any of this amount in cash or other benefits.

EXAMPLE 2

Same facts as Example 1, except that an employee may receive a cash payment equal to the unused reimbursement amount at the end of each year or upon termination of employment. The employer treats these as taxable compensation.

EXAMPLE 3

Again, the plan is the same, except that unused reimbursement amounts are paid in the form of a death benefit.

EXAMPLE 4

The employer has a plan purporting to be separate from the reimbursement plan. If the employee elects to participate, any amounts unused at retirement are forfeited; however, the employee may receive an amount equal to any forfeited amounts either in cash or in contributions to one of several retirement plans.

The IRS indicated that none of these three variations satisfies the requirements for tax-favored treatment. The cash payments and the death benefits are direct and obvious instances where an employee has a right to receive payments regardless of whether medical expenses are incurred. In the fourth example, the IRS would ignore the employer's description of the second plan as separate, and if viewed as a whole, the result is the same.

The IRS stated that all of the payments made would be taxable, including reimbursements for qualifying medical expenses, because the authorization of an ineligible payment makes the entire plan fail, not just the payment.

¶465 BANKRUPTCY PROTECTION FOR RETIREMENT ACCOUNTS

Although as described previously two individuals suffered defeats in tax cases when bankruptcy was a factor, 2005 brought significant good news for taxpayers concerned about protecting their retirement assets in bankruptcy. Even before the president signed the Bankruptcy Abuse Prevention and Consumer Protection Act of 2005 (Bankruptcy Act), two court decisions extended protection to certain retirement account assets.

The Supreme Court ruled in *Rousey v. Jacoway*, 544 U.S. ¶50,258 (2005) that creditors could not reach IRA assets of debtors in bankruptcy. Reversing the Eighth Circuit Court's decision, the Court held that IRA assets were protected if they met three requirements:

- The right to receive payment must be from a stock bonus, pension, profit sharing plan, annuity or similar plan or contract;
- The right must be "on account of illness, disability, death, age, or length of service;" and
- The right may be exempted only to the extent that it is reasonably necessary to support the debtor or his or her dependents.

This same test can be applied to other forms of retirement accounts such as 401(k) plans, although the Court did not address them. However, the Court's "on account of...age" requirement stated that part of the applicability of the test to IRAs stemmed from the fact that a penalty would be owed if the funds were withdrawn before the debtors reached age 59½ and would not thereafter, and also that distributions are mandatory for account holders older than age 70½. This has led some to question whether the protection would extend to Roth IRAs, where there is no tax or penalty on withdrawals up to the amount of after-tax contributions and no RMD.

Not long afterward, the Bankruptcy Court for the Western District of Pennsylvania held that 403(b) accounts would be protected from creditors in *In re Gould.* The debtor's plan stated that the debtor's "interest may not be sold, used as collateral for a loan, given away, or otherwise transferred." Further language indicated that creditors could not "attach, garnish, or otherwise interfere with" the account.

Bankruptcy Code Sec. 541(c)(2) states that if there is an enforceable restriction on the transferability of the debtor's interest in a trust outside of bankruptcy, then the restriction is also enforceable under bankruptcy law. Although the bankruptcy trustee argued that the statute did not apply because an annuity was not a trust, the Bankruptcy Court, while noting that there was a split of opinion among the courts, held that an express trust was not necessary to give ERISA plans this protection.

The Bankruptcy Act, which became effective October 17, 2005, extends bankruptcy protection to all tax-favored retirement savings plans, including those exempt from tax under Code Sec. 401, 403, 408, 408A, 414, 457, and 501(a). For IRA accounts, there is a $1 million limitation (as adjusted for inflation) on the protection, except for IRAs funded by rollovers from qualified plans. However, retirement plan loans cannot be discharged in bankruptcy.

> **CAUTION**
>
> Because the Bankruptcy Act was not due to take effect until several months after the two court cases described, the extent to which a retirement account is protected in bankruptcy will depend on when the bankruptcy filing was made. Filings before October 17, 2005, are not covered by the Act. In the case of an IRA, this means the difference between explicit protection of $1 million in IRA assets and protection only of a "reasonably necessary" amount. It is also important to know that although bankruptcy is a matter of federal law, what is exempt from the bankruptcy estate may be determined in part by state law.

STUDY QUESTION

---

15. All of the following court rulings and legislative acts extended the protection of retirement benefits in case of bankruptcy **except:**

   a. *Rousey v. Jacoway*
   b. *In re Gould*
   c. Bankruptcy Act
   d. All of the above extended protection of retirement benefits in bankruptcy

---

¶470   EMPLOYEE BENEFIT PLANS: AMENDMENTS AND NOTICES

.01   Reducing or Eliminating Pension Benefits

In the 2004 decision in *Central Laborers' Pension Fund v. Heinz*, 124 S.Ct. 2230, the Supreme Court held that an amendment to a multiemployer pension plan that imposed additional restrictions on the right to receive accrued early retirement benefits violated the "anticutback" rule under ERISA, found in Code Sec. 411(d)(6). Although future amendments of this sort were prohibited, the Court indicated that the IRS could decline to apply the decision retroactively. In 2005, the IRS issued rulings and proposed regulations that help clarify what changes to qualified pension plans will not violate this rule.

The IRS issued Rev. Proc. 2005-23 to explain when an amendment to a pension plan suspending some benefits would not be covered by this decision. The amendment must have been adopted before June 7, 2004, and the plan must also adopt a corrective amendment that would provide that the terms of any amendment under which benefits could be suspended did not apply to any benefits accrued as of June 7, 2004. The effective date of the corrective amendment must be no later than June 7, 2004.

Additional rules imposed by the IRS require that the reforming amendment give plan participants the option of a retroactive election to start receiving benefits on the effective date of the reforming amendment. Participants must be considered eligible to elect benefits if they were entitled to do so before the original amendment suspended them and they had not previously applied for benefits. They must be able to elect payments during an election period that begins when they receive notification of the option in the reforming amendment and lasts no less than six months. The plan must make reasonable efforts to locate all eligible participants.

The IRS and Treasury also finalized regulations describing reductions in plan benefits that do not violate the anticutback rule. The Economic Growth and Tax Relief Reconciliation Act of 2001 (EGTRRA) permits employers to reduce and even eliminate early retirement benefits retirement-type subsidies and optional forms of benefit if a participant's benefits are not affected in more than a *de minimis* manner.

If the change results in a different annuity starting date or a lower present value than the benefit that would be eliminated, the amount of the reduction cannot exceed the greater of:

- Two percent of the present value of the retirement subsidy under the eliminated optional form of benefit; or
- One percent of the participant's prior-year compensation.

The regulations apply to amendments that became effective after August 12, 2005.

One of the permissible methods of eliminating benefits allows employers to eliminate redundant optional forms, as long as participants' rights to remaining optional forms of benefit are not subject to materially greater restrictions. Benefits with an annuity starting date less than 90 days after the plan has been amended may not be eliminated.

A second allowable method is to eliminate noncore optional benefit types while retaining certain core options. These core options include a straight life annuity, a 75 percent joint and contingent annuity, a 10-year term certain and life annuity, and the most valuable option for a participant with a short life expectancy. Plans may substitute either a 50 percent or 100 percent joint and contingent annuity option for the 75 percent annuity. Amendments may not apply to optional forms of benefit that commence within four years of the amendment.

Finally, employers may eliminate some forms of benefits that have not been used by participants during a given look-back period. If a plan has at least 100 participants, any noncore form of benefit that has not been used in the past two years may be eliminated. If a plan has fewer than 100 participants, the look-back period may be extended up to three more years to provide a sample of 100 participants, but no benefit may be eliminated under this method if the plan has not had at least 100 participants during the five previous years.

The IRS has said that in some instances, multiple amendments may be treated as one amendment for the purpose of determining whether a prohibited cutback has taken place. In general, the effects of amendments within a three-year period will be combined for this purpose. Amendments taking effect the same day will also be treated as one amendment.

.02 Electronic Notification

Some information on employee benefit plans must be sent to plan participants and beneficiaries in writing. The IRS has issued proposed regulations on using electronic media (usually e-mail) to send this information in place of paper documents, covering a broad range of benefit plans. These include all qualified plans, qualified annuity contracts (including joint and survivor annuities), SEPs, SIMPLEs, Code Sec. 125 cafeteria plans, accident and health plans, educational assistance plans, qualified transportation fringe benefits, and HSAs. The regulations also cover the electronic transmission of elections or consents from participants and beneficiaries.

The regulations are designed to ensure that the communications are as easily read, understood, and answered as easily as the paper documents. The content of a communication and the medium through which it is delivered must be no less understandable to a recipient than if the communication were in writing. At the time delivery is made, the electronic transmission must alert the recipient to the significance of the transmission and instruct the participant on how to access the notice in a "readily understandable and accessible" manner. In addition, an electronic system must:

- Allow the participant effective access to transmit the election;
- Be reasonably designed to prevent individuals other than the participant from making an election;
- Provide the participant with a reasonable opportunity to review and make changes before the election becomes final; and
- Provide a confirmation within a reasonable time after the election has been made.

Participants must consent to receive electronic communications in writing, electronically, or by alternative authorized means, before a plan can begin sending electronic notices. Consent must be made in a manner "that reasonably demonstrates that the participant can access the notice in the electronic form that will be used to provide the notice." Participants must also receive disclosure statements that detail:

- The scope of consent;
- Their right to withdraw consent;
- Their right to receive written communications;
- Procedures for updating information; and
- How to access electronic communications.

¶475 LOOKING AHEAD

The IRS and the Office of Tax Policy issued the 2005-2006 Priority Guidance Plan in August of 2005. This document is essentially a "to-do list" of what the IRS hopes to accomplish in the year ahead. This list contains:

- 24 items listing guidance, revenue procedures, and proposed, temporary, and final regulations relating to retirement benefits; and

- Another 21 items concerning executive compensation, health care, and other benefits and employment taxes.

In addition, the Priority Guidance Plan has a month-by-month listing of regularly scheduled publications the IRS will issue up through June 2006.

Among the items listed on the Priority Guidance Plan that relate to deferred compensation are:

- Guidance on the tax treatment of distributions from Roth retirement plans;
- Guidance on benefits not permitted in a defined benefit plan;
- Final regulations setting forth the definition and requirements for a designated Roth contribution to a 401(k) plan;
- Guidance on annuity valuation issues in conversions from a traditional IRA to a Roth IRA;
- Guidance regarding accrual and vesting of benefits provided pursuant to qualified retirement plans;
- Regulations regarding the elimination of optional forms of benefit in defined benefit plans;
- Guidance on the impact of providing a 2½ month grace period for FSAs on HSAs; and
- Regulations on employer comparable contributions to HSAs.

This list is not a complete listing of relevant items, and issues that were not included in the Priority Guidance Plan may be addressed in response to future legislation. In September, Chief Counsel Donald Korb indicated that his office expects to deal with issues stemming from tax reform. As of this writing, the Tax Reform Panel had not submitted its recommendations, but it is a reasonable assumption that Congress will attempt to pass some legislation so that members can claim to be addressing issues of tax complexity.

¶480   CONCLUSION

The increasing number of tax provisions related to deferred compensation reflects Congress' intent to encourage individual saving for retirement and health care. This should remain true even if Congress is able to pass Social Security and Medicare reform. But even as Congress extends tax advantages to promote these purposes, the IRS seeks to restrain those advantages through regulations, letter rulings, and decisions favorable to its interpretations. The result is a substantial body of material for practitioners to deal with in advising clients on their health and retirement goals, but the rewards of having current and accurate knowledge on these issues are great for practitioner and client alike.

MODULE 2 — CHAPTER 5

New Tax Breaks from Congress: Energy Incentives, Hurricane Relief, and Phased-In Benefits

This chapter was prepared to provide an overview of major 2005 tax legislation, and the benefits individual taxpayers may realize from that legislation.

LEARNING OBJECTIVES

Upon completion of this chapter, you will be able to:

- Understand the basic provisions for individuals and small businesses of the Energy Tax Incentives Act of 2005;
- Determine which tax incentives apply to clients and how to claim them;
- Have a working knowledge of the tax provisions for individuals and small businesses in the Highway Act of 2005;
- Advise clients how to take advantage of any of the incentives applicable in the Highway Act;
- Understand the provisions of the Katrina Emergency Tax Relief Act of 2005 as well as the IRS's administrative relief for individuals and small business taxpayers both within and outside of the disaster areas;
- Advise taxpayers how to use the special tax deductions and credits available to victims, volunteers, and charitable donors after Hurricane Katrina; and
- Discuss and answer questions about how prior tax legislation will impact clients' 2006 tax liability.

¶501 INTRODUCTION

In 2005, Congress enacted significant tax legislation. After years of wrangling and political deals, an energy act was finally passed, giving incentives and tax opportunities to taxpayers to make energy-efficient and environmentally friendly choices. The Energy Tax Incentives Act of 2005 (2005 Energy Act) passed in July, and it will provide several years of intensive tax credits, deductions, and revenue raisers, followed by some longer-term benefits. Both businesses and individuals are affected and they will be able to take advantage of a variety of incentives that can impact their tax liability significantly. At about the same time, Congress passed the Highway Act of 2005, which included some excise tax provisions that will prove significant to many businesses. Both pieces of legislation were expected because President Bush had made both energy and the nation's transportation infrastructure high on his agenda.

By contrast, no one could have expected the devastation caused by Hurricane Katrina. In late August, when the storm hit, displacing hundreds of thousands of Americans and causing billions of dollars of damage, Congress and the IRS were forced to table other tax legislation and focus on appropriating for the clean-up and for relief to victims of the hurricane. The IRS responded almost immediately, with administrative remedies for victims available within days of the crisis. Congress acted quickly as well, appropriating more than $60 billion for relief efforts. Substantial tax-related provisions were signed by the president on September 23, 2005, in the Katrina Emergency Tax Relief Act of 2005 (KETRA). KETRA provides tax-related opportunities and incentives for victims of the storm to rebuild and begin again, volunteers to give their time more easily, good Samaritans to donate goods and services, and friends and families of those impacted to help their loved ones.

Also passed in 2005 was the Bankruptcy Abuse Prevention and Consumer Protection Act of 2005 (Bankruptcy Act). The Bankruptcy Act received considerable media attention at its passage in July. Critics vehemently decried the legislation as being heavy-handed and draconian, hurting lower- and-middle income taxpayers. Proponents were equally vocal, insisting the legislation finally closed loopholes that had allowed unscrupulous taxpayers to walk away from their debt without relinquishing valuable assets. The law is helpful to the IRS, giving the agency opportunities to recoup tax debt. Although the average bankruptcy debtor loses opportunities for debt forgiveness under the Bankruptcy Act, there are still ample administrative opportunities available for relief.

In 2005, as in every tax year, many tax provisions sunset, while others take effect. Some provisions passed way back in 2001, and others passed just a year ago, are only now having a significant impact. This chapter provides a timeline of what will happen when, and what taxpayers can expect as a result.

¶505 ENERGY TAX INCENTIVES ACT

For legislative sessions in four of the past years, Congress had been unable to reach an agreement on a tax title for energy. The logjam finally broke in 2005, and an energy bill was finally pushed through—but not without some compromise. The bill survived several revisions before finally being passed. Yet although the tax cuts are not as sweeping as were proposed in some previous versions, the savings will nonetheless prove significant. The president signed the Energy Tax Incentives Act of 2005 on August 8. The law contains $14.5 billion in tax cuts that will enable domestic energy conservation at every level. Small businesses and individuals in particular are eligible for new deductions, credits, and incentives.

The 2005 Energy Act takes a four-pronged approach to produce long-term, energy-saving initiatives. Of the four, two are geared toward individual taxpayers and small businesses: conservation and alternative energy. The remaining two involve improving the U.S.'s energy infrastructure and the production of domestic energy, but neither will have much of a direct impact on the average taxpayer.

The 2005 Energy Act is mammoth—and expensive. According to the Joint Committee on Taxation's 10-year estimates, it includes $940 million in excise tax reforms, $607 million in offsets, and more than $860 million in transportation tax breaks. To cover the cost, the 2005 Energy Act offsets its tax cuts with $3 billion in revenue raisers.

The array of conservation initiatives are those most likely to directly impact the greatest number of taxpayers. Generally, they encourage the widespread implementation of energy-efficient homes and businesses as well as alternative-energy, "green" vehicles. New installations as well as improvements will be rewarded, and more taxpayers will be eligible for the green vehicle tax break.

STUDY QUESTION

---

1. The four-pronged Energy Tax Incentives Act of 2005 focuses on all of the following energy-saving approaches **except:**
    a. Improving the U.S. energy infrastructure
    b. Conservation
    c. Development of new energy sources
    d. Green vehicles

NOTE

Answers to Study Questions, with feedback to both the correct and incorrect responses, are proved in a special section beginning on page 191.

.01   Residential Energy Property Credit

For most individuals, this credit will be the one they will get to apply. It rewards taxpayers for the purchase of large energy-efficient improvements and property. The credit is capped at $500 for each taxpayer and, up to that cap, is equal to the sum of two subcredits:

■   10 percent of significant energy-efficiency improvements to existing homes (called the **residential energy conservation property credit**); and

■   Residential property energy expenditures, at 100 percent (called the **residential property expenditures credit**).

The $500 cap is called a "lifetime" limit, although the credit is only available for two years; taxpayers may only apply the credit for property placed into service during 2006 and 2007. Stated in the negative (which is often useful in tax planning), property placed into service on or before December 31, 2005, or after December 31, 2007, will **not** be eligible for the credit.

STUDY QUESTION

---

2. The $500 maximum for the Residential Energy Property Credit comprises a total of _____ percent of residential property energy expenditures as well as _____ percent of significant energy efficiency improvements to existing residences.

   a. 10; 100
   b. 50; 50
   c. 100; 100
   d. 100; 10

Residential energy conservation property credit. This credit is the first part of the umbrella Residential Energy Property Credit. Only specific property qualifies for the credit. The property must meet certain energy conservation codes and must be part of the building envelope. The **building envelope** includes everything that separates the interior of a building from the outdoor environment, including windows, walls, foundation, basement, slab, ceiling, roof, and insulation. Unlike a homeowners' energy credit available in the early 1970s, the current credit does not include all energy-conservation measures, such as set-back thermostats and ceiling fans, because they are not part of the home's "envelope."

Sometimes referred to as the **improvement property credit,** the credit applies to property that qualifies under this 10 percent credit, including any insulation material or system primarily designed to reduce heat loss or gain, exterior windows, skylights, windows, and doors, and metal roofs coated with heat-reducing pigments. Certain limitations apply to the individual credits. For example, a taxpayer may not claim more than $200 of the $500 during the entire five-year duration for windows. The credit will only apply to improvements in a taxpayer's principal residence; second homes will not qualify. All qualifying property must be put into service by the taxpayer (that is, it must be first used during the 2006 and 2007 period in which it is effective; the purchase date does not necessarily control). Additionally, any property must be reasonably expected to be in use for five years. For example, seasonal installation of plastic heat-applied storm-window film, intended to last only until the spring when it is removed, does not qualify.

CAUTION

Many taxpayers have erroneously read that the 2005 Energy Act allows for a credit for the purchase of energy-efficient appliances such as dishwashers, clothes washers, and refrigerators under the Manufacturer's Credit for Energy Efficient Appliances. This is not true. The law extends the credit to manufacturers of the items, and only applies to qualifying appliances manufactured after December 31, 2005, and before January 1, 2008

To qualify as an energy improvement, the property purchased by the homeowner must not only be part of the building envelope but also must meet rigorous energy-conservation standards. The standards are found in the 2000 International Energy Conservation Code (IECC), as it was effective on August 8, 2005. Metal roofs that qualify will have to meet the Energy Star Program requirements.

COMMENT

It is likely that installation costs will not qualify toward the credit. Elsewhere in the 2005 Energy Act, labor costs are considered and statutorily qualify for the credit. The omission here is probably indicative of Congress's intent to apply the credit to the property and components alone.

EXAMPLE

Susan and Ron own a single-family home. In 2006, they redecorate their kitchen. As part of the change, they reinsulate the kitchen with qualified energy efficient insulation and energy efficient windows. They also install an energy-efficient refrigerator and dishwasher. Susan and Ron may take a credit on their 2006 tax return up to $200 for the windows (purchased for $2,000), and up to $300 for the insulation (at 10 percent of its cost). Neither the refrigerator nor the dishwasher is eligible for the credit because Susan and Ron merely bought the appliances and did not manufacture them.

STUDY QUESTION

3. All of the following are requirements for claiming the Residential Energy Conservation Property Credit *except:*

    a. Qualifying property must be energy-efficient building property affixed to the building.
    b. Qualifying property must be put into service during 2006 and/or 2007.
    c. Energy-efficient appliances do not qualify.
    d. Qualifying property must meet energy-conservation standards such as those of the IECC or Energy Star Program.

Residential energy property expenditures credit. This credit, when added to the residential energy property conservation credit, makes up the residential energy property credit. The key difference between this expenditures credit and the conservation property credit is that here, the qualifying property is more permanent in nature and its full cost, up to the overall

$500 lifetime maximum and certain amounts, listed immediately below, counts towards the credit. Three types of property qualify, and each has its own dollar limitations:

- Certain furnaces, including those that burn natural gas or propane, may be eligible for the credit, up to $150;
- Advanced main air circulating fans qualify for up to $50; and
- Energy-efficient building property, limited to $300 (**energy-efficient building property** is property like electric and geothermal heat-pumps, and central air conditioners).

As part of the residential energy property credit, all qualifying property must be put into use during 2006 and 2007. This means an expenditure is considered made when the property's original installation is complete. If the property is part of an overall-construction project, the expenditure is made when the original use of the constructed structure by the taxpayer starts.

> **EXAMPLE**
>
> Connie hires a contractor to install qualifying energy property into her home, which she is having renovated. Replacement windows are installed in December 2005; work on a new furnace/air conditioning system begins in December but isn't finished until January 2006. Connie pays 30 percent of the total job in November when the contract is signed, and the rest in February 2006 when all renovations are finished. Connie may take the credit for installation of the furnace and air conditioner because both are not ready for use until January. (Note that if the A/C system were installed in December 2005 instead, no credit is allowed even though arguably the system won't need to be used until hot weather rolls around in June. It was considered ready for use in December 2005). The window installation in December 2005 won't qualify, even though the entire contract will not be considered completed for payment purposes until February 2006. However, a gray area exists on whether each window in the house needs to be installed in 2006 to be allowed a credit, or whether the entire window replacement "job" needs to be finished in 2006.

To qualify, all property must meet any performance or quality standards imposed by the IRS at the time the property is acquired, erected, or constructed. For example, the standards qualifying air conditioners must meet are based on the unit's manufacturer's published data from tests run at 95 degrees Fahrenheit or may be based on the standards from the Air Conditioning and Refrigeration Institute. Heat pumps, fans, and furnaces must also meet stringent standards set by the industry and adopted by the IRS. All qualifying property must be installed for use in the taxpayer's principal residence and must be put into service by the taxpayer. Here, labor costs, including on-site assembly and installation, are included in the statute as eligible under the credit.

> **CAUTION**
>
> A taxpayer's basis in the property is reduced by the amount of the credit, and no property purchased with subsidized energy financing qualifies for the credit. This credit has no carryforward provision.

New rules in the law ensure that joint owners of property are not penalized with regard to the amount of the credit allowable. However, when the joint owners are married to one another and file a joint return, only one maximum $500 is allowed (because the joint owners must also make the home their principal residence, this is the most likely case).

The building envelope component and qualified energy property improvements made to condominiums and cooperative housing units qualify. A tenant-stockholder of a cooperative housing unit or a condominium complex will be considered to have incurred a ratable or proportionate share of the costs of the property installed, and may take the credit to the extent of his or her share.

> **EXAMPLE**
>
> Scott owns a condominium in a small condominium complex of 20,000 square feet with all equal-sized units. He and the four other tenant-shareholders for their condominium complex decide to replace their furnace. In 2006, they make the replacement and do so with a qualified energy-efficient natural gas furnace. Because the property is a furnace, the credit is limited to $150. Scott may claim $30 on his tax return ($150 maximum credit for the furnace ÷ five equal shares = $30 per tenant) toward the furnace.

When the business and nonbusiness uses of the property are mixed, special rules apply. If the qualifying property is used less than 80 percent of the time for nonbusiness use, only the percentage of the use attributable to that nonbusiness use may be used in calculating the credit.

A word about the AMT. Another significant benefit written into the energy credits available to individual homeowners is that the full credit may be taken against alternative minimum tax (AMT) liability. A growing number of individuals are subject to the AMT, in part because homeownership often gives rise to high real estate tax and mortgage interest deductions. The new energy credit, being unreduced by the AMT, will provide an incentive to all homeowners to install qualifying energy-saving property.

STUDY QUESTION

> **4.** The Residential Energy Property Expenditures Credit may not be carried forward to future tax years. ***True or False?***

.02   Residential Alternative Energy Expenditures Credit

For "going solar" or "fuel cell," a homeowner is rewarded by a tax credit significantly larger than for installing insulation, windows, and energy-efficient conventional furnaces and central air conditioning units. The residential alternative energy expenditures credit is available to individual taxpayers who install in their homes certain alternative-energy producing property (the 2005 Energy Act does not distinguish between principal homes and second homes here). Solar hot water, photovoltaic (solar-powered, electricity-producing property), and full cell property will be eligible for a new 30 percent credit.

This 30 percent credit is only available to property put into service during 2006 and 2007. The maximum credit for any tax year is $2,000 for each of the two categories of solar property (solar hot water and solar electricity), and $500 for each 0.5 kilowatt capacity for fuel cell property (with an unlimited cap). This means that for solar property, the total amount allowable is either 30 percent of the actual expense or $2,000, whichever is less, and there is no cap on the fuel cell property credit.

> **COMMENT**
>
> A taxpayer would have to install $6,667 on solar panels to claim the entire $2,000 for a category of solar energy production ($6,667 × 30 percent credit = $2,000). Generally, solar panel installation costs between $7,000 and $10,000, depending on the location and kilowatt output of the panels.

Unlike the Residential Energy Property Expenditures Credit, the Residential Alternative Energy Expenditures Credit is available on *any* property used by the taxpayer as a residence—including vacation homes—not only expenditures on a principal residence qualify for this credit.

Like the Residential Energy Property Expenditures Credit, however, taxpayers may include toward the Residential Alternative Energy Expenditures Credit labor cost for original installation, on-site preparation, or assembly, and joint property owners such as condominium owners may split the cost of the property with their neighbors, and take their ratable portion of this generous credit. Taxpayers must reduce their tax basis in the property by the amount of the credit.

Standards. Like most of the other energy credits in the 2005 Energy Act, in order for solar property to qualify for use for the credit, it must meet rigid certification standards, although interestingly, the heaters need not meet any particular efficiency rating. The nonprofit Solar Rating and Certification Corporation and comparable entities endorsed by the IRS are responsible for certifying eligible solar hot water heaters. Although there is no efficiency rating necessary for solar property to qualify, at least half of the property's energy must be generated from the sun. For photovoltaic property, any expenditures will qualify, regardless of how many kilowatt hours are generated by the solar energy expenditures or what percentage of the taxpayer's total energy consumption is covered by the expenditures. However, to maximize the tax break, taxpayers should check local and state regulations for efficiency or certification standards to ensure the products on which they settle will qualify.

> **CAUTION**
>
> This credit is not available for water-heating property that is used to heat hot tubs and swimming pools.

Fuel cells, which are essentially high-tech, electrochemical batteries, are commonly used in NASA space applications and in defense projects. Now taxpayers may use them to lower their tax bills, so long as the fuel cell employed generates at least 0.5 kilowatts of electricity using electrochemical processes and has an electricity-only generation efficiency greater than 30 percent. Fuel cell technology is still new to average consumers, can be extraordinarily expensive, and is not widely available. For taxpayers who are able to install fuel cell energy-producing property in their principal homes (portable generators will not likely qualify because they are not "installed"), the credit is 30 percent of cost of the property up to a maximum of $500 for each 0.5 kilowatt of capacity purchased by the taxpayer per year. Costs of labor for installation, as well as costs for wiring and piping, qualify toward the credit. There is no maximum for this credit, so the greater the number of kilowatts the taxpayer purchases, the greater the credit will be.

COMMENT

Originally, the energy alternative fuel property credit being put before Congress was only available to individuals, but an amendment to the 2005 Energy Act created a similar provision for businesses as part of the general Business Energy Tax Credits. Businesses that install solar energy property to generate electricity, heat or cool a structure, or provide hot water for a structure, as well as businesses that install fuel cell energy-producing property, may qualify for the credit. Public utility energy producers are not eligible for this credit.

STUDY QUESTION

5. The Residential Alternative Energy Expenditures Credit applies at a rate of _____ percent up to a maximum of _____ for solar hot water heaters and electricity producers placed into service during 2006 or 2007.

   a. 10; $3,000
   b. 20; $2,500
   c. 30; $4,000
   d. None of the above is the correct percentage or maximum dollar amount

.03 Energy-Efficient Commercial Buildings Deduction

Businesses can also take advantage of new energy conservation incentives. Similar and analogous provisions to those made available to consumers and individuals by the 2005 Energy Act are available to businesses.

Unlike those incentives for individuals, however, individual businesses (except for homebuilders) are entitled to a deduction rather than a credit. Therefore, the deduction only reduces taxable income rather than directly reducing their bottom-line tax liability. However, although it is a deduction that a business would eventually be allowed to write off anyway through depreciation deductions, it allows for the benefits to take place sooner. The energy-efficient commercial buildings deduction allows a business to take an immediate deduction for the full cost of the expenditure rather than taking depreciation, a little bit at a time each year.

The maximum deduction allowed is $1.80 per square foot, and is only available to property placed in service after December 31, 2005, and before January 1, 2008. Any property used in calculating the deduction must have its tax basis reduced by it, which can result in more taxable gain should the property be sold in the future and retain its value.

In order to qualify for the deduction, the costs must be associated with depreciable or amortizable property installed in a commercial building within the United States. The property must be installed as part of:

- The interior lighting system;
- The heating, cooling, ventilation, or hot water systems; or
- The building envelope, which includes everything that separates the interior of the structure from the outdoor environment.

To qualify for the full deduction, the overall cost-reduction plan must target all three systems.

The property must be installed as part of a plan to reduce the building's energy consumption **costs** by at least 50 percent in comparison to a **reference building** that meets minimum requirement standards. To reiterate, this standard does not require a 50 percent reduction in the building's energy **consumption,** and the 50 percent cost reduction is not compared to the building's current costs, but instead, to the costs of a hypothetical building standardized by the IRS. The standards can be found in *Standard 90.1-2001*, which is a standard published by the North American Society of Heating, Refrigerating, and Air Conditioning Engineers and the Illuminating Engineering Society of North America, and provides the minimum requirements for the design of energy-efficient buildings other than low-rise residential buildings. The standard has general acceptance in the relevant industries and has been incorporated by the International Energy Conservation Code (IECC) for 2003.

STUDY QUESTION

> 6. All of the following are requirements to qualify for the full energy-efficient commercial buildings deduction *except:*
>
>   a. The overall cost deduction plan must target property installed in the lighting, heating and cooling or water system, and building envelope systems.
>   b. The property must be installed as part of a plan to reduce the building's energy consumption costs by at least 50 percent compared to a reference building.
>   c. The costs must not be amortizable property.
>   d. The deduction may not exceed expenses totaling $1.80 per square foot.

.04   Energy-Efficient New Home Production Credit

A special credit is available for contractors who build new homes in the United States. For each home built that qualifies as energy-efficient, one contractor responsible for the home's construction (for example, the general contractor) may claim a $2,000 credit. A similar credit for $1,000 is available to contractors of manufactured homes that meet a 30 percent energy consumption reduction standard.

In order to qualify, the dwelling unit (which includes manufactured homes) must be certified to have an annual heating and cooling energy consumption that is at least 50 percent below that of a comparable dwelling unit, which also must be set by specified standards. The reduction is set by the building envelope, which must account for 10 percent of the reduction of energy consumption to qualify. The standards of a "comparable dwelling home" used for this credit are found in Chapter 4 of the 2003 International Energy Conservation Code (IECC), effective as it reads on the date the credit is enacted, with heating and cooling equipment efficiencies that correspond to the minimum allowed under regulations established by the Department of Energy under the National Appliance Energy Conservation Act.

The home must further meet certain certification guidelines set by the IRS and the Energy Department. The specifics of the certification requirements are not yet available; however, they must be in writing and must specify in a readily verifiable fashion the energy-efficient building envelope components and property, as well as the heating and cooling units in the home, and the properties' energy efficiency performance rating.

For the contractor to take advantage of the credit, the home must be substantially completed to be sold to a person for use as a residence 2006 and 2007.

STUDY QUESTIONS

7. The difference between the amount of the Energy-Efficient New Home Production Credit available to contractors for new homes and contractors for manufactured homes meeting a 30 percent energy consumption reduction standard is:

   a. $500
   b. $600
   c. $750
   d. $1,000

8. To qualify for the Energy-Efficient New Home Production Credit, the dwelling unit must be certified as having an annual heating and cooling consumption that is at least _____ percent below that of a comparable dwelling unit under the 2003 IECC.

   a. 50 percent
   b. 40 percent
   c. 30 percent
   d. 25 percent

.05 Alternative, "Green" Vehicles

Businesses and individuals alike are eligible for tax incentives for the purchase of environmentally friendly "green" vehicles. For most consumers, this means a tax break for buying a hybrid vehicle. However, they do include more exotic energy-efficient vehicles.

In 2005, any car deemed to be a "clean fuel" car by the IRS, purchased and put in service during the tax year, was entitled to a $2,000 deduction. Mostly this deduction went to mass-produced hybrid vehicles such as the Toyota Prius and the Honda Civic Hybrid. With the enactment of the 2005 Energy Act, however, the incentives changed. Available beginning in 2006 as a credit, the incentive will replace the deduction, which will now sunset at the end of 2005.

COMMENT

Because credits have a greater impact on tax liability than do deductions, taxpayers interested in maximizing the tax break should be encouraged to wait until 2006 to make any green vehicle purchase.

The comprehensive credit applies to a broader range of vehicles and taxpayers than did the pre-2006 deduction, encompassing hybrids, advanced lean-burn technology vehicles, vehicles powered by fuel cells, and alternative fuel vehicles (for example, hydrogen-powered cars). Only electric cars are not included. Sellers may claim the credit if the vehicle is sold to a government entity or a tax-exempt organization.

CAUTION

Many taxpayers and practitioners have misread the 2005 Energy Act, thinking that the law applies for the first time to lessees of environmentally friendlier vehicles. Laypersons and some industry professionals have initially concluded that the consumers got the credit, with the only exception being if they were tax exempt or a governmental entity. Unfortunately, the way that Congress wrote the law, it is the leasing company that gets the credit. Of course, optimism argues that because lessors will be able to claim the credit for the vehicle they will pass on the lower prices to consumers, but that has yet to be seen.

Hybrids and lean-burn vehicles. Unlike the prior deduction, which was a flat maximum rate of $2,000 for any qualifying hybrid, the amount a taxpayer may claim as a credit for the green vehicle will be dependent on the car the taxpayer buys. The new credit imposes a two-part test made up of:

- A fuel economy credit, which is based on the vehicle's rated fuel-economy, and
- A conservation credit based on the vehicle's estimated lifetime fuel savings.

The fuel economy credit is $400 for a car or light truck that gets 25 to 50 percent greater mileage than a comparable 2002 model, $1,600 for a vehicle that gets double the mileage of a comparable 2002 model, and $2,400 for a vehicle that gets 2.5 times the mileage. The conservation credit also varies from vehicle to vehicle and ranges from $250 to $1,000.

CAUTION

Taxpayers should be alert that under the 2005 Energy Act, the credit is phased out for hybrids and other lean-burn vehicles produced by any particular manufacturer following the second quarter after that manufacturer has sold more 60,000 of those vehicles. This provision is likely a step by Congress to aid American car manufacturing companies who were slower to jump on the hybrid and lean-burn trend. Many foreign-owned auto manufacturers have been selling hybrids and lean-burn vehicles for many years, and will reach the limits much faster. Taxpayers should also note that for light trucks and cars, the credit expires on December 31, 2010. For heavy hybrid trucks, the credit expires on December 31, 2009.

Fuel cell vehicles. The credit for fuel cell vehicles is much greater than that offered for hybrid and other lean-burn vehicles. For cars and light trucks, the credit can be as high as $12,000. The credit is created in two parts for cars and light trucks, and varies based on the vehicle's weight class and its fuel economy based on a comparison to a comparable 2002 model. The base credit begins at $8,000 for cars and falls to $4,000 beginning on January 1, 2010. For trucks weighing more than 26,000 pounds, the credit is $40,000. The fuel cell credit expires entirely on December 31, 2014.

Alternative fuel vehicles. Until the 2005 Energy Act, a deduction was available of between $5,000 and $50,000 for trucks, vans, and busses, which varied based on vehicle weight. Beginning in 2006, the incentive is a credit, and the maximum for it is $4,000 for cars and light trucks, varying incrementally by the cost of the vehicle. For heavy trucks weighing in excess of 26,000 pounds, the maximum credit is up to $32,000. Vehicles included under the general "alternative fuel" heading include those that are powered by: compressed natural gas, liquefied natural gas, liquefied petroleum gas, and liquid fuels that are 85 percent ethanol, but do not include hybrids or fuel-cell vehicles. The credit sunsets on December 31, 2010.

STUDY QUESTIONS

---

9. For green vehicles, under the 2005 Energy Act the incentive changes from a flat $2,000 for a qualifying hybrid to a fuel economy credit of up to ____ and a conservation credit of up to _____.

   a. $400; $250
   b. $1,000; $500
   c. $2,000; $750
   d. $2,400; $1,000

10. Which of the following is *not* a major difference between the clean fuel car incentive and the green vehicle incentive by the IRS?

   a. The clean fuel car incentive was a deduction, whereas the green vehicle incentive is a credit.
   b. The green vehicle incentive applies to a broader range of vehicles than did the clean fuel car incentive.
   c. For alternative fuel vehicles the prior incentive was based on vehicle weight, whereas the green vehicle incentive is based on the cost of the vehicle.
   d. All of the above are major differences.

¶510 SAFE ACCOUNTABLE, FLEXIBLE, AND EFFICIENT TRANSPORTATION EQUITY ACT

At about the same time Congress was passing the 2005 Energy Act, the members passed the Safe, Accountable, Flexible, and Efficient Transportation Equity Act of 2005 (2005 Highway Act). Despite the law's naming, the $286 billion legislation provides excise tax relief for businesses conducted on land, in water, as well as in the air. It is expected to fund highway, transit, and highway safety programs for fiscal years 2004 through 2009.

Unlike the 2005 Energy Act, which is full of tax breaks, the 2005 Highway Act has fewer tax incentives and a greater emphasis on business excise taxes and revenue raising. Although the law includes tax cuts expected to save taxpayers approximately $1.126 billion over 10 years, according to the Joint Committee on Taxation's estimates, to pay for itself, the 2005 Highway Act extends some taxes and raises others.

Two of the biggest revenue-raising provisions are part of a handful of extensions of transportation-related taxes. The greatest offsetting measure calls for the $495 million provision to tax all kerosene removals, other than to the wing of an airplane, as diesel fuel. All three nonfuel excise taxes and the motor fuel excise tax are all extended from 2005 to 2011 at their current rates.

The law does provide some tax breaks, however. Limousines weighing more than 6,000 pounds are now exempted from the gas guzzler tax. Tractors that weigh 19,500 pounds or less are excluded from the excise tax on heavy trucks and trailers. The excise tax on fishing poles and other fishing equipment has been capped at $10, and the occupational taxes for wholesalers, distributors, and importers of distilled spirits have been lifted. The biggest tax break, though, will be in the issuance of $15 million in tax-exempt bonds to finance transportation projects.

Most of the provisions in the 2005 Highway Act took effect on October 1, 2005.

STUDY QUESTION

11. Which of the following is *not* one of the transportation-related taxes that were extended under the 2005 Highway Act?

a. Kerosene removal tax
b. Motor fuel excise tax
c. "SUV" tax
d. All of the above were extended

¶515 KATRINA EMERGENCY TAX RELIEF ACT OF 2005

In late August 2005, much of the Gulf region of the United States was all but destroyed by the wrath of the largest hurricane to hit the United States in recorded history. Hurricane Katrina literally leveled cities, displacing hundreds of thousands of gulf residents and costing billions in cleanup and reconstruction. After the magnitude of the storm was realized, government agencies and Congress, as well as individual taxpayers and businesses, came to the aid of the area and its residents.

Within days of Hurricane Katrina, Congress appropriated $10.6 billion for rescue and relief efforts. No one was shocked when that amount was woefully inadequate, and Congress went back to work to appropriate another $51.8 billion. During that time, the IRS stepped in and offered administrative relief to taxpayers affected by the storm by offering extended deadlines, setting up a toll-free number for taxpayer assistance, and providing a host of other remedies. Congress solidified many of the IRS's measures in late September in the Katrina Emergency Tax Relief Act of 2005 (KETRA). KETRA gives businesses and individuals victimized by Hurricane Katrina temporary tax breaks with the intention of getting their lives and businesses back on track. According to Joint Committee on Taxation reports, the measure will cost more than $6 billion.

Most of the provisions in KETRA are specific to victims of Hurricane Katrina, and several vary depending on the location of the taxpayer prior to the storm. Those taxpayers who resided in the hardest hit areas (the **core disaster areas**), are extended even greater relief than those living and working in less-damaged locales. Other provisions apply to all taxpayers, regardless of geography, who choose to donate money, leave from work, goods, their home spaces, and their time to help rebuild the region.

> **COMMENT**
>
> KETRA is full of tax opportunities for victims of Hurricane Katrina to begin the process of rebuilding their lives. Additionally, opportunities abound for taxpayers to claim tax incentives for relief related to Hurricane Katrina, with the added benefit of civic philanthropy.

.01 Extended Tax Deadlines

KETRA extended the time to file and pay taxes for taxpayers in the disaster areas to February 28, 2006. Any taxpayer living within the disaster area, whose records or tax professionals were in the disaster area, or whose business was in the disaster area may file any tax returns for which the expiration date was not after August 25, 2005 until February 28, 2006. This includes income tax returns, estate and gift tax returns, and excise and employment taxes as well.

.02 Preserving Tax Benefits

Relocating and the loss of work for individuals in the disaster area had the potential of disrupting the tax status for thousands. In order to aid those still reeling, KETRA allows taxpayers in the Hurricane Katrina disaster areas to use their 2004 income to calculate the Child Credit and the Earned Income Tax Credit (EITC). The rules for this benefit are specific, and taxpayers should note their eligibility. To qualify, the taxpayer must have resided in a designated Hurricane Katrina core disaster area or have lived in the general disaster area, and been displaced from their principal place of residence. The benefit may be used for the taxpayer's tax year that includes August 25, 2005. The taxpayer's income for 2005 must be less than 2004 to claim the EITC portion.

KETRA also authorizes the IRS to adjust any tax law application for taxpayers who qualify for the benefit to ensure that taxpayers do not lose any deduction, credit, or experience any change in filing status by reason of temporary Hurricane Katrina-related relocation.

COMMENT

The Joint Committee on taxation illustrated this provision by explaining that the IRS will have the authority to overlook the residency requirements for dependency exemptions.

STUDY QUESTION

---

12. To what date did the KETRA grant an extension for filing any tax returns (income tax, estate or gift tax, excise tax, and employment tax) for Hurricane Katrina victims?

    a. January 1, 2006

    b. February 28, 2006

    c. April 15, 2006

    d. December 31, 2006

.03 Casualty Losses

KETRA lifts all restrictions and limitations on claiming casualty losses. This means the general rule that nonbusiness casualty losses are usually deductible only to the extent they exceed 10 percent of the taxpayer's adjusted gross income, and a $100 floor has been eliminated for losses attributed to Hurricane Katrina.

This provision essentially functions to treat Katrina losses differently from other casualty losses. Hurricane Katrina losses are disregarded when the taxpayer calculates other casualty losses because other, non-Katrina attributed losses are still subject to the 10 percent threshold and the $100 floor.

EXAMPLE

In June of 2005, Gary's home was damaged by a fire. His home was in New Orleans. On August 25, his home was flooded and further damaged by Hurricane Katrina. Gary may claim casualty losses for both events, but the cost of the fire damage must exceed 10 percent of Gary's adjusted gross income and the $100 floor, whereas the Katrina damage need not.

As with all presidentially declared disasters, victims of Hurricane Katrina have the option of amending their previous year (2004) income tax returns to claim the casualty loss for the storm, and expedite the use of the deductions. Only taxpayers who itemize may claim these deductions.

.04   Early Distributions from IRAs and Pensions

Taxpayers who take early distributions from IRAs, pensions, and other retirement accounts are generally hit with a 10 percent early withdrawal penalty. The rules are relaxed for specific, special situations, and KETRA makes Hurricane Katrina one of those situations. Under KETRA, Hurricane Katrina victims may withdraw up to $100,000 per taxpayer from an IRA, pension, 401(k) or other, similar plan, without incurring the 10 percent penalty. The distributions must be made between August 25, 2005, and January 1, 2007, and victims must have had their principal home in the Katrina disaster area on August 25, 2005, and had suffered an economic loss to qualify.

For pension holders, KETRA raises the limit of maximum amounts taxpayers can borrow from $50,000 to $100,000. The distributions must be made between September 23, 2005, and January 1, 2007, to qualify.

For taxpayers who take the special distributions and are able to replace the funds within three years, the funds will not be taxed as income but will instead be given rollover treatment. If the taxpayer does not replace the funds within the three-year period, the distribution will be taxed as income. However, for those taxpayers, KETRA has an additional safeguarding provision: Income not replaced within three years will be taxed ratably over a three-year period. Of course, taxpayers will be able to elect out of the three-year ratable taxation treatment.

PLANNING TIP

Family members and friends of Hurricane Katrina's victims may also take advantage of the law's retirement account provisions. Qualified distributions made to a taxpayer to assist a victim (not the taxpayer taking the distribution) will also be treated specially under KETRA.

KETRA also has a special provision for taxpayers who were in the process of homebuying. Taxpayers who withdrew funds from their retirement accounts between February 28, 2005, and August 25, 2005, to purchase a home, and that purchase was interrupted by Hurricane Katrina, will be allowed to replace the funds without a penalty if the funds are replaced by February 28, 2006.

> **COMMENT**
>
> Taxpayers who expect to remain unemployed by Hurricane Katrina may want to defer the early IRA distribution to 2006, then elect out of the three-year averaging, so that the distribution is taxed as income at one time when the taxpayer's income is at its lowest.

STUDY QUESTION

13. All of the following are revisions under KETRA for retirement account distributions and loans to Hurricane Katrina victims *except:*

  a. Withdrawals from IRAs, pensions, 401(k)s, or similar retirement plans will not incur the 10 percent early withdrawal penalty.

  b. Repayments to retirement plans will be given rollover treatment.

  c. The maximum loan amounts from pension benefits increased from $50,000 to $100,000 until January 1, 2007.

  d. All of the above are KETRA provisions for Hurricane Katrina victims.

.05   Extended Nonrecognition Replacement Period

For taxpayers who receive insurance proceeds from damaged or destroyed property, taxable gain is usually created by those proceeds. The gain can go unrecognized so long as the property for which the proceeds were disbursed is replaced within a certain replacement time period. For businesses, this period is usually two years. For individuals, the period is normally four years. In both cases, KETRA has extended these periods to five years, as long as the replacement property is located within a Hurricane Katrina disaster area. This nonrecognition benefit is elective, and taxpayers should individually decide whether using it is best for them.

> **CAUTION**
>
> For taxpayers whose insurance gain will not exceed the $250,000/ $500,000 homesale exclusion, it will make better financial sense to recognize the gain and use the exclusion that is available to all taxpayers. This works because using the replacement property rules requires a carryover basis. Those tax-payers whose gain is in excess of the homesale exclusion should consider using replacement benefit for the excess portion of the gain only.

.06   Mortgage Revenue Bonds

KETRA has a provision making state and local government-issued mortgage revenue bonds more common for low-interest mortgages, ensuring that they are more readily accessible to more people. Normally, the bonds are only available to first-time homebuyers at below-market mortgage rates. KETRA waives the first-time homebuyer requirement for a **qualifying Hurricane Katrina recovery residence,** which is defined in KETRA as any principal residence in a Hurricane Katrina core disaster area or any other principal residence in a general Hurricane Katrina disaster area that on August 28, 2005, was rendered uninhabitable by Hurricane Katrina. The new residence must be financed through 2007 (meaning the loan cannot expire prior to December 31, 2007) to qualify and must be located in the same state as the prior principal residence destroyed by the storm. Eligible taxpayers may receive up to $150,000 in loan proceeds to repair a Hurricane Katrina-damaged home.

.07   Discharge of Indebtedness

Generally, having debt forgiven is a taxable event. When a taxpayer is discharged from his or her responsibility to pay a debt, income is realized, because the taxpayer is no longer expected to repay that debt and funds otherwise earmarked for debt repayment are available. For Hurricane Katrina victims whose principal residence was located in a core Hurricane Katrina disaster area on or after August 25, 2005, KETRA allows discharge of indebtedness without taxation. The same rule applies to taxpayers with any other principal residence in the general Hurricane Katrina disaster areas that suffered economic loss as a result of the storm. Any discharge must be made by January 1, 2007, to qualify.

Taxpayers who would qualify for this tax break should check with their mortgage lender. After Hurricane Katrina, some mortgage companies announced they planned to forgive outstanding mortgages in the cases where the qualifying home was underinsured.

.08   Work Opportunity Tax Credit

Another opportunity available to all businesses is the Work Opportunity Tax Credit (WOTC). The WOTC is credit that encourages employers to hire economically challenged and high-risk individuals. The credit is equal to 40 percent of the first $6,000 paid to the qualifying employee. KETRA creates a new class of qualifying individuals, **Katrina employees,** defined as workers whose principal place of abode was in a core disaster area on August 28, 2005. Any business hiring a Katrina Employee may claim this credit, regardless of the business' location, so long as the employee was not employed by that business on August 28, 2005. For businesses outside of the core disaster area, the hire must be made by December 31, 2005. For businesses within the core area, the deadline is extended to December 31, 2007.

> **EXAMPLE**
>
> On August 28, 2005, Karen was a nurse whose principal place of abode was in New Orleans, Louisiana. On October 15, 2005, Karen is hired by a hospital in Boston, Massachusetts. That hospital may claim a credit for 40 percent of the first $6,000 paid to Karen.

.09 Employee Retention Credit

For smaller businesses, KETRA provides another layer of opportunity through the employee retention credit. This new credit is meant to encourage small business taxpayers in the core disaster area to retain workers on their payrolls. Like the WOTC, this credit is 40 percent of the first $6,000 paid to each eligible employee after August 28, 2005 and through December 31, 2005. To be eligible for this credit, the employer's place of business must have been located in the core disaster area on August 28, 2005, and the business must have been rendered inoperable by Hurricane Katrina. Only employers with an average of 200 or fewer employees for the prior tax year may take this credit, and the credit is only available for the duration of the time the business was inoperable.

.10 Charitable Contributions

Although KETRA's main focus is on helping the victims of Hurricane Katrina begin to rebuild and plan again for the future, Congress and the IRS realized that Americans from all over the nation would be donating their time, money, and energy to aiding those victims of the storm. To make the process of giving a little easier, KETRA and the IRS have provided several ways for taxpayers to reduce their tax liability while they help.

Raising the income percentage limitation for individuals. Normally, an individual's deductible charitable contributions for any one year cannot exceed 50 percent of that taxpayer's adjusted gross income. The theory behind this limit is to prevent wealthy individuals with ample assets or tax-exempt income from paying no tax by sheltering all of their taxable income through charitable giving. To encourage these individuals to open their purses wider during the Katrina disaster, Congress lifted the 50-percent income limit on cash charitable deductions for the remainder of 2005.

Cash donations (including checks but not property, including stock) made between August 28, 2005 and December 31, 2005, are allowed as an itemized charitable deduction with no income limitation. Further, itemized deductions for charitable contributions will not be reduced by the otherwise required phaseout of part of the deduction for high-income taxpayers. As in the past, any deduction in excess of income may be carried over to a future year.

PLANNING TIP

This provision, although appearing in KETRA, need not have any connection with Hurricane Katrina. Any and all monetary donations to qualified charities during the prescribed time period will qualify for the base exemption. This is a unique opportunity for taxpayers to significantly impact their tax liability while benefiting their alma maters, church, community, or other favorite charities in addition to donations earmarked for Katrina relief.

EXAMPLE

Doug, a 1993 college graduate, wants to donate a monetary gift to his alma mater. In October 2005, Doug makes a significant contribution worth 80 percent of his allocable income to the school. Despite the gift being greater than 50 percent, Doug may take a charitable deduction for the whole amount.

Mileage reimbursement. For many taxpayers, in the aftermath of Hurricane Katrina, the desire to donate time in lieu of (or in addition to) monetary contributions to relief efforts led them to leave their homes and go to the disaster areas to help in rescue, cleanup, and rebuilding efforts. Usually, taxpayers who use their personal vehicles for charitable uses may claim a tax deduction for 14 cents-per-mile for every mile driven in lieu of claiming actual expenses.

KETRA raises the statutory mileage rate for individuals who use their personal vehicles to aid in Hurricane Katrina relief efforts. For charity work related to Hurricane Katrina, taxpayers may deduct up to 70 percent of the standard business mileage rate per mile. For most taxpayers, this will be 70 percent of 48.5 cents per mile, or 34 cents-per-mile. The 48.5 cents-per-mile business rate is in effect for miles driven between September 1, 2005, and December 31, 2005. Prior to September 1, 2005, the standard business mileage rate was 40.5 cents-per-mile, which means that taxpayers who will claim this deduction for services donated between August 25, 2005, and August 31, 2005, may only claim 29 cents-per-mile.

After December 31, 2005, the new mileage rates for 2006 will apply, and taxpayers who are still using their vehicles for Hurricane-Katrina-related charitable relief efforts must adjust their deductions accordingly. The IRS will release the 2006 mileage rates at the end of 2005. The mileage rates may be lower than the 2005 rates, and Katrina volunteers will have to adjust their deductions accordingly.

Parking fees and tolls may also be deducted separately by taxpayers claiming the statutory standard mileage rate for any charity work. This is the case for Hurricane Katrina efforts as well.

Taxpayers will have to substantiate that the miles driven were indeed in connection with Hurricane Katrina. The Joint Committee on Taxation suggests that at a minimum, taxpayers will have to provide written records evidencing the following:

- The number of miles driven;
- The dates the mileage was incurred;
- The name of the organization for which the volunteer work was completed needing the use of the vehicle;
- The locations the taxpayer used the vehicle on behalf of the organization for Katrina relief services; and
- The service's relationship to Hurricane Katrina.

Providing housing to Katrina victims. In response to the scores of gulf-region residents displaced by the storm's destruction, good-Samaritan Americans have been opening their homes to victims and offering lodging. KETRA rewards this special charity by allowing individuals who take in displaced victims a special personal exemption. Both homeowners and renters are eligible for the exemption, which is $500 per qualified displaced person housed, free-of-charge, for at least 60 days.

The exemption limit caps at $2,000 for 2005 and 2006 total for both years, which effectively limits the exemption to four evacuees. To qualify, the housing must be rent-free and must be in the taxpayer's principal residence. The displaced victims' principal residence must have been located in a disaster area on August 28, 2005, to be eligible. Income-based phaseouts will not apply to this exemption, which is available regardless of whether the taxpayer providing the housing itemizes his or her deductions.

Dependents and a spouse will not qualify as an eligible displaced person. Other nondependent family-members, such as aunts, uncles, cousins, and even parents are eligible. To substantiate the exemption, the taxpayer must provide the displaced person's tax identification number on his or her tax return.

> **EXAMPLE**
>
> Terri, Charlie, and their two children house three qualifying victims displaced by Hurricane Katrina from September 1, 2005, to December 15, 2005. The victims live rent-free, and until move-in, were strangers. Susan and Charlie may take an additional $1,500 exemption—$500 per victim—on their 2005 tax return, in addition to the four personal exemptions to which they would normally be entitled.

Corporate charitable donation limit lifted. Generally, the charitable contribution deduction for a corporation is capped at 10 percent of the corporation's taxable income for the year in which the contribution was made. Any excess may be carried over into succeeding tax years for up to five years. However, between August 28, 2005, and December 31, 2005, the 10 percent limitation is removed for donations made to qualified Code Sec. 170(b)(1)(A) charities. The donations must be monetary and made in connection with Hurricane Katrina relief. In application, this will allow corporations to more readily match contributions made by employees to relief efforts.

The corporation will have to elect to have this treatment apply to its donations in order to be eligible for the special benefit. Also, unlike the lifting of the income limitation for charitable contributions by individuals, corporations can only apply the exemption from the limitation to contributions earmarked specifically for Hurricane Katrina relief efforts.

Donating employee leave. After the terrorist attacks of September 11, 2001, the IRS created a program by which employees could donate their unused leave time back to their employers. The employers could take the funds from the donated days otherwise necessary to pay for the leave and contribute them to a qualified charity. The employer could take a deduction for the amount donated as well as having to pay less in employment taxes, and the employee would have less income to report, thus lowering his or her tax liability. In the aftermath of Hurricane Katrina, the IRS has again allowed for donated leave. The program will function the same way for Hurricane Katrina donations as it did post-September 11th.

> **CAUTION**
>
> It is important for taxpayers to note that employees will not be able to claim a charitable deduction for the leave time they donate.

Although most of the IRS's administrative remedies were codified in KE-TRA, some were not. They are still effective, though, and provide additional opportunities for individuals and businesses to lessen their tax liabilities while providing help. For example, the employee donated leave program has been reinstated.

STUDY QUESTION

14. Ways in which companies may help victims of Hurricane Katrina while the employers use available tax relief include all of the following *except:*

   a. Hiring Katrina employees

   b. Matching employee contributions without being subject to the 10 percent charitable contribution cap

   c. Using donated employee leave to contribute to qualified charities and deducting the donation

   d. All of the above are ways for companies to help

¶520 BANKRUPTCY ABUSE PREVENTION AND CONSUMER PROTECTION ACT OF 2005

For all of the tax opportunities legislatively afforded taxpayers in 2005, certainly a significant number were also removed. Beginning October 17, 2005, taxpayers looking to file for bankruptcy found a new set of rules by which they had to play as set by the Bankruptcy Abuse Prevention and Consumer Protection Act of 2005. In one sense, the 2005 Bankruptcy Act was touted by experts as being the first tax cut of 2005 by saving taxpayers the cost associated with others' bankruptcies. But for individuals faced with bankruptcy, the rules will be much more stringent for debt discharge.

.01 Eliminating Superdischarge

The tax provisions in the title heavily favor the IRS and other taxing authorities, affording them additional priorities and protections. Most notably in the tax-related provisions, the law eliminates **superdischarge,** a term for a Chapter 13 windfall in which judges allowed bankruptcy debtors to discharge tax debt from fraudulent or misfiled returns, which is normally not allowed. Tax debts from failure to file a return or from fraudulently filed returns will not be dischargeable in light of the Bankruptcy Act.

.02 IRA Protection

Although it is unlikely that taxpayers plan for bankruptcy, those that plan cautiously may fare better than those on whom bankruptcy surprises altogether. This is in part due to the way the Bankruptcy Act treats IRAs, some ERISA plans, and some government and church retirement plans. Generally, retirement accounts are provided broad protection in bankruptcy. Debtors will be able to shield $1 million in IRA funds from the bankruptcy estate, and the amount is adjusted for inflation. Even better news for debtors is that the limit only applies to IRAs, and any amounts rolled into IRAs from other qualified accounts will not be subject to the limitation.

Educational IRA protection. Education IRAs and Code Sec. 529 plans are also exempted form the bankruptcy estate. For funds deposited between 365 days and 720 days prior to the bankruptcy petition filing will be exempted, up to $5,000. Any funds placed in the account within a year of the petition will not be exempted.

¶525   EXPIRING PROVISIONS FOR 2005

On December 31, 2005, without action from Congress (which may occur after the first publication of this course), many popular tax incentives will be sunsetting. This means that taxpayers get one final crack in 2005 at using these provisions as they are applicable to their credit. In 2006, they are scheduled to exist no more. These sunsetting provisions are described here.

.01   Sales Tax Itemized Deduction

For 2004 and 2005, the American Jobs Creation Act of 2004 (2004 Jobs Act) allows individual taxpayers to elect to deduct either their state and local income taxes or their state and local sales taxes. Only taxpayers who itemize can take the deduction. Although lawmakers from states with no state income taxes are lobbying hard to make the optional deduction permanent, no legislation has yet to surface from committee consideration. Taxpayers who are planning to take the deduction in 2005 and not use the standard tables provided by the IRS should consider accelerating some anticipated 2006 purchases into December 2005.

.02   Higher Education Expense Deduction

Individuals may take an above-the-line deduction for qualified tuition and related expenses in tax years beginning after December 31, 2001, and before January 1, 2006. In 2004 and 2005, the maximum deductible amount is $4,000 for taxpayers with adjusted gross income not exceeding $65,000 ($130,000 for joint filers). Taxpayers whose income exceeds that limit but does not exceed $80,000 ($160,000 for joint filers) in 2004 and 2005 may deduct up to $2,000 in qualified expenses. The deduction is allowed for expenses paid during a tax year, in connection with an academic term beginning during the year or the first three months of the next year. Especially if the individual does not qualify for the Hope or lifetime learning credit, arrangements should be made to pay tuition for the spring semester before 2006 in order to qualify for the higher education deduction. If year-end legislation extends this deduction, the taxpayer can always reevaluate at that time whether to pay in 2005 and 2006.

.03   Educators' Deduction

Teachers should save their receipts for unreimbursed school-related expenses. Eligible teachers and other educators (including instructors, counselors, principals, and aides) are entitled to a deduction of up to $250 for qualified expenses on their 2005 return. This deduction is scheduled to sunset at the end of 2005. However, several proposals have been floated in Congress to extend it.

.04   Higher AMT Exemption

No one believes that the present AMT exemption amounts will not be extended to 2006, but as of press time for this course, legislation has yet to be passed to do so. Without the extension, Treasury reports that more than two-thirds of taxpayers with incomes between $100,000 and $200,000 could be liable for the AMT in 2006. A family with two children earning $67,980 could have AMT liability. The plan at the start of the year was to address the AMT as part of the reform legislation that would develop out of President Bush's Tax Reform Panel's recommendations. That report has been postponed.

¶530   NEW PROVISIONS FOR 2006 FROM PAST LEGISLATION

Starting on January 1, 2006, several provisions become effective even though they were in fact enacted almost five years ago, as part of the Economic Growth and Tax Relief Reconciliation Act of 2001 (EGTRRA).

01.   Pease Deduction Phaseout

Before 2006, higher-income individuals whose adjusted gross income (AGI) exceeds a threshold level must reduce the amount of their otherwise allowable itemized deductions. This itemized deduction limitation (the so-called Pease deduction named after a congressman who sponsored the provision) will be repealed in stages over a five-year period from 2006 through 2010. Under the phase-in of the repeal of the itemized deduction limit for tax years beginning after 2005, the limitation will be reduced by one-third in 2006 and 2007; two-thirds in 2008 and 2009; and is repealed for 2010.

Under the limitation, itemized deductions that would otherwise be al-lowable are reduced by the lesser of 3 percent of the amount of the taxpayer's AGI in excess of an inflation-adjusted threshold amount (for 2005 it is $145,950 for joint filers, $72,975 for a married individual filing separately) or 80 percent of the itemized deductions otherwise allowable for the tax year. For purposes of this limitation, itemized deductions do not include the deduction for medical expenses, investment interest, casualty or theft losses, or allowable wagering losses.

Higher-income individuals who find themselves close to the threshold amounts of AGI in 2005 should consider shifting their itemized deductions to 2006 by deferring payment of deductible expenses if they use the cash accounting method. They would lose less of the amount of itemized deduc-tions due to the benefit of reductions in the itemized deduction limitation for 2006.

.02   Designated Roth 401(k) Contributions

Starting in 2006, employees will be able to designate all or part of their contributions to their 401(k) plans to be made on an after-tax basis, which will make most distributions tax free. The Economic Growth and Tax Relief Reconciliation Act of 2001 (EGTRRA) first authorized these accounts but delayed their effective date until tax years beginning after December 31, 2005. The IRS is issuing rules now to give employers plenty of time to amend their plans. No plan sponsor is forced to amend its plan, but no employee may elect after-tax Roth contributions without that amendment. Proposed regulations (NPRM REG-152354-04) spell out the requirements.

STUDY QUESTION

---

15. All of the following tax provisions were scheduled to expire at the end of 2005 *except:*

  a. High AMT deduction
  b. Pease deduction
  c. Sales tax itemized deduction
  d. All of the above were scheduled to expire

¶535   CONCLUSION

There is always an ebb and flow to tax legislation and opportunities. Indi-vidual taxpayers can only hope to take advantage of incentives as they come available and use them to the extent they are allowed before the incentives are repealed or replaced. At times the replacement will provide better tax liability relief for taxpayers, and at other times it will inevitably result in a higher tax bill. Planning ahead and knowing how to use the 2005 legislation, or legislation from prior years that impacts 2005 or 2006, is the best way to maximize tax benefits.

CPE NOTE

When you have completed your study and review of chapters 3, 4 and 5 which comprise this Module, you may wish to take the Final Exam for this Module. CPE instructions can be found on page 221.

The Module 2 Final Exam Questions begin on page 229. The Module 2 Answer Sheet can be found on pages 247 and 249.

For you convenience, you can also take this Final Exam online at www.cchtestingcenter.com.

MODULE 3 — CHAPTER 6

Compliance with Circular 230

This chapter explores Circular 230 and the IRS's rules of practice. In 2005, the IRS revised the Circular 230 rules for tax shelter opinions. These changes and more, which may come in the future, require practitioners to be up-to-date with the rules of practice before the IRS.

LEARNING OBJECTIVES

Upon completion of this chapter, you will be able to:

- Describe the final Circular 230 regs for tax shelter opinions;
- Identify how practitioners are adjusting to the new rules for tax shelter opinions;
- Understand other key requirements of Circular 230;
- Describe the work of the IRS's Office of Professional Responsibility;
- Identify who may engage in "limited practice" before the IRS; and
- Discuss possible future regulation of unlicensed return preparers.

¶601 INTRODUCTION

Every time the IRS has revised Circular 230, the proposed changes have generated controversy. Many of the revisions have been fueled by changes in the industry. The emphasis on using Circular 230 as a tool to combat tax shelters and abusive transactions emerged in the 1990s when the shelter industry exploded. The IRS is using every tool at its disposal to terminate shelters. One tactic is to go after the firms and practitioners that design, market, and sell shelters.

IRS Commissioner Mark Everson said this about tax shelter abuses:

The vast majority of tax practitioners are responsible, and they are doing their jobs correctly. But the decline in ethics that took place over the '90s, this hurt not just the taxpayers who may be taking positions they shouldn't have taken, but it also hurt other tax practitioners, because the more aggressive practitioners were taking business away from the people who were trying to act responsibly.

¶605 PRACTICE BEFORE THE IRS

.01 Practice Defined

Practice before the IRS is defined as making a presentation to the IRS concerning a client's rights, privileges, or liabilities under federal tax law. This definition includes the following activities:

- Preparing and filing documents;
- Communicating with the IRS; and
- Representing a client at conferences, hearings, and meetings.

.02 Who May Practice

Attorneys. Any attorney not currently under suspension or disbarment may practice before the IRS. The attorney must file a written statement that he or she is currently qualified as an attorney and is authorized to represent his or her client.

CPAs. Any certified public accountant not currently under suspension or disbarment may practice before the IRS. The CPA must file a written statement that he or she is currently qualified as a CPA and is authorized to represent his or her client.

Enrolled agents. Any enrolled agent not currently under suspension or disbarment may practice before the IRS.

Enrolled actuaries. The rules for enrolled actuaries are similar to attorneys, CPAs, and enrolled agents; however, practice is more limited in scope. Practice as an enrolled actuary is limited to representation with respect to certain issues. Many of these issues involve employee plans.

Limited practice. The IRS also allows some individuals to engage in "limited practice," explained in detail later in the chapter.

¶610 FINAL RULES FOR TAX SHELTER OPINIONS

A debate that raged on for so many years that seemed like it would never end finally did in 2005. On June 20, 2005, the final Circular 230 Rules of Practice for tax shelter opinions took effect. The revised version of Circular 230 effectively turns the old rules upside down. According to the IRS, the main purposes of the bold revisions to Circular 230 are to regulate tax shelter opinions issued for penalty protection and issue standards for giving these opinions to clients.

One of chief complaints about the final Circular 230 regs for tax shelter opinions is about their perceived vagueness. Many of the key terms that are instrumental for practitioners attempting to comply with the new rules are ambiguous and are not defined elsewhere. In addition, many practitioners believe that the final regs, which were designed to reign in a small group of tax shelter advisors and promoters, punish mainstream practitioners as well.

Another complaint is complexity. Navigating the various categories of opinions and the requirements that attach to them is a complex process. Many practitioners are complaining that the complexity of the final Circular 230 tax shelter regs makes tax practice as complex, if not more complex, than the Tax Code.

On top of those complaints, many practitioners believe that the final regs do not allow them to provide complete and accurate advice to their clients. A practitioner's ability to give responses to short follow-up questions based on a change in facts or on limited issues is especially hampered by the new regs.

The response from Treasury and the IRS has not exactly eased the minds of many practitioners. IRS officials call Circular 230 a "living document" that is subject to later modification. The literal language of the final regs scares many practitioners because key provisions include stiff penalties for failure to comply with them, including being permanently disbarred from practicing before the IRS and having an entire firm sanctioned. Attempting to allay practitioner fears, the IRS's Office of Professional Responsibility (OPR) has promised to apply Circular 230 "reasonably." IRS Chief Counsel Donald Korb offered this piece of advice to practitioners: Use "common sense" when interpreting Circular 230 as it applies to tax shelter opinions.

.01   "Covered" Opinions

Under Circular 230, opinions that address tax shelters and similar transactions are called **covered opinions.** If a written opinion falls within the definition of a covered opinion, a stringent set of rules apply to the factual and legal assumptions in the opinion. The definition of covered opinion is any written advice about:

- A "listed transaction (or substantially similar transaction);"
- Any plan or engagement that has as its principal purpose tax avoidance or evasion; or
- Any plan or engagement that has tax avoidance or evasion as a significant purpose if the written advice is:
  - A reliance opinion;
  - A marketed opinion;
  - Subject to conditions of confidentiality; or
  - Subject to contractual protection.

The definition of a covered opinion contains several terms that must be defined themselves.

- *Listed Transactions*—transactions that the IRS has identified as patently abusive. Examples are Son of BOSS, SILO transactions, abusive foreign tax credit transactions and inflated basis "CARDS" transactions.
- *Principal purpose of tax avoidance or evasion*—if tax avoidance or evasion exceeds any other purpose, the transaction will be characterized as having as its principal purpose tax avoidance or evasion.
- *Reliance opinion*—an opinion that concludes at a confidence level of more likely than not that one or more significant federal tax issues could be resolved in the taxpayer's favor.
- *Marketed opinion*—an opinion written by a practitioner who knows or should know that the opinion will be used to promote, market, or recommend a partnership, entity, investment plan or arrangement.
- *Subject to conditions of confidentiality*—written advice that limits disclosure to protect the practitioner's strategies.
- *Subject to contractual protection*—an opinion that gives a client the right to full or partial refund of fees if all or some of the intended tax consequences addressed within the opinion are not sustained is subject to contractual protection. An opinion is also subject to contractual protection if fees for the opinion are contingent upon the realization of tax benefits.
- *Principal purpose*—whether one purpose of an opinion exceeds another purpose is a subjective determination.
- *Significant purpose*—whether tax avoidance or evasion is a significant purpose is open to interpretation. In addition, an opinion may be issued for one reason, but the client may use it for another purpose without the knowledge of the practitioner.
- *More likely than not*—a greater than 50 percent likelihood of the position being upheld.
- *Significant federal tax issue*—an issue for which the IRS has a reasonable basis for a challenge.

STUDY QUESTIONS

> **1.** Any plan that provides written advice prepared under conditions of confidentiality is considered a:
>
>   **a.** Contractual protection
>   **b.** Marketed opinion
>   **c.** Covered opinion
>   **d.** Reliance opinion

2. An issue having a reasonable basis for challenge by the IRS is known as:

    a. A listed transaction

    b. Subject to contractual protection

    c. A reliance opinion

    d. A significant federal tax issue

NOTE

Answers to Study Questions, with feedback to both the correct and incorrect responses, are proved in a special section beginning on page 191.

Requirements for covered opinions. If a practitioner determines that an opinion is a covered opinion, Circular 230 gives detailed requirements that must be followed. The requirements cover the identifying of facts and issues, applying assumptions, relating the law to the facts and reaching conclusions on those facts and issues. In a nutshell, Circular 230 requires practitioners to:

- Identify and consider all relevant facts;
- Avoid basing the opinion on unreasonable factual assumptions;
- Identify all factual assumptions in a separate section of the opinion;
- Ignore "unreasonable" factual representations;
- Consider all significant federal tax issues;
- Relate the law and judicial doctrines to the facts;
- Come to a conclusion regarding the likelihood of the taxpayer prevailing to explain why no conclusion has been reached;
- Set forth the reasons for the conclusion; and
- Identify any outside opinions the practitioner relied upon in issuing the opinion and the conclusions of those opinions.

Excluded advice. A few important items are excluded from the definition of a covered opinion:

- Written advice prepared after a the taxpayer has filed a return for the transaction;
- Written advice that does not concern a listed transaction or a principal purpose transaction and:
  - Is included in documents filed with the SEC; and
  - Is given to a client during the course of an engagement if the practitioner is expected to provide subsequent advice that satisfies new Circular 230.

Negative advice. Written advice given to a client that explains that a federal tax issue will be not be resolved in the client's favor, known as **negative advice,**

is generally not considered a covered opinion. However, negative advice may fall within the purview of a covered opinion if the written advice:

- Reaches a conclusion favorable to the taxpayer at any level regarding the client's tax issue; or
- Relates to a listed transaction or a principal purpose transaction.

Preliminary advice. Advice that is intended only to be a precursor to a later, more detailed analysis is considered **preliminary advice.** It is rarely given on the assumption that the client will be using it for penalty protection. Preliminary advice is not considered a covered opinion under the Circular 230 tax shelter regs.

In-house counsel. Advice from in-house counsel is excluded from the definition of a *covered opinion.* The practitioner must be acting in his or her capacity as an employee of his or her employer solely for determining the tax liability of the employer. Although in-house advice is excluded from the definition of covered opinion, practitioners cannot give tax advice based on unreasonable factual or legal assumptions, unreasonably rely on taxpayer assertions or fail to consider all relevant facts.

"Legend out" language. Many practitioners believe that the best way to avoid being penalized for violating Circular 230 is to place disclaimers or **legends** on every tax-related letter, e-mail, or written communication sent to a client. The placing of disclaimers on written communications is often referred to as "legend out" an opinion.

A typical disclaimer cautions the client that the opinion cannot be relied on for avoiding penalties that the IRS may impose on the taxpayer. To comply with Circular 230, the disclaimer must also be prominently disclosed on the communication. At a minimum, Circular 230 requires that the disclaimer is placed in a separate section in a typeface that is the same size or larger than the typeface used in the advice.

Clients need to understand that legend out language is not an excuse for sloppy advice. Practitioners must reassure clients that the quality of the advice is still excellent but its scope is limited because of the new Circular 230 rules.

Circular 230, Section 10.35(b)(4), provides that "written advice is not treated as a reliance opinion if the practitioner prominently discloses in the written advice that it was not intended or written by the practitioner to be used, and that it cannot be used by the taxpayer, for the purpose of avoiding penalties that may be imposed on the taxpayer." Here are some sample legends out based on Section 10.35(b)(4):

Additional issues may exist that could affect the federal tax treatment of the transaction or matter that is the subject of this advice and this advice does not provide a conclusion with respect to such issues. With respect to issues outside the limited scope of this advice, the advice is not written and cannot be used for penalty protection.

Please be advised that based on current IRS rules and standards the advice contained herein is not intended to be used, nor can it be used, for the avoidance of any tax penalty that the IRS should access related to this matter. That said, please do not hesitate to contact me if you have any questions regarding this matter.

Treasury and the IRS are not exactly thrilled about practitioners legending out every communication. Top Treasury officials have told practitioners that the placement of disclaimers on every communication defeats the purpose of Circular 230, which ensures that clients are provided with a thorough, well-informed opinion. Default legending out of every written piece of advice was never the intent of Treasury and the IRS.

Legend out language must be prominently disclosed in the communication. At a minimum, this means the language should be placed in a different section from the main text. Legend out language cannot be placed in a footnote. The language also must be in the same size typeface, or larger, of the main text of the communication.

Many practitioners are questioning if legend out language can be added to the boilerplate confidentiality lingo that appears in emails. Whether that would be considered a footnote is debatable. Ending the correspondence with a closing and a signature before the "legend out" language probably would not work. Placing the legend out language in the last paragraph probably would be adequate.

STUDY QUESTIONS

3. When might negative advice be considered a covered opinion?
- **a.** When the tax issue eventually is settled in the taxpayer's favor
- **b.** When the advice related to a listed transaction
- **c.** When it is preliminary and a later analysis follows
- **d.** None of the above

---

4. What is a requirement for legend out language under Circular 230?

    a. It must appear in the same section of the communication as the material it disclaims.

    b. It must appear in a type smaller than the item it disclaims.

    c. It must appear in a separate section of the document specifically designed for that purpose.

    d. It must appear on every communication in order for its scope to be proven comprehensive.

.02 Limited Scope Opinion

Circular 230 does offer one option to issuing covered opinions. A practitioner may issue a **limited scope opinion** to clients. Instead of issuing an opinion on all related federal tax issues, a limited scope covers only a few federal tax issues. The practitioner must prominently disclose that the limited scope opinion:

- Is limited to one or more federal tax issues addressed in the opinion;
- Does not cover additional issues that exist that may affect the federal tax treatment of the subject matter of the opinion;
- Does not consider or provide a conclusion regarding noncovered issues; and
- Cannot be used for penalty protection for noncovered issues.

.03 Practitioners with Supervisory Authority

Under Circular 230's tax shelter opinion rules, a practitioner who is in charge of a firm's tax practice "must take reasonable steps to ensure that the firm has adequate procedures in effect for all members, associates, and employees for purposes of complying" with Circular 230. Therefore, a practitioner in charge of a tax practice must not only personally stay vigilant against Circular 230 violations but also have a system in place to guard against violations.

¶615 BOND OPINIONS

At the same time the IRS issued final Circular 230 regs for tax shelter opinions, it also released proposed regs for bond opinions. The bond opinion proposals are controversial because many practitioners believe they will disrupt the municipal bond markets. Traditionally, bond opinions were an exception to the definition of tax shelter for Circular 230. The final Circular 230 tax shelter regs remove that exception.

    The IRS has revised the proposed bond opinion regs several times in response to concerns from practitioners and local and state governments. Under the latest version, issued in June 2005, a state or local bond opinion is written advice concerning:

- The excludability of interest on a state or local bond from gross income under Code Sec. 103;
- The status of a state or local bond as a qualified zone academy bond under Code Sec. 1379E;
- One or more federal tax issues reasonably related and ancillary to tax-exempt bonds; and
- Any combination of the above.

The IRS has outlined some examples of federal tax issues related to and ancillary to tax-exempt bonds. These include application of Code Sec. 55 to a state or local bond; whether a state or local bond has been reissued for federal tax purposes; treatment of original issue discount or premium on a state or local bond under the Tax Code; and whether the entity that is borrowing the proceeds of the state or local bond is a 501(c)(3) organization.

Bond lawyers have expressed concern that the use of penalty protection disclaimers (legend out language) may not be acceptable to investors or underwriters of tax-exempt bonds. Many bond lawyers are also leery that the proposed regs could capture preliminary advice and negative advice. Moreover, they could treat routine bond transactions as tax shelters.

¶620   OTHER CIRCULAR 230 REQUIREMENTS

With all the controversy about the new tax shelter opinion letter rules in Circular 230, it's easy to forget that Circular 230 encompasses a lot more. Circular 230 set out the standards of practice every tax professional must follow if he or she wants to enjoy the privilege of representing clients before the IRS. Tax shelters are high-profile cases but they make up a small percentage of the problems practitioners encounter with Circular 230. Now that the IRS has finalized the Circular 230 rules for tax shelters, it is likely to update some of the other rules.

.01   Section 10.20: Obligation to Provide Information to the IRS

If the IRS makes a request for information, practitioners generally are obliged to submit the information unless he or she believes that the material is privileged or the request is of doubtful legality. The practitioner's belief must be in good faith and it must be reasonable.

Practitioners must promptly advise their clients of any noncompliance with the tax laws that the practitioners discover. Clients also must be alerted if a practitioner discovers an omission. The IRS has proposed tweaking this requirement to require the practitioner to advise the client of the manner in which the error or omission may be corrected. The practitioner would also have to inform the client of the consequences of not taking corrective action.

Under Section 10.22, practitioners must exercise due diligence in:

- Preparing, approving, and filing returns, affidavits and documents with the IRS;
- Determining the accuracy of oral or written representations made to the government; and
- Determining the accuracy of oral or written representations made to clients.

.02 Work Product of Another

The IRS has proposed clarifying the impact of relying on the work product of another person. Under proposed amendments to Section 10.22, a practitioner would be presumed to have exercised due diligence if he or she relies on the work product of another and the practitioner used reasonable care in engaging, supervising, training, and evaluating that person.

.03 Requested Information Unavailable

There is no current exception to the requirement to submit documents or information on request to the IRS when the practitioner or his or her client does not have the information. The IRS has proposed clarifying what to do in this situation. A practitioner should promptly respond to a proper request for documents by either submitting the information or explaining why the information cannot be provided to the IRS. If the information is not within the control of the practitioner or his or her client, the practitioner would be called upon to identify any persons who may have the information.

.04 Section 10.30: Soliciting Business

Circular 230 sets out some broad standards practitioners must follow when soliciting business. Tax professionals authorized to practice before the IRS cannot make an uninvited solicitation of employment in matters related to the IRS. Solicitation includes in-person contacts and telephone conversations, as well as any other means of communications. The restriction; however, does not apply when a practitioner is:

- Seeking new business from an existing or former client in an unrelated manner;
- Communicating with family members;
- Making known the availability of professional services to other practitioners, as long as the person or the firm contact is not a potential client;
- Soliciting business by mail; and
- Engaged in noncoercive in-person solicitation when the practitioner is acting as an employee, member, or officer of a religious, charitable, social welfare, or educational organization.

Circular 230 allows solicitations to be made through professional lists, tele-phone directories, print media, mailings, radio, and television. The method of communication cannot cause the communication to become untruthful, deceptive, or unduly influencing. Practitioners must retain copies of all direct mail communications for at least 36 months. Radio and television solicita-tions must be prerecorded.

The IRS is considering clarifying some of the solicitation requirements. Proposed amendments would permit practitioners to contact potential business clients using any means not specifically barred by statute or rule. The prohibition against deceptive solicitation would be expanded to include private as well as public solicitations. The definition of **communication** would be updated to include e-mails and fax transmissions.

.05   Targeted Mail Solicitations

Targeted mail solicitations must be clearly identified. These are generally solicitations to those whose unique circumstances are the basis for the so-licitation. The communication must disclose the source of information the sender used to select the recipient.

STUDY QUESTION

---

5. Which of the following is an *acceptable* method for practitioners in soliciting clients?

   a. Live radio solicitations

   b. Soliciting via telephone conversations with other practitioners' cli-ents who are before the IRS and who will accept second opinions about their position

   c. Targeted mail solicitations

   d. Sending solicitations to former associates who might interest their new firm in using the practitioner's services

---

.06   Advertising Fees

Every potential client wants to know how much the practitioner's services are going to cost. Circular 230 authorizes practitioners to disclose the fol-lowing types of fees:

- Fixed fees for specific routine services;
- Hourly fees;
- Range fees for particular services;
- Fees charged for an initial consultation; and
- Availability of a written schedule of fees.

.07 Section 10.33: Best Practices

In addition to the controversial changes about tax shelter opinions, the IRS also has added a new list of **best practices** for tax advisors in Section 10.33. The best practices are aspirational. They are practices that tax professionals "should" follow rather than "must" follow. Failing to comply with them does not automatically result in a disciplinary action, such as suspension or disbarment from practice before the IRS. Practitioners with supervisory authority have additional aspirational responsibilities.

08. Checklist

The following checklist has been prepared based on the "best practices" outlined in Circular 230. This checklist will help practictioners review the fundamentals of the new Circular 230 rules not only to consider tax shelter opinions but also to provide the highest quality of work to their clients.

General Considerations

- ☐ Did I communicate clearly with the client regarding the terms of engagement?
- ☐ Did I establish the facts?
- ☐ Did I determine which facts are relevant?
- ☐ Did I evaluate the reasonableness of any assumptions or representations?
- ☐ Did I relate the law to the relevant facts?
- ☐ Did I arrive at a conclusion supported by the law and the facts?
- ☐ Did I advise my client on the consequences of the conclusion?
- ☐ Did I act fairly and with integrity when practicing before the IRS?
- ☐ Did I provide my client with the highest quality representation?

Covered Opinions

- ☐ Did I issue a "covered opinion?"
- ☐ Does the opinion cover a listed transaction?
- ☐ Is the opinion a reliance opinion?
- ☐ Is the opinion a marketed opinion?
- ☐ If so, did I follow all of the standards for covered opinions?
- ☐ Am I competent in the area of tax law in which the opinion is based?
- ☐ Have I included all of the necessary disclosures?
- ☐ Have I disclosed any compensation arrangement if disclosure is required?
- ☐ Have I disclosed any referral agreement?
- ☐ Have I prominently displayed "legend out" language?

B. John Williams, former IRS Chief Counsel, reminded practitioners in Washington, D.C., in September 2005 that clients are always on notice to provide the necessary facts. The first job of the practitioner is to determine what facts are needed and to ascertain the necessary facts. Opinions must have factual integrity. An opinion based on untrue information is worthless.

Williams reminded practitioners that they must still determine what facts are needed. For example, the practitioner may need to find the transaction's nontax business purpose.

.09   Section 10.50: Censure, Suspension, and Disbarment

Practitioners who violate Circular 230's rules may be censured (publicly reprimanded) or have their privilege to practice before the IRS suspended or revoked.

Determining whether a practitioner's conduct has crossed the line from merely being unprofessional to being disreputable is a subjective process. Under Circular 230, conduct that may make a practitioner liable for disciplinary action includes:

- Conviction of any criminal offense under the tax laws;
- Conviction of any criminal offense involving dishonesty or breach of trust;
- Conviction for any felony that makes the practitioner unfit to practice before the IRS;
- Willful failure to file a return;
- Evading or counseling to evade federal taxes;
- Misappropriating client funds;
- Attempting to improperly influence an IRS employee;
- Knowingly aiding another person to practice before the IRS who is disbarred or suspended; and
- Lack of due diligence.

STUDY QUESTION

6. Which of the following is *not* a penalty imposed by the IRS for violators of Circular 230 standards?

   a. Imprisonment
   b. Censure
   c. Disbarment from practice
   d. All of the above are IRS penalties

> **EXAMPLE**
>
> Minh operates a small tax practice and has three employees preparing returns. Minh always reviews their work and signs the returns as the preparer. One of her clients had made several trips over the last year. The return preparer accepted the client's characterization of the trips as business trips and did not ask for any substantiation, which was contrary to company policy. The return preparer gave the return to Minh to review and sign. Minh assumed that the return preparer had verified the accuracy of the client's information. Minh's company had a good reputation and no history of filing inaccurate returns. When the IRS audited the return, the agent discovered that the trips were not business trips. Minh urged the IRS not hold her responsible because her employee had disregarded company policy. In consideration of Minh's policy and, in the absence of a history of inaccurate returns, the IRS determined that Minh had not knowingly submitted false information. However, Minh was the person who signed the return and could not disclaim responsibility for the accuracy of the return. The IRS concluded that Minh had failed to exercise due diligence.

Failure to file. The punishment for failure to file a return is often censure. The particular facts and circumstances, such as the amount owed, whether estimated taxes were paid, evidence of evasion, and other evidence, will be weighed by the IRS. If the practitioner has informed the IRS of his or her failure to file, filed returns and paid any liability, his or her conduct will likely help to avoid a harsher sanction. For example, the IRS may monitor the practitioner for several years to ensure that the practitioner does not fall back into his or her bad habit of not filing returns.

> **EXAMPLE**
>
> Amelia is an enrolled agent and a sole practitioner. She failed to file her income tax return. Amelia told the IRS that she gave her clients first priority and consequently had no time to file her own return. Moreover, she claimed that her payment of estimated taxes, which exceeded her personal tax liability, showed that she acted in good faith. Nonetheless, the IRS sanctioned her for failing to file. Amelia's willful failure to file was a violation of a known legal duty. Although Amelia was entitled to some credit for her estimated payments, making those payments did not offset her failure to file a return.

Delay. Deadlines arrive all too soon and many practitioners can fall behind in their work through no fault of their own. However, if a practitioner actively seeks to delay a meeting, hearing, or conference with the IRS with no explanation, he or she is likely risking disciplinary action.

EXAMPLE

Over the course of two months, Juan cancelled five conferences with an Appeals officer. Early in the morning on the day of each conference, Juan would telephone the Appeals officer and tell the officer that he had to cancel the meeting because of scheduling problems or prior commitments. The Appeals officer tried to contact Juan about rescheduling but he was always unsuccessful. When Juan was questioned by Appeals, he could not recall the specific reasons for the cancellations. According to the IRS, Juan had established a pattern of behavior that showed no consideration for the Appeals officer's time. Juan had no objective reason for the delays and he showed no interest in rescheduling appointments. The IRS censured Juan and warned him that future delays could result in more serious disciplinary action.

Disbarment by another authority. If a practitioner loses his or her license to practice law or work in her or her profession, the individual cannot practice before the IRS.

False opinions. Providing a false opinion on federal tax law is grounds for disciplinary action. The practitioner may have acted with knowledge or he or she may have acted recklessly or through gross incompetence. Reckless conduct is a highly unreasonable omission or representation showing an extreme departure from the standards of ordinary care. Gross incompetence includes conduct that reflects gross indifference, preparation that is grossly inadequate, and consistent failure to perform obligations for the client. Generally, behavior is reflected in a pattern of conduct.

False opinions can arise from:

- A knowing misstatement of fact or law;
- Illegal conduct; and
- Concealment of matters required by law to be revealed.

Abusive language. The stress of dealing with clients and IRS employees can sometimes cause practitioners to lose their cool. Unprofessional language directed at an IRS employee can result in disciplinary action.

> **EXAMPLE**
>
> Lao called the IRS to discuss a client's case. The case had been close to being resolved several times in the past but at the last minute there was always some sticking point. Lao and the IRS agent could not agree on the next course of action and, in frustration, Lao said to the agent, "How about me coming down there and jerking you around a while!" The agent terminated the call. Later that day, Lao telephoned the agent and apologized for his remark. The agent reported Lao's comments to his supervisor. Sometime later, Lao received a letter from the IRS. The agency reprimanded him. His comments were abusive to the agent and similar future conduct would not be tolerated.

STUDY QUESTIONS

7. If Jonathan Howard loses his state bar license to practice law:

   a. He may not practice before the IRS for the remainder of the calendar year or the date of his reinstatement by the state bar, whichever is later.

   b. He may not represent new clients before the IRS but may continue representing existing clients in the midst of actions by the IRS.

   c. He cannot practice before the IRS.

   d. None of the above; practice before the IRS is not dependent on retaining his license with the state bar.

8. Which of the following is **not** a source of false opinions?

   a. Concealment of matters required by law to be disclosed

   b. Knowing misstatement of fact or law

   c. Illegal conduct

   d. All of the above are sources of false opinions

¶625 REVITALIZED IRS OFFICE OF PROFESSIONAL RESPONSIBILITY

The IRS has made implementing the new standards of Circular 230 one of its top four enforcement priorities. To ensure the provisions are followed, the IRS has beefed up the office in charge of enforcing Circular 230: the IRS Office of Professional Responsibility (OPR). IRS Commissioner Everson said OPR was a "backwater" and "wasn't doing the kind of work it ought to be" before the agency increased its budget and doubled its staff.

As a result, OPR now has the manpower to carry out its duties, including:
- Investigating violations of Circular 230
- Compliance efforts;
- Sanctioning a practitioner if a violation has in fact occurred; and
- Educating practitioners about Circular 230.

.01   Sanctions by the OPR

OPR may sanction practitioners for different types of misconduct. The IRS has identified four broad categories of misconduct that may subject a practitioner to disciplinary action. They are:
- Misconduct while representing a taxpayer;
- Misconduct related to the practitioner's own return;
- Giving a false opinion, recklessly or through gross incompetence; and
- Misconduct not directly involving IRS representation.

Best practices do not end when a client leaves the office. Cutting corners, whether accidentally or deliberately, with your own return can land you in hot water with OPR. The IRS recently highlighted some examples of personal misconduct that can lead to disciplinary action:
- The IRS suspended a CPA after an audit revealed improper personal expenditures claimed as business deductions and untimely filed income tax returns;
- An enrolled agent was suspended after making misleading statements on federal employment tax returns; and
- The IRS suspended indefinitely an attorney for failing to file returns for multiple years and failing to pay significant delinquent tax debts.
  OPR receives allegations of violations in one of two ways:
- An IRS employee will make a referral to the OPR after establishing a pattern of misconduct on the part of a practitioner; or
- A member of the general public, usually a client, will send OPR a letter alleging misconduct.

The IRS encourages individuals who have a complaint about a practitioner to file their complaint in writing. Individuals should provide the IRS with as much detail as possible about the allegations of misconduct. If the taxpayer has any supporting documents, copies of the documents should be included in the correspondence. The IRS also wants to know whether the practitioner is an attorney, CPA, enrolled agent, or unenrolled return preparer.

.02   Possible Changes Ahead

The Taxpayer Protection and Assistance Act of 2005 (Sen 832) would direct the Treasury Secretary and not the IRS Commissioner to appoint the director of OPR. The director would report to the Commissioner and would be considered a senior level official within the agency, comparable to the status given to the National Taxpayer Advocate.

B. John Williams, former IRS Chief Counsel, told practitioners in Washington, D.C., in September 2005 that an important issue is how OPR will apply the new rules. Williams expects OPR to handle more cases with tax shelter issues and improper factual analysis.

¶630 LIMITED PRACTICE BEFORE THE IRS

The IRS permits some individuals to engage in "limited practice" before it. Of course, taxpayers can represent themselves. An individual may also represent another taxpayer if they are in a special relationship with one another, such as immediate family members of employee and employer. The representative must present satisfactory identification and proof of his or her authority to represent the taxpayer.

Here are some examples:
- An individual may represent a member of his or her immediate family. The IRS defines *immediate family* to include the individual's spouse, child, parent, brother, or sister;
- An employee may represent his or her employer. The employee must be a full-time employee;
- A general partner can represent the partnership; and
- An officer of an association, corporation, or other organized group can represent the entity

.01 Government Officers and Employees

Generally, an officer or employee of the federal government cannot practice before the IRS. He or she may represent a member of his or her family. A government officer also may represent a person for whom he or she is serving as a guardian. If the government officer or employee is the executor of an estate, he or she may represent the estate. Of course, the officer or employee can represent his or her organization before the IRS.

Traditionally under Circular 230, partners of former officers or employees of the federal government may not represent anyone before the IRS on a matter in which the officer or employee personally and substantially participated. A proposed amendment would remove this prohibition.

STUDY QUESTION

> **9.** A government officer or employee may not serve as the executor of an estate. ***True or False?***

.02   Power of Attorney

A taxpayer's representative must show proof that the taxpayer has authorized him or her to act as his representative. The IRS requires taxpayers to complete and submit a power of attorney. Form 2848 is used to appoint a representative. The representative also must file a declaration stating that he or she is currently eligible to practice before the IRS and is an attorney, CPA, enrolled agent, enrolled actuary, family member, corporate, association or organization officer, employee of the taxpayer, or an unenrolled return preparer. A power of attorney must identify the types of tax matters for which the representative may act on behalf of the taxpayer. If a representative desires to act on a taxpayer's behalf only through correspondence with the IRS, he or she must still submit a power of attorney even though no actual personal appearance is made.

EXAMPLE

Chantal, a small business owner, wants to appoint Justin, an enrolled agent, to represent her before the IRS in a dispute over employment tax liability. Chantal completes Form 2848, and in the section "Tax Matters," she indicates the type of tax, which in her case, would be "employment." Chantal also indicates the numbers of any tax forms applicable to her case and the tax years involved in the dispute.

A taxpayer's representative **must** have a power of attorney to:
- Waive of restriction on assessment or collection of a deficiency;
- Waive of notice of disallowance of a credit or refund claim;
- Consent to extending the collection or assessment period of a tax;
- Execute a closing agreement;
- Receive a taxpayer's refund check; and
- Sign the taxpayer's return.

The IRS generally will accept a power of attorney that is not on Form 2848 so long as the tax matters for which the representative can act are apparent. If they are not, the taxpayer will have to complete Form 2848.

> **EXAMPLE**
>
> Lori is a noncommissioned officer in the U.S. Army. She completed a general power of attorney authorizing her friend David to represent her in her financial matters. David is not an attorney, CPA, enrolled agent, or enrolled actuary. He is also not a member of Lori's immediate family. David must obtain permission from the IRS Office of Professional Responsibility (OPR) to represent Lori. If OPR grants permission, Lori will have to execute Form 2848 to specify the types of tax matters for which David can act on her behalf.

Refund checks. A taxpayer can authorize his or her representative to receive refund checks. However, that is all the taxpayer can authorize. A taxpayer cannot permit his or her representative to endorse or otherwise cash his or her refund check.

Taxpayer's signature. Generally, a taxpayer's representative cannot sign the taxpayer's personal income tax return unless the taxpayer gives this authority to the representative. In addition, there must be a reason why the taxpayer cannot sign, for example, if the taxpayer is gravely ill or injured. Form 2848 or a copy of an earlier executed power of attorney must be forwarded to the IRS along with the taxpayer's return.

Revoking a power of attorney. A taxpayer may revoke a power of attorney by alerting the IRS in writing. The signed revocation statement must contain the name and addresses of each representative whose power to act on behalf of the taxpayer is being revoked. The revocation should be sent to the office of the IRS where the power of attorney was filed. Generally, a new power of attorney revokes an existing power of attorney if it is granted by the taxpayer to another representative for the same tax matters. However, the old power of attorney is not revoked if the new power does not state that it is revoked.

A representative may withdraw from acting on the taxpayer's behalf. The representative can submit a signed revocation statement with the IRS. The statement should be filed with the office of the IRS where the power of attorney was filed.

A power of attorney may authorize the representative to appoint another person to act on the taxpayer's behalf. If substitution is permitted, the original representative must notify the IRS of the change and the identity of the new representative. The new representative must declare that he or she is eligible to serve.

Disclosure of information. Granting a power of attorney is different from designating someone to exchange information with the IRS. A designee has much less authority. He or she may request and receive tax information relating to the taxpayer's return. This information includes copies of notices, correspondence, and account transcripts. A designee may work with the IRS to resolve a mathematical error. However, the designee cannot represent the taxpayer before the IRS in examination, collection, Appeals, or other substantive issues. Form 8821, "Tax Information Authorization," tells the IRS who a taxpayer wants to be informed about his or her personal tax information. Taxpayers can also check the "yes" box in the "Third Party Designee" area on their Forms 1040. Taxpayers using "check the box" must give their designee a five-digit identifying number.

> **EXAMPLE**
>
> Carl recently retired and moved in with his adult daughter Sophie. Carl wants Sophie to be informed about his tax accounts. Carl can either complete Form 8821 or "check the box" on his Form 1040.

"Check the box" authority automatically expires after one year from the due date (not including extensions) of the return. For 2006 1040 returns, the authorization for most people will automatically end on April 16, 2007 (because April 15 is a Sunday). Otherwise, taxpayers can write to the IRS if they want to terminate the authorization earlier. Taxpayers wanting to revoke a designee identified on Form 8821 must alert the IRS. They can send a letter or a copy of executed Form 8821 with the word "Revoked" across top of the document.

A third-party designee can be a person, corporation, firm, organization, or partnership.

¶635   REGULATION OF UNLICENSED RETURN PREPARERS

According to the National Taxpayer Advocate (NTA), more than 50 percent of taxpayers pay a return preparer to prepare their federal income tax returns. NTA estimates that there are 1.2 million known tax preparers in the United States. Of these, roughly one-third are not regulated by any licensing body.

Proposed legislation in Congress would require these individuals to successfully pass a national certification exam and register with the IRS. Only registered individuals would be able to represent taxpayers before the IRS. However, critics of the proposed legislation point out that many return preparers do not want to represent clients before the IRS, preferring to focus on return preparation.

.01   Examination and Continuing Education

The Taxpayer Protection and Assistance Act (Sen 832) would give Treasury one year to create an initial examination and continuing education requirements for **enrolled preparers.** The exam would test the individual's technical knowledge and competency to prepare individual and business federal tax returns and the Earned Income Tax Credit (EITC). The exam would also cover professional responsibility.

Return preparers who successfully pass the exam would be eligible to practice before the IRS for three years, after which they would have to renew their credentials. Part of the renewal process would be the successful completion of continuing education. Return preparers who do not comply with the renewal and continuing education requirements could risk suspension or disbarment. Administrative law judges appointed by the Treasury Secretary would hear these cases and make disciplinary decisions.

STUDY QUESTION

---

10. The Taxpayer Protection and Assistance Act would require all of the following *except*:

   a. Development of continuing education requirements for enrolled preparers
   b. Renewal of credentials by enrolled preparers every three years
   c. Preparation by the Treasury Department and successful test completion by enrolled preparers of an initial examination
   d. All of the above are requirements of the act

.02   Problems with Terminology

Some tax professional groups are complaining about the terminology in the proposed legislation. The National Association of Tax Professionals (NATP) told Congress that using the label **enrolled preparer** will only confuse taxpayers. "We continually hear from taxpayers that they do not know what an Enrolled Agent is or what they do," the NATP reported. The proposed label of enrolled preparer will "detract from the value of the Enrolled Agent credential," NATP said. NATP suggested that Congress change the label from enrolled preparer to **licensed tax return preparer** or **registered tax return preparer.**

NATP has also recommended that Congress consider a graded system of registration with different classes of registration. For example, a return preparer could be a "Class A" preparer authorized to prepare individual and business returns. A "Class B" preparer would be authorized only to complete individual returns, and a "Class C" preparer would be authorized only to complete business returns.

NATP and other groups have also protested that the proposed legislation may unfairly single-out return preparers for problems with EITC compliance. The perceived rampant abuse of the EITC is one of the driving forces for return preparer registration. However, as NATP told Congress, "A quick review of disbarment and suspension cases as well as civil and criminal tax cases will reveal that most prosecuted perpetrators of fraud, schemes, and other forms of tax system abuse are already licensed and authorized to practice before the IRS." Registration also will not deter individuals who have no qualms about working outside the law.

¶640   CONCLUSION

As the IRS stresses, Circular 230 is a "living document." It has changed over the years as practice before the IRS has changed. The most recent and controversial changes, the new tax shelter regs, responded to what the IRS perceived as rampant abuses in the tax profession. More revisions are likely in the future as the IRS responds to additional changes in the profession. Knowing, understanding, and adhering to Circular 230 are the only ways to stay in compliance.

MODULE 3 — CHAPTER 7

IRS Ramps Up Enforcement to Crack Down on Abuses

This chapter was prepared as guidance to practitioners about the IRS's renewed emphasis on enforcement and the various techniques the agency is using to combat tax evasion, tax shelters, and abusive transactions.

LEARNING OBJECTIVES

Upon completion of this chapter, you will be able to:

- Describe the IRS's enforcement techniques;
- Understand the compliance areas feeding the "tax gap";
- Identify areas of serious noncompliance;
- Define a tax shelter;
- Explain key features of two tax shelter settlement initiatives; and
- Understand how criminal prosecution has become another IRS weapon in the tax-shelter wars.

¶701 INTRODUCTION

"Service plus enforcement equals compliance." That phrase has been repeated almost every day by IRS Commissioner Mark Everson since his term began. According to Everson, each element, service, and enforcement must be present to ensure the taxpayers are able to understand and comply with their tax obligation. Neither service nor enforcement alone will support our tax system. "When a doctor, a dentist, a construction worker, or anyone else is audited, word gets around. And some people who might be tempted to play fast and loose will think twice," Everson said.

In Everson's view, the pendulum swung too far to the service side during the late 1990s and early 2000s. It was during this same period that corporate governance went awry. In addition to accounting scandals that rocked corporate America, the tax shelter industry was moving along at full steam. With the IRS primarily concerned about service, tax shelter promoters were free to do as they pleased.

Everson decided that the pendulum needed to swing back to enforcement. He has made it his central objective to strengthen IRS enforcement. Combating abusive tax shelters is the centerpiece of Everson's enforcement campaign. Everson has shifted the IRS's focus to high-risk areas, developed "settlement initiatives" for abusive tax shelters, shared information on tax shelters with foreign countries, and referred many tax shelter cases to the Justice Department for criminal prosecution.

¶705 ENFORCEMENT TAKES TOP PRIORITY

The IRS's enforcement activities are stymied by lack of funding. Everson says that lack of funding is the number one obstacle to increasing the IRS's enforcement presence. Everson has repeatedly called upon Congress to increase the agency's funding for enforcement efforts.

Although the IRS's budget has increased over the past few years, funding is never as sufficient as the agency wants. In FY 2005 President Bush asked for a $500 million increase in IRS funding, but Congress only approved a $48 million increase. Nevertheless, in 2005, the IRS's overall budget towered at $10.236 billion, with $6.39 billion devoted exclusively to enforcement.

.01 Tax Gap Fuels Enforcement Efforts

The IRS's emphasis on enforcement is motivated by the "tax gap." The tax gap is simply the difference between what taxpayers should pay and what they actually pay on a timely basis. For Tax Year 2001, all taxpayers paid $1.76 trillion on time. That's about 85 percent of the total amount due leaving a tax gap of more than $300 billion. According to the IRS, enforcement is able to recover about $55 billion.

The tax gap has three components:
- Underreporting;
- Nonfiling; and
- Underpayment.

Underreporting. The largest component of the tax gap is underreporting. It accounts for more than 80 percent of the tax gap. For individual underreporting, more than 80 percent comes from understated income and not overstated deductions. Most understated income comes from business activities and not wages or investments.

Pass-through entities, such as partnerships and S corps, are popular ways of operating a business. The IRS discovered that more taxpayers are not reporting net income from pass-through entities. The IRS also found compliance problems with sole proprietorships. Reporting of proprietor income and expenses, such as gross receipts, bad debts, and vehicle expenses, is down.

Third party reporting and/or withholding, the IRS reported, encourages compliance. Less than 1.5 percent of individuals misreport income reported on their W-2s.

Nonfiling and underpayment. Nonfiling and underpayment are much smaller pieces of the overall tax gap. They account for about 10 percent each.

National research program. The IRS's estimate of the size of the tax gap is based on preliminary statistics from the NRP study. The NRP was launched in 2001 to give the IRS a current snapshot of compliance. Before the NRP, the IRS was using taxpayer statistics from 1988 to measure compliance.

From 2001 to 2004, the NRP selected approximately 50,000 returns annually for review and examination. The NRP especially looked at returns from higher-income individuals, particularly taxpayers filing Schedule C as sole proprietors.

The IRS will use the NRP data to update the statistical formulas it uses to select returns for audit. The IRS explained that when these updated formulas become available for use, IRS employees will be better positioned to select returns for examination that have the greatest likelihood of underreporting. Using such an approach better ensures that IRS audits are focused on the returns most in need of examination. This not only improves IRS efficiency, but it also assures taxpayers that others are paying their fair share. It also lessens the likelihood that those with accurate tax returns will receive the same degree of scrutiny.

"No one should think we can totally eliminate the gap. That would take Draconian measures and make the government too intrusive. We have to strike the right balance," Everson said.

STUDY QUESTION

> 1. Which of the following components accounts for more than 80 percent of the tax gap?
>   a. Nonfiling
>   b. Underreporting
>   c. Underpayment
>   d. None of the above accounts for the major share of the tax gap; all three contribute almost equally

> **NOTE**
>
> Answers to Study Questions, with feedback to both the correct and incorrect responses, are proved in a special section beginning on page 191.

.02   Record Enforcement in 2004

In FY 2004, the IRS recovered a record $43.1 billion in enforcement revenue. The FY 2004 total is an increase of $5.5 billion compared with the $37.6 billion in enforcement revenue recovered in FY 2003. According to Everson, every dollar invested in the IRS's enforcement budget yields four dollars in enforcement revenues. The IRS expects to report even better success when the 2005 results are in.

Here are some highlights from the IRS:

- Audits of higher-income taxpayers, which the IRS defines as taxpayers earning $100,000 or more, topped 195,000 in 2004;
- Total audits of all individual taxpayers topped 1 million for the first time since 1999;
- One in six large corporations was audited in 2004;
- The number of levies executed to collect assessed deficiencies topped 2 million; and
- The IRS recommended more than 3,000 cases to the Department of Justice for criminal prosecution.

Although the overall audit rate has increased, Everson believes it should be higher. Everson especially wants to boost audits of small businesses. Audits of small businesses decreased from 13,860 in FY 2003 to 7,290 in FY 2004.

.03 Problems with Small Businesses

Everson's concerns about the decline in small business audits have been confirmed by the Treasury Inspector General for Tax Administration (TIGTA). TIGTA reviewed the audit statistics in IRS's Small Business/Self-Employed (SB/SE) Division and discovered severe declines in audits of small corporations and S corps. The audit rates for small corporations and S corps examined from FY 2001 to FY 2004 dropped significantly from the prior four-year period. TIGTA emphasized, however, that recent examination initiatives may reverse the trend.

TIGTA found virtually no examination oversight of small corporations from 2001 to 2004. For 2003, for example, small corporations filed approximately 2.3 million Forms 1120, yet the audit rate was 0.32 percent (or 7,360 returns). S corps were subject to even less scrutiny, with only 0.19 percent audited among the 3.4 million Forms 1120S filed (or 6,460 returns).

Not only were fewer small corporation returns audited, but those audited resulted in more "no-change" returns than ever before. Approximately 43 percent of small Form 1120 filers that were examined had no change to the tax reported (of which 70 percent had no adjustments). S corps had the same good fortune, with 42 percent of the returns examined resulting in no changes.

TIGTA noted that the Discriminant Index Function (DIF) formulas used to score the small corporate returns for audit potential have not been revised since the 1980s. As a result, DIF fails to consider even publicly announced IRS compliance strategies such as abusive schemes, unreported income, and structured transactions.

Despite all of its statistics, TIGTA had some encouraging words for the IRS. The IRS has initiatives underway, such as the Compliance Initiative Projects (CIP), from which some returns already entered the audit stream in 2004. TIGTA also pointed to new hiring of almost 1,000 revenue agents in FY 2005 as a positive step to address a "longstanding human capital crisis." Nevertheless, TIGTA found there is insufficient evidence yet to evaluate whether recent IRS actions will be effective in reversing the decline in the number of audits.

Some small business representatives complain, however, that the recent IRS focus on small business is not be to applauded. Some have even accused the IRS of a "witch hunt" to cover up its own failings in providing reasonable examination policies toward small business. Likely, the debate will continue for at least a few more years until an equilibrium satisfactory to both side is found.

.04   LMSB Enforcement Efforts

Deborah Nolan, Commissioner of the IRS's Large and Mid-Size Business Division (LMSB), agrees with Everson's calls for increased enforcement efforts. Under Nolan's leadership, LMSB has begun to aggressively investigate tax shelter promoters. As June 2005, Nolan said that LMSB was involved in 271 ongoing investigations of tax shelter promoters.

LMSB has also become more aggressive in asserting penalties against taxpayers. According to Nolan, the number of penalty cases has increased since Everson's enforcement campaign.

Nolan has expressed concern about the potential rise of abusive tax shelter transactions by pass-through entities. Filings by pass-through entities now compose more than half of all LMSB filings. LMSB is likely to increase its audit coverage of pass-throughs. According to Nolan, LMSB is developing a model for identifying characteristics of pass-through entities that indicate abuse.

.05   Use of Civil Injunctions Grows

The IRS is increasingly using civil injunctions to combat tax evasion. Civil injunctions have been served on promoters of tax scams and fraudulent return preparers.

The IRS has used civil injunctions against:

- Abusive trusts;
- Misuse of "corporation sole" to set-up bogus religious organizations;
- Frivolous arguments to evade employment taxes;
- Claims of personal housing and living expenses as business deductions;
- "Zero-income" tax return filers;
- Abuse of the disabled access credit; and
- Claims that only foreign-source income is subject to U.S. taxation.

The IRS starts the injunction process with an investigation. If it discovers abusive activity, and the Department of Justice agrees, it files suit against the promoter or return preparer. The IRS asks the court to order the promoter or return preparer to refrain from the fraudulent activity. A court may issue a temporary restraining order, a temporary injunction, or a permanent injunction. The IRS is currently investigating more than 1,000 promoters for possible referral to the Justice Department and conducting individual examinations on thousands of tax scheme participants.

"I encourage the public to bring questionable promotions and abusive preparers to our attention," Kevin Brown, Commissioner of the IRS Small Business/Self-Employed Division, said. "We give serious attention to every referral we receive."

.06   Simultaneous Civil and Criminal Cases

Traditionally, if a case was referred to the Department of Justice for criminal investigation, the IRS would not pursue civil penalties until the criminal case was resolved. Because of this policy, the IRS sometimes would not refer a case for criminal prosecution so it could impose civil penalties.

This policy is no longer in effect. As a result, criminal referrals to the Department of Justice jumped 20 percent from 2003 to 2004. Criminal prosecutions also rose in 2004.

According to the new litigation policy, attorneys for the IRS and DOJ will litigate the case from the civil and criminal sides simultaneously. On top of the intended deterrent effect of the new litigation policy, the simultaneous proceedings attempt to strain the defendant taxpayer's resources to increase the government's chances for success in court.

STUDY QUESTIONS

> **2.** The National Research Program focused especially on returns for:
>
> **a.** Large corporations whose underpayments have the highest dollar value
> **b.** Low-income individuals more likely to participate in the "underground economy"
> **c.** Sole proprietors filing Schedule C
> **d.** None of the above was the focus
>
> **3.** What segment of business was subject to the least audit scrutiny in 2003, according to the Treasury Inspector General for Tax Administration?
>
> **a.** S corporations
> **b.** Large C corporations
> **c.** Limited liability companies
> **d.** Family limited partnerships
>
> **4.** The TIGTA cited the continuing decline in revenue agents as feeding a "long-standing human capital crisis" in the IRS. ***True or False?***

¶710   TAX SCAMS

The focus of IRS enforcement runs to gamut, from the ultra-sophisticated tax shelter to the flim-flam tax scams that promise the "less-sophisticated" similar riches. In both instances, the underlying characteristic is fraud.

Taxpayers are always on the lookout for ways to minimize their tax liabilities. Lurking in the shadows of legitimate tax practitioners are a host of unscrupulous promoters and tax preparers. A small percentage of taxpayers will believe anything a promoter tells them to justify eliminating their tax bills.

Whereas some taxpayers actively seek out scam artists, others taxpayers run into them accidentally. Many are taxpayers who want to complete their returns but are attracted by the promise of huge tax savings and refund checks. The offers are too enticing to refuse.

Scams that promise to eliminate taxes are too good to be true. Unfortunately, many taxpayers leave their common sense at home. In the end, everyone loses. Taxpayers sucked into these schemes not only have to pay the taxes they owe, but also have to pay interest and penalties. Promoters and practitioners risk not only being permanently barred from practicing but also fines and imprisonment.

.01   The Dirty Dozen

Tax scams are easy abuses for the IRS to detect. The IRS labels these tax scams as the "Dirty Dozen."

The Dirty Dozen list for 2005 warns about some old yet still prevalent scams, such as:

- Misuse of trusts;
- Frivolous arguments
- Return preparer fraud
- "Claim of Right" doctrine;
- Corporation Sole scams; and
- Offshore transactions.

A new addition to the IRS's warning list is identity theft. The IRS has discovered that several identity theft scams are tax related. Many of these scams involve scammers pretending to be IRS examiners. A typical scam involves a request for the individual's personal financial data. The IRS never uses e-mail to contact taxpayers about their accounts.

Identify theft also is perpetrated by tax preparers themselves. The IRS has become aware of several tax preparers who have simply misappropriated their clients' personal information to file false tax returns without the clients' knowledge.

The IRS has also noticed a considerable rise in the use of tax-exempt organizations to shield income or assets. The IRS is especially troubled by the contribution of historic façade easements to a tax-exempt conservation organization. The typical donation often nets the taxpayer a sizeable deduction compared to the value of the property. In many cases, historic preservation laws already prohibit alteration of the home's façade. The contribution to the organization is essentially a sham.

Tax-exempt credit counseling organizations that claim that they can fix credit ratings have also come under fire. Many of the credit counseling agencies charge high fees for little or no results.

Finally, the last two "schemes" to round off the "dirty dozen" are for the truly gullible because they are invariably picked up when returns are first scanned into the IRS computer system. Using a "no gain" deduction in one, filers attempt to eliminate their entire adjusted gross income by deducting it on Schedule A with the words, "No Gain Realized" included in the filing. In the last scheme, filers skip the "need" for taking a deduction altogether, placing zeros in all lines of the return.

.02 Some Enforcement Victories

In Washington State, the DOJ recently targeted a husband and wife team of promoters who the government accused of selling sham trusts and other shelters. The government alleged that the couple helped clients to create sham trusts to eliminate or reduce federal tax liability. In its complaint, the government sought a court order directing the couple to turn over the names, addresses, and telephone numbers of their clients.

In Georgia, a federal court issued an injunction halting a scheme sold over the Internet to customers in 41 states. The promoter claimed that his "Tax Buster" scheme would enable customers to avoid income taxes by "renouncing" their Social Security numbers and claiming to be "sovereign citizens."

A federal court in Tennessee has permanently barred the owner of a tax preparation business from preparing income tax returns or claims for refund. Without her clients' knowledge, the tax preparer either made up or vastly inflated itemized deductions. This inflated the preparer's fees, which were linked to the tax refund on the return.

In North Carolina, a federal court issued a permanent injunction barring an individual from selling two tax fraud schemes. In one scheme, taxpayers transferred their assets to a "corporation sole" and falsely claimed it was a church. Under the "claim of right" scheme, customers claimed their wages were exempt from tax. The Justice Department launched lawsuits against promoters around the country involved in the same schemes.

STUDY QUESTIONS

---

5. A new, tax-related scam becoming part of the Dirty Dozen is:

  a. Return preparer fraud
  b. Identity theft contacting taxpayers about IRS information via e-mail
  c. Offshore transactions
  d. All of the above are new entries to the Dirty Dozen

6. All of the following are enforcement victories against scam promoters described here **except:**

  a. Renouncing taxpayers' Social Security numbers and claiming to be sovereign citizens not subject to income tax
  b. Overly inflated itemized deductions listed on claims by a tax preparer in Tennessee without clients' knowledge
  c. Transferring assets to a "corporation sole" billed as a church
  d. All of the above are scams described here

¶715 DEFINITION OF A TAX SHELTER

Much of the IRS's enforcement work is focused on abusive tax shelters. These are multimillion-dollar transactions that have cost the government billions in lost tax revenues. Although the monetary costs are known, it is difficult to precisely define a tax shelter. According to the IRS, an abusive tax shelter generates little or no income and "generally offers inflated tax savings which are disproportionately greater than your actual investment placed at risk." A tax strategy or scheme that shelters income from normal taxation is abusive when its significant purpose is the avoidance or evasion of federal income tax."

On the other hand, a legitimate tax shelter is designed to produce income and has a risk of loss proportionate to the expected tax benefit. It is difficult to draw an often fine line between a tax shelter that is abusive and a tax shelter that is legitimate.

The 2004 Jobs Act significantly increases penalties and sanctions on promoters, investors, and others engaged in abusive transactions. To curb the growth of shelters, lawmakers voted to raise penalties for failing to register shelters, maintain investor lists, and disclose participation. Congress also enacted a new accuracy-related penalty for understatements arising from listed and reportable transactions.

.01 Reportable Transactions

There are six categories of reportable transactions. The concept of **transaction** is broad. It includes all the facts surrounding the expected tax treatment of an investment, entity, plan, or arrangement. A reportable transaction may be a series of steps that are carried out as part of a plan. A reportable transaction may consist of a series of transactions entered into the same tax year. The transactions are: (1) listed transactions, (2) confidential transactions, (3) transactions with contractual protection, (4) loss transactions, (5) transactions with a significant book-tax difference, and (6) transactions involving a brief asset holding period. The IRS has made some revisions to transactions in these groups.

.02 Listed Transactions

If a transaction is "listed," the transaction must be disclosed to the IRS by the participating taxpayer. The IRS alerts the public that a transaction has been identified as a listed transaction through guidance. The IRS also maintains a list of these abusive tax shelter transactions.

Listed transactions almost always fall under the definition of **technical tax shelters:** tax transactions that are highly technical in nature and are often marketed by an accounting or law firm. The tax benefits that accrue from technical tax shelters are generally based on "strained, technical readings of the Tax Code, regulations, or rulings." In many cases, the purported benefits from these transactions were never intended because the transactions do not reflect the substance of the law. Other technical tax shelters are based on faulty interpretations of the law that is not supported by legislative history or judicial interpretation.

¶720 LEGISLATION AIDING THE ENFORCEMENT EFFORT

.01 2004 Jobs Act

On October 22, 2004, the American Jobs Creation Act of 2004 (2004 Jobs Act) was signed into law. Although the 2004 Jobs Act was primarily aimed at replacing the FSC-ETI provisions, the act contains a hodgepodge of tax cuts, revenue raisers, and tax loophole closers. Several provisions signaled a clear attack on tax shelters by Congress. Here are some highlights:

- Increased disclosure of reportable transactions;
- Extended statute of limitations for unreported listed transactions;
- New penalty for failing to disclose tax shelters;
- New accuracy-related penalty;
- No deductions for interest paid to IRS;
- New penalty for failure to provide information on tax shelter;
- Modified penalty for failing to maintain investor lists;
- Increased penalty on tax shelter promoters; and
- Increased threshold on substantial understatements by corporations.

.02   Pending Legislation

Despite the tough new penalties added by the 2004 Jobs Act, some members of Congress feel that the legislation does not go far enough in penalizing tax promoters and participants. Senators Carl Levin, D-Mich., and Norman Coleman, R-Minn., have introduced the Tax Shelter and Tax Haven Reform Act of 2005. The bill aims to curb abusive tax shelters by:

- Increasing the Code Sec. 6700 penalty on abusive tax shelter promoters to the greater of either 150 percent of the promoters' gross income from the activity or the amount assessed against the taxpayer;
- Codifying the economic substance doctrine;
- Requiring federal bank regulators and the SEC to work with the IRS to develop examination techniques to detect abusive tax shelters promoted by financial institutions;
- Allowing the IRS to disclose tax return information relating to abusive tax shelters and tax evasion to the SEC, federal banking agencies, and the PCAOB;
- Providing a single rule that would prohibit tax practitioners from charging fees according to the amount of tax losses;
- Creating a Whistleblowers Office within the IRS and providing incentives for turning in promoters and unscrupulous practitioners;
- Directing Treasury to develop new standards for issuing tax shelter opinions; and
- Denying tax treaty benefits to offshore tax havens.

Although it is anyone's guess whether the bill will be eventually passed, it is certain that the 2004 Jobs Act did not put an end to the tax shelter industry. Cracking down on corporate wrongdoing is popular in Washington, and the bill may have a good chance of being passed.

¶725   SETTLEMENT INITIATIVES

.01   Son of BOSS

In May of 2004, the IRS announced a settlement initiative, a groundbreaking new strategy in the war on tax shelters, for transactions known as **Son of BOSS transactions.** Such transactions were the offspring of the bond-and-option sales strategy (BOSS) tax shelter. The IRS identified such a tax shelter as abusive and reportable in 2000. Taxpayers who participated in Son of BOSS transactions could elect to fess up to their wrongdoing and accept the terms of the settlement initiative.

From the IRS's standpoint, the settlement initiative made sense in terms of administrative efficiency. The IRS knew that Son of BOSS tax shelters were aggressively marketed by a consortium of law firms, accounting firms, and investment banks to numerous businesses and wealthy individuals in the late 1990s and early 2000s. The IRS discovered more than 1,000 taxpayers known to have participated in the transaction. Using data provided by the Justice Department, the IRS estimated that a total of more than 1,800 taxpayers had engaged in the shelter.

Instead of expending enormous amounts of the agency's time and revenue litigating the more than 1,000 cases in court and tracking down an additional 800 estimated participants, why not try to get the known participants to come forward with a tough, yet rewarding, settlement offer? Recognizing the Herculean task of litigating these 1,000-plus known cases in the courts with a good chance of conflicting results, the IRS opted to go with the settlement offer. However, one simple question remained: Would it work?

Taxpayers often would prefer to settle with the IRS rather than litigate in court. Traditionally, taxpayers had a considerable amount of wiggle room during settlement negotiations with the IRS. The IRS would often concede penalties or settle for less than 100 percent of the tax owed.

The Son of BOSS settlement changed the rules. Investors had to concede 100 percent of the claimed tax losses, all applicable interest, and pay a penalty unless they had previously disclosed their participation.

As a reward for participating in the settlement initiative, the IRS would reduce the penalty against the taxpayer depending on the facts and circumstances and allow the taxpayer to deduct out-of-pocket transaction costs.

Taxpayers opting out of the settlement were dealt with much more harshly. All losses and out-of-pocket costs were disallowed and taxpayers assessed the maximum penalty possible, which could go as high as 40 percent.

Program results. Initially, the IRS estimated that the Son of BOSS settlement initiative would bring in $6 billion in unpaid taxes. After the deadline for participating in the settlement initiative passed, the IRS reported a "strong turnout" by taxpayers.

The IRS reported in March 2005 that 1,165 taxpayers elected to participate in the Son of BOSS settlement initiative. They coughed up $3.2 billion in taxes, interest, and penalties. The approximately 1,200 participants reflected an 85 percent participation rate in the settlement initiative by taxpayers known by the IRS to have engaged in the Son of BOSS transactions. In addition, more than 300 taxpayers previously unknown to the IRS came forward as well. According to the IRS, 90 percent of the settlement participants were high-income individuals. The remaining 10 percent were corporate taxpayers.

By July 2005, the IRS reported that more than 1,200 taxpayers had participated in the settlement initiative. More than 1,500 taxpayers came forward because of the settlement initiative. The total amount collected by the IRS in taxes, interest, and penalties rose to roughly $3.7 billion.

For the 750 taxpayers choosing not to participate, IRS officials promised a vigorous litigation strategy. Many cases are now in various stages of the audit process. The first of potentially more than 100 cases involving Son of BOSS tax shelters is underway. The long-awaited *Jade Trading, LLC v. U.S.* began opening arguments in the Court of Federal Claims sitting in Atlanta, on September 6. Although the IRS has acknowledged that there was some opportunity for profit in the transaction, the agency contends the buy-and-sell transactions of the call options could be collapsed into a single transaction, and are therefore abusive. Relying largely on factual arguments, the IRS has argued in court documents that although profits are possible under the arrangement, they are unlikely and "atypical."

The IRS has identified over a dozen Son of BOSS promoters as well. For the identified promoters, criminal sanctions are a definite possibility. IRS officials have been expressing a newfound willingness to consider criminal charges for arranging abusive technical tax products that rise to the level of fraud against the government.

States benefit from Son of BOSS. The Son of BOSS settlement initiative also paid off handsomely for states. The IRS shared information from more than 1,000 Son of BOSS cases with approximately 34 states. This information enabled states to recapture several hundred million dollars from taxpayers who amended their state tax returns.

The California Franchise Tax Board was one of the largest initial beneficiaries of the IRS's settlement initiative. As of March 2005, the state agency collected more than $132 million. Some of the other big winners were New York, which collected over $45 million, and Maryland, which collected nearly $8 million as of March 2005.

STUDY QUESTION

> 7. What type of taxpayer most often elected to participate in the Son of BOSS settlement initiative?
>
>   **a.** Middle-income individuals who used the tax scam unknowingly
>   **b.** Corporate taxpayers
>   **c.** High-income individuals
>   **d.** Trusts

.02   Executive Stock Option Scheme

Basking in the glow of its success with the Son of BOSS settlement, the IRS decided the time was ripe to go forward with another settlement. The IRS had uncovered a large number of high-level executives and corporations that engaged in a scheme designed to hide millions of dollars of income. In February 2005, the IRS announced a new settlement for participants in abusive executive stock option schemes.

A typical scheme would start with a corporation amending its stock option plan to permit the corporation to grant stock options to an executive. The corporation would grant the stock options to the executive, who, in turn, would then transfer the options to a related entity, typically a family limited partnership, in exchange for a long-term, unsecured promissory note with a balloon payment at maturity. Subsequently, the related entity would exercise the options and sell the stock.

The goal of the scheme was to freeze the income recognized by the executive at the time the options were transferred. Normally, the exercise of stock options by an executive would trigger taxable compensation equal to the difference in the stock's fair market value (FMV). As a result of the transaction, recognition of the income received by the corporation was postponed until the related entity began making payments on the note.

Several features of such transactions were problematic:

- An executive participating in the scheme would avoid paying millions of dollars in taxes until many years later at preferential capital gains rates;
- The transaction hurt shareholders. Corporations would often fail to deduct the compensation received by the executive after amending their stock option plans to permit the transaction. Consequently, the corporation's income and tax liability would increase; and
- Corporations paid lucrative fees to promoters for setting-up the transactions. As a result, shareholders would end up footing the bill for the executive's untaxed compensation.

The IRS uncovered 42 corporations and an even larger number of individuals that participated in the abusive transaction. After the final tallies came in, participating taxpayers, including many leading publicly traded companies and high-profile executives, allegedly hid more than $700 million of income from the IRS.

Settlement terms. The terms of the Son of BOSS settlement were harsh, and, not wanting to reverse course, the IRS offered equally harsh terms for executives and corporations identified in the executive stock option settlement initiative.

Under the terms of the settlement initiative, participating executives had to:

- Recognize compensation equal to the FMV of the stock when exercised minus the costs of exercising the option in year exercised;

- Pay the employee's share of FICA tax on the recognized compensation income gain up to the amount that the deferred obligation exceeds the amount recognized as compensation;
- Pay interest on the deferred obligation as it is paid or accrued and the portion of any annuity payment not excludable under Code Sec. 72; and
- Disclose the corporation's identity.

As a reward for coming forward, the IRS agreed not to challenge the deduction, capitalization, or amortization of costs associated with the transaction. The IRS also reduced the accuracy-related penalty under Code Sec. 6662 from 20 percent to 10 percent.

Corporations had to disclose the taxpayer identification numbers of executives who received stock. Corporations also had to pay both:

- The employer's share of FICA tax income; and
- The employee's share of FICA tax for an executive who chose not to participate in the settlement initiative.

As with executives, the IRS agreed not to challenge a corporation's deduction, capitalization, or amortization of costs associated with the transaction.

Program results. After the May 23, 2005, cutoff date to elect participation in the settlement passed, the IRS quickly announced that the executive stock option settlement initiative, much like its Son of BOSS predecessor, had a high participation rate. Of the 124 executives suspected of participating in the shelter, 80 executives came forward. Another 15 executives reached agreement with the IRS through audits, and 10 executives were determined by the IRS not to have participated in the scheme.

Forty-six corporations were identified by the IRS as participants in the scheme. Thirty-three elected to participate in the settlement initiative. In addition, the settlement initiative brought four new companies and seven executives out of the woodwork that were unknown to the IRS. The IRS promised a tough litigation policy for the corporations and 19 executives that elected to *not* participate in the settlement initiative.

.03 Collaboration with the SEC

The IRS is also working more closely than ever before with the Securities and Exchange Commission (SEC) to uncover abusive tax shelters.

The IRS released guidance this summer detailing when and how tax shelter penalties must be disclosed to the SEC. Taxpayers are warned that if the required penalty disclosures are not made to the SEC, the IRS will assess additional penalties.

According to Rev. Proc. 2005-51, the following tax shelter penalties must be disclosed to the SEC:

- The Code Sec. 6707 penalty for failing to disclose a listed transaction;
- The Code Sec. 6662A accuracy-related penalty of 30 percent for a reportable transaction understatement if the relevant facts of the transaction were not disclosed under the Code Sec. 6011 regs;
- The Code Sec. 6662 accuracy-related penalty of 40 percent for a gross valuation misstatement if the person would have been subject to the 30 percent accuracy-related penalty of Code Sec. 6662A if not for the exclusionary rule of that code section; and
- The Code Sec. 6707A(e) penalty for failing to disclose the above three penalties to the SEC.

The IRS will treat the nondisclosure of the first three penalties as failure to disclose a listed transaction. The taxpayer will be penalized again by the IRS for nondisclosure of those three penalties.

To meet the IRS's new requirements, a taxpayer must disclose the penalty to the SEC in Item 3 (Legal Proceedings) on Form 10-K; and either:

- In the fiscal year the taxpayer received notice of the penalty, or
- In the year the taxpayer actually pays the penalty in full before receiving notice.

.04   Individual Settlement Offers

Although only certain tax shelters with broad characteristics and application are being selected for "IRS settlement programs," that emphasis doesn't mean that the IRS and the Justice Department are not settling many situations on a case-by-case basis. In fact, settlements are the IRS's preferred method of resolution. Nevertheless, the terms have not been generous, with the IRS fully aware that the Service has many taxpayers over the proverbial barrel. Many taxpayers are settling because of the strong legal arguments they believe the IRS has in its favor. Taxpayers are also worried about the negative publicity that litigation would bring to themselves and their companies.

One settlement representative of many made in 2005 involved a contingent liability shelter. Early in the year, the IRS secured a big win in settlement, ending a long-running dispute about a contingent liability tax shelter. The taxpayer agreed to pay the full amount of a multimillion-dollar liability, plus a 20-percent penalty, to avoid a 40-percent penalty.

In 1999, Hercules Inc. engaged in a contingent liability shelter and claimed a $154 million loss. According to the IRS, the company had received an opinion from its outside tax advisor that it was more likely than not to prevail if the investment was challenged on audit. The IRS challenged the transaction and started litigation. Not long thereafter, however, the IRS announced that Hercules conceded 100 percent of the loss from the contingent liability shelter, resulting in a $30 million tax liability. Hercules also agreed to pay a 20-percent accuracy-related penalty of approximately $6 million. In return, the IRS agreed not to seek a 40-percent penalty for a gross valuation misstatement.

The settlement followed recent IRS losses in two contingent liability cases: *Black & Decker* in federal district court and *Coltec Industries Inc.* in the federal claims court. The IRS used the settlement to reaffirm its position that contingent liability transactions are patently abusive. Chief Counsel Donald Korb said the recent court losses—which the IRS stressed were lost in trial courts and not on appeal—had not kept the agency from pursuing listed transactions. Korb also discussed the government's settlement philosophy: "The decision to accept Hercules settlement offer reflects our commitment to resolving controversies involving listed transactions without litigation—provided the ultimate goal of enforcement is not compromised."

.05   More Settlement Initiatives to Come?

The IRS is actively examining other possible transactions that may be suitable for a settlement initiative. Insiders have been speculating that the next settlement initiative crafted by the IRS may involve tax-exempt organizations. These speculations appear to be supported by remarks by Chief Counsel Donald Korb that the agency is examining abuses in the tax-exempt organization community as a possible candidate for the next settlement initiative.

STUDY QUESTION

---

8. If a taxpayer fails to disclose penalties for failing to disclose a listed transaction, reportable transaction understatement, and gross valuation misstatement, the IRS will:

    a. Offer amnesty from prosecution if all penalties and tax liabilities are paid

    b. Penalize the taxpayer again under Code Sec. 6707A(e) for the nondisclosure of the penalties

    c. Suspend the requirement to disclose the penalties on the taxpayer's Form 10-K for the next fiscal year

    d. None of the above is the IRS response to the nondisclosure

---

¶730 HIGH-PROFILE SHELTER ENFORCEMENT— THE KPMG AGREEMENT

The fact that IRS enforcement efforts are designed to generate tax revenues far in excess of taxes and penalties collected from the particular taxpayers targeted in any single case was driven home in spades recently in connection with its settlement agreement with the national accounting firm of KPMG.

KPMG, LLP's, record settlement shows that the government will not settle simply for civil penalties in its campaign against abusive tax shelters. The indictment of nine individuals for conspiracy to commit tax fraud and the imposition of a record fine of $456 million indicate the strength of the government's resolve.

Justice Department and IRS officials said the case was the largest criminal tax fraud case in history. KPMG generated at least $11 billion in phony tax losses and cost the IRS more than $2.5 billion in taxes. The indicted individuals—eight former KPMG employees and one outside attorney—could serve five years in jail and be fined up to $100,000 if convicted.

IRS Commissioner Mark used this opportunity to speak broadly on the IRS's enforcement theme. He said that the tax system:

> ...Can't tolerate flagrant abuse of the law and professional obligations by tax practitioners, particularly those associated with so-called blue chip firms like KPMG, which by virtue of their prominence set the standard of conduct for others. Accountants and attorneys should be the pillars of our system, not the architects of its circumvention.

The actions taken against KPMG and its former employees, including the $456 million fine, involve only the government and do not provide any relief directly to taxpayers who used the firm's services.

.01 High-level Professionals

The government's indictment focused on key managers who were responsible for the fraudulent activities. The indicted individuals included a former deputy chairman of the firm, two former heads of KPMG's overall tax practice, and three former heads of KPMG's tax shelter practice who provided services to wealthy individuals. KPMG fired many of the individuals after the Senate Permanent Subcommittee on Investigations shined a spotlight on the firm's questionable actions. KPMG and an attorney with the law firm of Sidley Austin Brown & Wood were accused of generating false and fraudulent opinion letters that claimed the tax shelters "more likely than not" would withstand any IRS challenge.

.02 Fraudulent Actions

As part of its agreement to avoid being indicted, KPMG admitted to defrauding the government by devising, marketing, and implementing fraudulent tax shelters, fraudulently concealing the tax shelters, making sham attorney–client privilege claims, and preparing and filing fraudulent tax returns that showed phony tax losses. KPMG admitted that it drafted false and fraudulent statements of facts underlying the shelters, issued opinions that contained false and fraudulent statements that KPMG and its clients knew were not true, and impeded the IRS by failing to produce documents and misrepresenting its role in the shelters.

KPMG also admitted making false claims that the shelter transactions were legitimate investments that clients entered into the transactions for investment purposes only. For one of the tax shelters, the firm admitted lying about the duration of the transaction and the clients' motivation for ending the transaction. The firm also admitted that the clients' motivation was to get a tax loss.

Several banks provided funds for investors to engage in the abusive transactions. KPMG admitted that these were sham loans that had nothing to do with any investment and that at least one bank never even serviced the purported loans.

The $456 million penalty includes $100 million in civil fines for failing to register the tax shelters with the IRS, $128 million in criminal fines to disgorge fees earned by KPMG, and $228 million in criminal restitution for taxes lost by the IRS because KPMG refused to provide documents and information before the statute of limitations ran on investors. The agreement requires the firm not to take a deduction for the $456 million penalty and to pay half of any insurance settlement to the IRS. In defending lawsuits by investors, KPMG agreed not to make any claims that contradict its admissions.

.03 Economic Substance Legislation

Sen. Max Baucus, D-Montana, the ranking member on the Senate Finance Committee, has called on Congress to codify the economic substance doctrine to curb abuses. Baucus said that KPMG "knowingly broke the law and then blatantly lied about it to Congress, the IRS, and the Department of Justice. KPMG's conduct has undermined the integrity of our voluntary self-assessment tax system." KPMG's admissions "underscore the need for strong anti-tax shelter laws," Baucus added.

STUDY QUESTION

> **9.** The resulting indictments and $456 million fine imposed on KPMG were actions in lieu of directing penalties and prosecutions of the firm's clients. *True or False?*

¶735 OTHER CRIMINAL ACTIONS

The IRS and the Justice Department are aggressively pursuing criminal prosecution of shelter promoters and advisors:

- A former banker has pleaded guilty to conspiracy, tax evasion and other crimes in a billion-dollar tax shelter case. The promoter, who worked for a German bank in the U.S., sold a shelter known as BLIPS. According to news reports, BLIPS peaked in the late 1990s and early 2000s. The bank's BLIPS transactions allegedly exceeded $3 billion. The shelter allegedly generated more than $1 billion in bogus losses. IRS Commissioner Mark Everson said in a statement after the guilty plea was announced:

  > These transactions went well beyond aggressive tax planning. They are part of a larger and very sad story about criminal activity driven by greed, plain and simple.

- After nearly seven days of evidence, a federal jury took less than a day to find a Hawaiian business owner guilty of five counts of filing false tax returns and four counts of tax evasion. According to the evidence presented at trial, the business owner failed to report and pay taxes on more than $10 million in business compensation. To hide the money received from his business, the owner used various schemes. Evidence introduced at trial showed the owner directed many of his customers to pay him directly for the delivery of goods. The owner also simply deposited the sales from certain goods into personal bank accounts over which he had sole control and possession.
- The Justice Department filed charges against a Florida promoter who sold purported voluntary employees' beneficiary association (VEBA) plans to employers. The promoter allegedly told employers that his VEBA plans allowed employers to make unlimited tax-deductible contributions to certain welfare benefit plans. However, the Justice Department alleges the plans were little more than abusive tax shelters designed to provide employers with a vehicle to disguise deferred compensation paid to high-level employees as employee benefits. The IRS estimates that the promoter's scheme cost the Treasury Department nearly $7 million in revenue over a period of five years.

- A federal grand jury in Seattle returned an indictment charging two defendants with conspiring to defraud the United States by impeding the collection of income taxes, failure to file tax returns, and criminal contempt for violating a permanent injunction. The indictment alleges the defendants instructed their clients to transfer assets and income to trusts and corporations that the defendants set up. The defendants allegedly had told their clients that because of the manner in which their tax shelter was constructed that neither they nor the entity would have to file a return.

¶740 FINALIZATION OF CIRCULAR 230

A debate that raged on for so many years that seemed like it would never end finally did. June 20, 2005, was the effective date for the final Circular 230 Rules of Practice before the IRS. The revised version of Circular 230 effectively turns the old rules upside down.

.01 Twofold Purpose of the Revisions

According to Treasury, the main purposes of the bold revisions to Circular 230 are to regulate tax shelter opinions issued for penalty protection and to issue standards for giving these opinions to clients. Tough new Circular 230 is a reaction to the rampant promotion of tax shelters during the late 1990s and early 2000s.

.02 Criticism Abounds

One of chief complaints about the Circular 230 rules concerns their vagueness. Many of the key terms that are instrumental for practitioners attempting to comply with the new rules are ambiguous and are not defined elsewhere in the document. In addition, many practitioners believe that the final rules, which were designed to reign in a small group of tax shelter advisors and promoters, punish mainstream practitioners as well.

Many practitioners believe that the result of the new rules is that they do not allow tax advisors to provide complete and accurate advice to their clients. Practitioners' ability to give responses to short follow-up questions based on a change in facts or on limited issues is especially hampered by the new rules.

The responses from Treasury and IRS have not exactly eased the minds of many practitioners. In responses to requests for revisions, IRS officials have called Circular 230 a "living document" that is subject to later modification. The literal language of the final rules scares many practitioners because key provisions include stiff penalties for compliance failures, including being permanently disbarred from practicing before the IRS and sanctions against an entire firm. Attempting to allay practitioner fears, the IRS's Office of Professional Responsibility (OPR) will apply Circular 230 "reasonably." IRS Chief Counsel Donald Korb offered this piece of advice to practitioners: use "common sense" when interpreting Circular 230.

STUDY QUESTION

> **10.** Key provisions of the revised Circular 230 feature all of the following **except:**
>
>   **a.** Vague or ambiguous terminology
>   **b.** Stiff compliance penalties
>   **c.** Tax advisors' ability to advise clients thoroughly is hampered
>   **d.** All of the above are features

¶745 CONCLUSION

The IRS and Treasury consider 2005 a watershed year in its battle against tax shelters, abusive transactions, and just plain tax fraud. Government officials see 2006 as promising even more success. The 2006 budget is giving the IRS the dollars to back up its renewed audit and enforcement efforts.

Many of those tax shelter investors and promoters who did not take the IRS's settlement terms within the 2004 and 2005 settlement program deadlines will be seeing their cases finally brought to trial in 2006. At least in their court briefs, they argue adamantly that the IRS has been overreaching and that many of the transactions of which they are accused were actually simply good, albeit aggressive, tax planning. The outcome of these cases, now on court calendars in key jurisdictions throughout the nation, will determine the extent of IRS's victory in penalizing those who had used tax shelters in the late 1990s and early 2000s.

The verdict is already in, however, on how the IRS's aggressive litigation has affected present taxpayer behavior. The majority of taxpayers, especially public corporations, now approach tax planning in a very conservative manner. They will not be seen buying into the speculative tax deals of the past. The question remains, however, how far the pendulum has swung to the side of caution and how long it will take to swing back to the center.

Tax officials addressing tax bar association meetings in Washington, D.C., over the most recent year have repeated several themes that succinctly summed up the current attitude of the IRS and Treasury. They proclaimed that the government's tax shelter enforcement efforts had "turned a corner" and that taxpayers were much more reluctant to engage in abusive transactions:

- Treasury Deputy Assistant Secretary (Tax Policy) Eric Solomon observed that taxpayers are much less willing to enter into shelter transactions;

- IRS Chief Counsel Donald L. Korb reported that the settlement initiative for the Son of BOSS tax shelter was a "watershed event"; and
- IRS Commissioner Mark W. Everson noted that the most significant IRS accomplishment during his tenure has been the recognition that enforcement is an "essential function" and not a "dirty word."

Commissioner Everson noted improvements in IRS enforcement activities, including: over 1 million returns audited; a doubling of audits of high-income taxpayers; an increase in audits of corporations with assets exceeding $10 million; and higher revenues from document matching. Everson perhaps summed it up best when he concluded that giving advice on abusive transactions has developed "from clever lawyering and accounting to theft from the government."

CPE NOTE

When you have completed your study and review of chapters 6 and 7 which comprise this Module, you may wish to take the Final Exam for this Module. CPE instructions can be found on page 221.

The Module 3 Final Exam Questions begin on page 239. The Module 3 Answer Sheet can be found on pages 251 and 253.

For you convenience, you can also take this Final Exam online at www.cchtestingcenter.com.

TOP FEDERAL TAX ISSUES FOR 2006

Answers to Study Questions

MODULE 1 — CHAPTER 1

1. c. Correct. This group is the third of the expense types deducted from DPGR to determine QPAI.
a. Incorrect. The expense categories are what determine net receipts, so they may not be subtracted from DPGRs to arrive at QPAI.
b. Incorrect. Only COGS related to DPGR are subtracted from DPGR in calculating QPAI.
d. Incorrect. One of the choices is the third expense category subtracted from DPGR to calculate QPAI.

2. d. Correct. All three choices are activities from which DPGR are derived.
a. Incorrect. U.S. engineering or architectural services for U.S. construction projects are activities from which DPGR are derived.
b. Incorrect. Construction performed domestically is an activity from which DPGR are derived.
c. Incorrect. Any lease, rental, license, sale, exchange, or other disposition of these items is an activity from which DPGR are derived.

3. b. Correct. For 2005 the maximum deduction is equal to 3 percent of the taxpayer's QPAI or taxable income without regard to Code Sec. 199.
a. Incorrect. The deduction is not calculated directly using the taxpayer's gross receipts or total DPGR.
c. Incorrect. QPP income is one of the activities from which DPGR are derived, not the amount from which the deduction is calculated. Code Sec. 199 property is QPP.
d. Incorrect. One of the choices lists the alternatives with which the deduction is calculated.

4. d. Correct. The deduction limit is 50 percent of actual wages paid and reported for the tax year.
a. Incorrect. The deduction limitation is greater than 10 percent of wages.
b. Incorrect. The limitation of the manufacturing deduction is not a maximum of 25 percent.
c. Incorrect. The wage limitation for the manufacturing deduction is not 30 percent.

5. d. Correct All three choices are part of the facts and circumstances test of the Treasury Department and IRS for determining whether a purchase, sale, exchange, or lease has occurred, but none of the choices is "controlling" in making the determination.

a. Incorrect. The delivery medium of the transaction does not control whether the Treasury Department or IRS considers the transaction to be a purchase.

b. Incorrect. Services provided with disposition of software do not result in qualifying gross receipts.

c. Incorrect. The classification of the software is not controlling of when a transaction is considered to be a purchase is a sale, exchange, or lease.

6. False. Correct. DPGR do not include gross receipts from software offered for use online for a fee.

True. Incorrect. The online usage fees are not includable in DPGR.

7. c. Correct.. The benefits and burdens of ownership are the determining factor in eligibility for DPGR.

a. Incorrect. The rule applies regardless of whether the customer supervises or controls the contractor.

b. Incorrect. The rule applies even if the contractor is considered a producer under Code Sec. 263A.

d. Incorrect. Only one taxpayer may claim the property's DPGR.

8. a. Correct. There is no minimum useful life for manufactured products in the substantial in nature test.

b. Incorrect. The relative cost of the domestic MPGE activity is part of the facts and circumstances surrounding the MPGE activity.

c. Incorrect. The nature of the property is considered in the substantial in nature test.

d. Incorrect. One of the choices is not considered in the substantial in nature test.

9. d. Correct. Any of the three methods may be used by a taxpayer whose gross receipts are less than $5 million.

a. Incorrect. The simplified deduction method is applicable to any taxpayer having average annual gross receipts of less than $25 million.

b. Incorrect. This method is available to all taxpayers.

c. Incorrect. The taxpayer may employ the small business simplified deduction method as outlined in Rev. Proc. 2002-28 for taxpayers whose average annual gross receipts total less than $5 million.

10. c. Correct. Although there are exceptions to this rule for warranties and de minimis gross receipts from embedded services, this is the rule of thumb.
a. Incorrect. The DPGR is not split in half.
b. Incorrect. The de minimis amount of gross receipts from embedded services is not 25 percent.
d. Incorrect. One of the choices describes the rule of thumb.

MODULE 1 — CHAPTER 2

1. a. Correct. Notice 2005-10 covers the definition of cash dividends, the requirements for domestic reinvestment plans, permitted and nonpermitted investments, and election and reporting requirements.
b. Incorrect. Notice 2005-23 does not address the Homeland Investment Act terms.
c. Incorrect. Notice 2005-38 concerns other aspects of the 2004 Jobs Act.
d. Inorrect. Notice 2005-64 involves disallowed deductions under the 2004 Jobs Act.

2. d. Correct. Notice 2005-64 provides guidance on key issues that affect a corporation's computation of its tax liability and also addresses increases in bank debt and the treatment of dividends paid to intermediary pass-through entities.
a. Incorrect. Notice 2005-10 covers the definition of cash dividends, the requirements for domestic reinvestment plans, permitted and nonpermitted investments, and election and reporting requirements.
b. Incorrect. Notice 2005-23 is not part of the guidance for the Homeland Investment Act.
c. Incorrect. Notice 2005-38 concerns other aspects of the 2004 Jobs Act.

3. c. Correct. Notice 2005-38 explains the impact of mergers, acquisitions, and other corporate transactions on the calculation of the base period amount and the ceiling on amounts that qualify for the deduction. The notice also addresses the effect of intercompany debt between related parties, the foreign tax credit "gross-up," and the disallowance of certain expenses.
a. Incorrect. Notice 2005-10 covers the definition of cash dividends, requirements for domestic reinvestment plans, permitted/nonpermitted investments, and election and reporting requirements.
b. Incorrect. Notice 2005-23 does not pertain to terms of the Homeland Investment Act.
d. Incorrect. Notice 2005-64 addresses secondary issues and details of the deduction but is not the essential guidance for determining the deduction.

4. True. Correct Calendar-year taxpayers have the choice of electing 2004 or 2005.
False. Incorrect. Taxpayers that use the calendar year can claim the deduction either for 2004 or 2005.

5. c. Correct. Amounts treated as dividends under Code Secs. 367 or 1248 (gain on sale of stock in foreign corporation treated as dividend) do not qualify for the special rate.
a. Incorrect. Code Sec. 316 dividends are one of the qualifying dividend types.
b. Incorrect. Code Sec. 332 dividends qualify for the special rate.
d. Incorrect. One of the choices does not quality for the lower rate.

6. c. Correct. The translation occurs at the spot rate on the date of distribution of the dividends.
a. Incorrect. The date of receipt is not the date of conversion.
b. Incorrect. The end of the corporation's accounting period is not the date of conversion.
d. Incorrect. One of the choices is the time of the conversion.

7. d. Correct. All three amounts are included in base period dividends.
a. Incorrect. Property dividends are included in base period dividends.
b. Incorrect. Deemed repatriations under Code Sec. 956 are included in base period dividends.
c. Incorrect. Distributions of previously taxed income are included in base period dividends.

8. a. Correct. The limit is allocated among the corporations in proportion to current and accumulated E&P that are not previously taxed.
b. Incorrect. The size of the E&P is not a determinant of the allocation.
c. Incorrect. The allocation is not a corporate decision.
d. Incorrect. The allocation is affected by previous taxation of E&P.

9. a. Correct. The deduction reduces the taxpayer's foreign tax credit limitation, so it will be advantageous to take the deduction for dividends from low-tax countries.
b. Incorrect. If taxpayers claim the deduction, they lose the credit that reduces their tax liability for **dividends from high-tax countries.**
c. Incorrect. The credit is not as tax-advantaged for dividends from low-tax countries.
d. Incorrect. One of the choices is beneficial in specifying which dividends carry the deduction.

10. b. Correct. Notice 2005-38 clarifies that gross-up rules do not apply to dividend payments qualifying for the 85 percent deduction.
a. Incorrect. Code Sec. 78 outlines the gross-up rules but does not discuss the 85 percent deduction.
c. Incorrect. Code Sec. 965 prohibits a foreign tax credit for the deductible portion of the dividend but does not describe exclusions from the gross-up rules.
d. Incorrect. Notice 2005-64 does not provide guidance on the gross-up rules.

11. d. Correct. None of the choices is required for reinvestment under a DRP.
a. Incorrect. Investments do not have to be completed in the election year.
b. Incorrect. The Treasury Department did not institute a tracing or segregation approach to repatriated dividends.
c. Incorrect. Using funds for nonpermitted investments does not affect the eligibility of the dividends.

12. b. Correct. Pro-rata portions are used if the taxpayer does not identify which dividend payments to carry the deductible and nondeductible amounts.
a. Incorrect. A single dividend is not required to be used.
c. Incorrect. It is permissible to designate a portion of a dividend as qualified to avoid exceeding the ceiling.
d. Incorrect. One of the choices is the treatment of the dividend chosen to carry the 85 percent deduction.

13. d. Correct. All three choices are relevant facts and circumstances.
a. Incorrect. The extent of the investment is relevant.
b. Incorrect. Compliance is relevant.
c. Incorrect. The plan's specificity about anticipated investments is relevant.

14. b. Correct. The safe harbor amount for completing or committing to the required investments is 60 percent.
a. Incorrect. A greater percentage is required.
c. Incorrect. The safe harbor amount differs from 75 percent.
d. Incorrect. A lower percentage of completed or committed investments is required.

15. c. Correct. The spun-off corporation is treated as though it existed for the same period as its shareholder.
a. Incorrect. The spun-off corporation is treated as though it had a history of distributing dividends.
b. Incorrect. The dividends history is not so granted.
d. Incorrect. One of the choices reflects the dividends history of the spun-off corporation.

MODULE 2 — CHAPTER 3

1. c. Correct. In this simple formula, AMT = Tentative AMT − Regular tax liability.
a. Incorrect. The taxpayer's AGI does not directly figure in the determination of the AMT tax liability.
b. Incorrect. AMT differs from "regular" tax in more ways than just the standard deduction.
d. Incorrect. One of the choices completes the simple formula for determining AMT liability.

2. d. Correct. The third step in determining AMT liability is to add back all itemized deductions disallowed under AMT.
a. Incorrect. Subtracting state and local refund amounts comes much later in the process than the third step.
b. Incorrect. The AMTI must be determined before the exemption may be subtracted from it, and many deductions allowed on the regular tax return must be subtracted to arrive at AMTI.
c. Incorrect. The adjustment occurs much later in the process than this third step.

3. True. Correct. The final step in arriving at the taxpayer's AMTI is the adjustment to taxable income for TPIs and other business adjustment items.
False. Incorrect This adjustment to taxable income follows those for disallowed itemized deductions and refunds of state and local taxes.

4. a. Correct. By examining in advance of tax season which itemized deductions will be add-backs in calculating the AMT, practitioners can advise taxpayers about avoiding situations that could generate those "excessive" deductions or preferences.
b. Incorrect. Finding additional deductions to take on future Form 1040 returns actually works against strategies for avoiding the AMT, because many such deductions are added back in determining the AMT liability.

c. Incorrect. Maximizing amounts of deductions to take on the Form 1040 actually works against strategies for avoiding the AMT, because many such deductions are added back in determining the AMT liability.

d. Incorrect. One of the choices reflects a useful approach to minimize or avoid the AMT.

5. d. Correct. All three choices represent add-backs of deductions allowable on Form 1040 and associated schedules but disallowed in figuring the AMT liability.

a. Incorrect. A state sales tax deduction claimed on line 9 of Form 1040 in lieu of deducting property taxes is an add-back for AMT purposes.

b. Incorrect. The only interest deduction allowed under the AMT is one for a mortgage whose proceeds are actually used to build, buy, or substantially improve a taxpayer's primary or secondary residence. Home equity loans not applied to such purposes do not qualify for an interest deduction under the AMT.

c. Incorrect. Form 1040 allows deduction of itemized medical expenses when they total 7.5 percent of the taxpayer's AGI, but the AMT requires the total itemized medical expenses to be in excess of 10 percent of the AGI.

6. a. Correct. The amount of federal tax due is compared to the tax liability once the AMT is calculated, but the regular federal tax liability is not an add-back as the AMT is calculated.

b. Incorrect. Foreign income tax paid may not be claimed under the AMT and thus is an add-back for calculating the AMT liability.

c. Incorrect. Personal property tax paid may be deducted from regular federal income tax on Form 1040 but is an add-back for the AMT.

d. Incorrect. One of the choices is not an add-back.

7. c. Correct. Only 42 percent of the 50 percent gain exclusion must be added back for AMT calculation of AMTI.

a. Incorrect. All miscellaneous itemized deductions from line 26 must be added back to calculate AMTI.

b. Incorrect. All the interest earned from private activity municipal bonds (specified private activity bonds) must be added back to determine AMTI.

d. Incorrect. One of the choices does not reflect the amount of add-back required to calculate the AMTI.

8. d. Correct. The foreign tax credit is the only credit fully allowed under the AMT and is now known as the AMT-FTC.

a. Incorrect. The research credit is not fully allowed for business taxpayers under the AMT. Rather, those deductible from regular income tax must be capitalized and amortized over 10 years for AMT calculations.

b. Incorrect. The new markets tax credit is not fully deductible under the AMT.
c. Incorrect. The mining exploration credit is not a full deduction under the AMT. Expenses must be capitalized and amortized over 10 years.

9. a. Correct. Exemption amounts are reduced by 25 cents for every dollar that AMTI exceeds the maximum amounts listed by filing status in Table 1.
b. Incorrect. The reduction is not 50 cents per dollar in excess of the amount of AMTI exceeding the maximum listed for the filing status of the taxpayer in Table 1.
c. Incorrect. The reduction for AMTI in excess of the maximum per filing status is not 75 cents on the dollar.
d. Incorrect. A lower reduction applies for AMTI in excess of the maximum by filing status.

10. c. Correct. Multiple-person households may have itemized deductions that are add-backs under the AMT, such as more sales taxes and qualifying medical and dental expenses.
a. Incorrect. Couples do not have more tax breaks under the regular tax system. In fact, until the passage of Working Families Tax Relief Act of 2004, married couples filing jointly faced discriminatory taxation in that their standard deduction was not twice that of single filers. Unless Congress chooses to extend the relief, married taxpayers will again face the "marriage penalty" in 2009 and beyond.
b. Incorrect. The only tax credit applicable to the AMT is the foreign tax credit, and there is no reason why married taxpayers are more likely to have foreign tax credits than are single filers.
d. Incorrect. The Tax Policy Center statistics state that 48 percent of married couples are subject to the AMT as opposed to just 3 percent of single taxpayers.

MODULE 2 — CHAPTER 4

1. a. Correct. Single taxpayers earning more than the $110,000 limit for Roth IRAs or married taxpayers earning in excess of $160,000 may still participate in designated accounts.
b. Incorrect. Designated Roth accounts do not feature a salary reduction for contributions, just as Roth IRAs do not
c. Incorrect. Contributions are made with after-tax earnings for both designated Roth accounts and Roth IRAs.
d. Incorrect. Employers are not required to offer designated Roth account plans, nor do they offer Roth IRAs.

2. b. *Correct.* Matching contributions are taxable as if the participant had received cash.

a. *Incorrect.* Contributions to designated accounts have a maximum of $15,000 (with a $5,000 catch-up contribution possible for workers older than age 50) or 100 percent of compensation—just the same as traditional 401(k) and 403(b) plans.

c. *Incorrect.* Funds may not be transferred either to or from designated Roth accounts.

d. *Incorrect.* One of the choices is a significant disadvantage in funding the plans.

3. b. *Correct.* To be a qualified distribution, contributions may not be withdrawn for five years after the end of the tax year in which the contributions were made.

a. *Incorrect.* This is not the required holding period for qualified distributions.

c. *Incorrect.* The holding period is shorter than 10 years.

d. *Incorrect.* One of the choices is the required minimum period before plan participants may take a distribution without the funds being treated as part of gross income.

4. a. *Correct.* Designated account holders must begin to take RMDs at age 70½ or upon retirement, whichever is later. Roth IRAs do not require distributions at any age.

b. *Incorrect.* Early withdrawals may be used for these purposes without being included in gross income.

c. *Incorrect.* As with other plans requiring RMDs, the excise tax is 50 percent.

d. *Incorrect.* One of the choices is a disadvantage of withdrawals from the accounts.

5. True. *Correct.* Taxes catch up to traditional plans, and when retirees begin taking distributions, the original contributions and well as accumulated earnings composing those payments will be taxable.

False. *Incorrect.* Because contributions can accumulate sizable earnings over the decades, retirees may owe significant taxes on the contributions and accumulated earnings. The taxes owed in retirement will total more than the deduction at the time the contributions were made.

6. d. Correct. All three choices are potential problems in having rollovers sent to the participant rather than using a trustee-to-trustee rollover directly between account custodians.

a. Incorrect. This problem occurs because the rollover distribution must be deposited within 60 days from the date the former account custodian issues the distribution.

b. Incorrect. This problem arises because the plan participant actually receives 20 percent less in the distribution than he or she must deposit in the new account to avoid taxation.

c. Incorrect. This problem arises because only one such rollover may be taken per year, and the taxpayer must remember to use trustee-to-trustee transfers for any other plan changes.

7. False. Correct. The distribution for educational costs must be taken in the year in which the expenses occurred, but a distribution for medical expenses may be taken regardless of the date on which the expenses occurred.

True. Incorrect. A distribution used for higher educational expenses must be taken in the year that the expenses are incurred, but distributions used to pay nondeductible medical expenses may be taken regardless of when the expenses were actually incurred.

8. d. Correct. All three situations would be reasons why she would not incur a penalty.

a. Incorrect. Deemed distributions for participants older than 59½ are considered normal, nonpenalized distributions.

b. Incorrect. Plan participants who are at least 55 are not assessed the 10 percent early distribution penalty.

c. Incorrect. If she is permanently disabled, the distribution becomes a regular one that has no penalty.

9. c. Correct. The total of distributions taken for the year must equal the RMD by no later than April 15 of the following year.

a. Incorrect. The deadline is not before the end of the year.

b. Incorrect. January 1 is not the deadline for taking RMDs.

d. Incorrect. One of the choices is the deadline.

10. b. Correct. HSAs are the updated version of Archer MSAs.

a. Incorrect. Flexible spending accounts actually predate Archer medical savings accounts.

c. Incorrect. HRAs are the newest deferred compensation option for medical expenses.

d. Incorrect. One of the choices is an updated version of the Archer medical savings accounts.

11. c. Correct. The additional contribution for participants age 55 and older is $700 in 2006 and will increase to $1,000 for years beginning in 2009.
a. Incorrect. The additional contribution is more than $500.
b. Incorrect. A different amount applies to additional contributions available to participants starting at age 55.
d. Incorrect. A smaller amount is allowed for additional contributions to HSAs for participants age 55 and older.

12. b. Correct. HRAs are employer-funded.
a. Incorrect. HSAs are employee-funded up to a maximum per year of $2,650 for singles and $5,250 for joint filers in 2005.
c. Incorrect. FSAs are employee-funded plans, and participants lose their contributions if they are not used promptly.
d. Incorrect. Archer MSAs are employee-funded IRA-like investment plans for health care costs, and participants can deduct their contributions.

13. c. Correct. Comparable contributions may be the same amount or the same percentage of the employee's HDHP deductible.
a. Incorrect. Comparable contributions are not concerned with eventual usage of benefits.
b. Incorrect. Self-only and family coverage are separate categories, and employers may contribute to one category without being required to contribute to the other.
d. Incorrect. One of the choices describes the two types of comparable contributions.

14. b. Correct. Contributions to partners' HSAs differ from those for employees and may not be deducted by the partnership. They must be reported on Schedule K-1 of Form 1040.
a. Incorrect. Contributions to partners' HSAs differ from those by employers to employees' plans.
c. Incorrect. Partners and S corp shareholders are not covered by the comparability rules.
d. Incorrect. One of the choices was the rule for partners' HSAs.

15. d. Correct. Both court cases and the Bankruptcy Act itself furthered protection of tax-favored retirement plans from the reach of creditors.
a. Incorrect. The Supreme Court denied creditors access to IRA assets of debtors in bankruptcy in this case.
b. Incorrect. Pennsylvania's Western District Bankruptcy Court protected the debtor's 403(b) account in this case.

c. *Incorrect.* The Bankruptcy Act extended bankruptcy protection to assets in tax-favored retirement savings plans.

MODULE 2 — CHAPTER 5

1. c. *Correct.* The 2005 Energy act does not focus on developing new sources of energy.
a. *Incorrect.* Although not affected the average taxpayer directly, one prong of the 2005 Energy Act is improving the nation's energy infrastructure.
b. *Incorrect.* Conserving energy is one of the four prongs of the 2005 Energy Act, encompassing credits for energy-efficient home improvements and residence remodeling using energy-efficient materials.
d. *Incorrect.* Encouraging taxpayers to purchase one of a broader range of alternative-energy vehicles than its predecessor deduction for hybrids is one of the four prongs of the 2005 Energy Act.

2. d. *Correct.* The Residential Energy Property Credit combines up to 100 percent of the cost of residential property energy expenditures in the residential property expenditures credit with 10 percent of the cost of significant energy efficiency improvements in the residential energy conservation property credit up to an overall cap of $500.
a. *Incorrect.* The credit does not allow these percentages for the residential energy conservation property credit and the residential property expenditures credit.
b. *Incorrect.* The maximum percentages of the two credits are not the same.
c. *Incorrect.* The Residential Energy Property Credit does not include the entire cost of either type of expenditure.

3. a. *Correct.* Energy-efficient building property qualifies for the Residential Energy Property Expenditures Credit, not the Residential Energy Conservation Property Credit. The difference is that energy-efficient building property is more permanent in nature and its full cost applies to the $500 maximum.
b. *Incorrect.* The property must be placed into service between January 1, 2006, and December 31, 2007.
c. *Incorrect.* Manufacturers of these appliances, not the consumers who purchase them, are eligible for the credit for energy efficiency.
d. *Incorrect.* Products and materials are subject to meeting these standards to be considered qualifying property.

4. True. *Correct.* The credit has no carryforward provision.
False. *Incorrect.* The credit may not be applied to tax liabilities in years following 2007.

5. c. Correct. The credit applies to 30 percent of the costs of alternative energy property up to a maximum of $4,000 if property placed into service fits both of the categories eligible for the credit.
a. Incorrect. The percentage is higher and the maximum credit is greater for the Residential Alternative Energy Expenditures Credit.
b. Incorrect. Neither the percentage nor the cap matches the one available for the credit.
d. Incorrect. One of the choices includes the correct percentage of costs and maximum credit available.

6. c. Correct. Costs must be associated with depreciable or amortizable property to qualify.
a. Incorrect. The cost reduction plan must target all three of these systems.
b. Incorrect. The plan must reduce the costs (and not the consumption itself) by at least 50 percent compared to a reference building standardized by the IRS
d. Incorrect. The maximum deduction is $1.80 per square foot for property placed in service during 2006 and/or 2007.

7. d. Correct. New home building contractors may claim a $2,000 credit, whereas manufactured home builders may claim $1,000.
a. Incorrect. The difference in the credits is greater.
b. Incorrect. The difference between credits for new home contractors and manufactured home contractors is another amount.
c. Incorrect. The difference between the credits is another amount.

8. a. Correct. The difference between the comparable dwelling unit and a qualifying dwelling unit must be at least 50 percent of heating and cooling consumption.
b. Incorrect. The qualifying dwelling unit must have a different percentage in lower heating and cooling consumption.
c. Incorrect. Another percentage applies to the difference between a qualifying dwelling unit and a comparable one.
d. Incorrect. The percentage difference is higher.

9. d. Correct. A vehicle that gets 2.5 times the mileage of a comparable nongreen vehicle and the most estimated lifetime fuel savings qualifies for $2,400 fuel economy credit and $1,000 conservation credit.
a. Incorrect. The credits exceed these totals.
b. Incorrect. A different amount is available for the fuel economy credit to the extent that the green vehicle's fuel economy exceeds a comparable model and its estimated lifetime fuel savings is optimal.

c. Incorrect. The fuel economy and conservation incentives have different maximum credits.

10. d. Correct. All three choices are major differences between the clean fuel car deduction and the green vehicle credit.
a. Incorrect. The incentive changed from a deduction to a more preferred credit under the 2005 Energy Act.
b. Incorrect. The range of vehicles has expanded with the green vehicle incentive to include more exotic energy-efficient vehicles than the clean fuel cars under the prior incentive.
c. Incorrect. Until the 2005 Energy Act, the incentive for clean fuel vehicles was based on vehicle weight for trucks, vans, and busses, whereas the new incentive varies by the cost of the vehicle.

11. c. Correct. There is no SUV tax under the rules affected by the 2005 Highway Act.
a. Incorrect. The kerosene removal tax was extended from 2005 to 2011.
b. Incorrect. The motor fuel excise tax was extended from 2005 to 2011.
d. Incorrect. One of the choices was a tax not extended under the 2005 Highway Act.

12. b. Correct. The extension ends on February 28, 2006.
a. Incorrect. The extension is longer in duration.
c. Incorrect. April 15, 2006, is not the end of the extension period but rather the regular due date for 2005 federal income taxes for all taxpayers.
d. Incorrect. The extension ends sooner than the end of 2006.

13. d. Correct. All three choices are special allowances under KETRA for victims of the hurricane.
a. Incorrect. Withdrawals by hurricane victims of up to $100,000 will not be subject to the early withdrawal penalty.
b. Incorrect. If taxpayers are able to replace the funds within three years, the distribution will be given rollover treatment (i.e., the 60-day maximum period to hold distributions without penalty is eliminated).
c. Incorrect. KETRA raises the maximum amounts taxpayers can borrow, but to qualify, the distributions must occur before January 1, 2007.

14. d. Correct. All three choices describe ways in which companies can assist hurricane victims.
a. Incorrect. The Work Opportunity Tax Credit (WOTC) encourages employers to hire economically challenged and high-risk individuals. The credit

is equal to 40 percent of the first $6,000 paid to the qualifying employee. KETRA creates a new class of qualifying individuals, Katrina employees.

b. Incorrect. Between August 28, 2005, and December 31, 2005, the 10 percent limitation is removed for donations made to qualified Code Sec. 170(b)(1)(A) charities. The donations must be monetary and made in connection with Hurricane Katrina relief.

c. Incorrect. Employees can donate their unused leave time back to their employers. The employers can take the funds from the donated days otherwise necessary to pay for the leave and contribute them to a qualified charity. The employer can take a deduction for the amount

15. b. Correct. The Pease deduction will be repealed over a five-year period from 2006 through 2009.

a. Incorrect. The present AMT exemption amounts were due to end before 2006.

c. Incorrect. The choice of electing to deduct state and local income tax payments or state and local sales tax was slated to end in 2005.

d. Incorrect. One of the choices is not set to expire before 2006.

MODULE 3 — CHAPTER 6

1. c. Correct. Advice subject to conditions of confidentiality limits disclosure to protect the practitioner's strategies is considered a covered opinion.

a. Incorrect. A contractual protection is concerned with granting a client a refund of fees if the tax consequences of the opinion are not sustained. It is not necessarily written under conditions of confidentiality.

b. Incorrect. A marketed opinion is developed by a practitioner who knows that the opinion will be used to promote an entity or arrangement, so it is not confidential.

d. Incorrect. A reliance opinion is not necessarily written under conditions of confidentiality.

2. d. Correct. The issue is a significant federal tax issue if the IRS has a reasonable basis for challenge.

a. Incorrect. A listed transaction is definitely subject to IRS challenge because the IRS has identified it as patently abusive.

b. Incorrect. Contractual protection concerns a client's right to full or partial refund of practitioner fees in a dispute with the IRS about the tax consequences of an opinion, not the chances of successful challenge by the IRS.

c. Incorrect. A reliance opinion features a confidence level for taxpayer success with federal tax issues rather than the chances for the IRS of sustaining its position.

3. b. *Correct.* Negative advice that relates to a listed transaction or principal purpose transaction may fall into the scope of a covered opinion.

a. *Incorrect.* The outcome of the issue is not considered in determining whether negative advice is a covered opinion.

c. *Incorrect.* Such advice is preliminary advice as is not considered a covered opinion.

d. *Incorrect.* One of the choices is a situation in which negative advice is considered a covered opinion.

4. c. *Correct.* Legends must appear in a separate section of the communication in a typeface at least as large as that used in the advice.

a. *Incorrect.* The legend out language should not appear in the same section as the advice.

b. *Incorrect.* The size of the type should be as large or larger than the advice to which it refers.

d. *Incorrect.* The IRS and Treasury Department do not favor placing disclaimers on every communication..

5. c. *Correct.* Usually these mailings are directed to "targets" whose circumstances pertain to the basis of the solicitation.

a. *Incorrect.* Radio solicitations must be prerecorded.

b. *Incorrect.* Practitioners should not discuss matters related to the IRS in this unsolicited fashion.

d. *Incorrect.* Such solicitation to other practitioners who are potential clients violates standards of Section 10.30 of Circular 230.

6. a. *Correct.* Imprisonment is not one of the sanctions discussed for violating Circular 230 standards, although perpetrating a fraud is a criminal offense.

b. *Incorrect.* Censure, or public reprimand, is an IRS penalty for violations of Circular 230.

c. *Incorrect.* Violators may be disbarred or suspended from practice before the IRS.

d. *Incorrect.* One of the choices is not an IRS penalty for violating Circular 230 standards.

7. c. *Correct.* If a practitioner loses his or her license to practice in his or her profession, that practitioner may not practice before the IRS.

a. *Incorrect.* This is not the IRS penalty for losing his license with the bar.

b. *Incorrect.* The sanction does not differentiate between new and existing clients.

d. Incorrect. One of the choices is the correct sanction, and licensure is related to the privilege of practicing before the IRS.

8. d. Correct. All three choices are sources of false opinions by a practitioner.
a. Incorrect. Concealment is a possible source of false opinions.
b. Incorrect. Knowing misstatement is a source of false opinions.
c. Incorrect. Illegal conduct may give rise to false opinions.

9. False. Correct. The government employee may serve as an estate executor.
True. Incorrect. A government officer or employee may serve as the executor.

10. d. Correct. All three choices are requirements of the act.
a. Incorrect. The Treasury Department would be required to establish CE requirements.
b. Incorrect. Enrolled preparers would be required to renew their credentials.
c. Incorrect. Treasury would be required to develop the initial examination, which would have to be successfully completed by enrolled preparers.

MODULE 3 – CHAPTER 7

1. b. Correct. Underreporting is the largest component of the tax gap, accounting for more than 80 percent of the tax compliance problem.
a. Incorrect. Nonfilers represent about 10 percent of the tax gap.
c. Incorrect. Underpayments represent only about 10 percent of the tax gap.
d. Incorrect. One of the choices constitutes the "lion's share" of the tax gap problem.

2. c. Correct. Higher-income individual filers, especially ones filing Schedule C as sole proprietors, received close examination by the NRP.
a. Incorrect. Large corporations' returns were not the major focus of the NRP study.
b. Incorrect. The NRP did not especially examine returns of low-income filers.
d. Incorrect. One of the choices was the special focus of the NRP.

3. a. Correct. Only 0.19 percent of S corp returns were audited among the 3.4 million Forms 1120S filings.
b. Incorrect. One in six large corporations was audited in 2004, showing the increased attention large corporations have received during this decade.
c. Incorrect. Limited liability companies did not compose the least-audited business entity according to the TIGTA.
d. Incorrect. FLPs were not cited by the TIGTA as the least-audited business entity.

4. False. *Correct.* TIGTA cited the hiring of almost 1,000 revenue agents in FY 2005 as addressing the human capital crisis in the IRS.
True. *Incorrect.* The number of revenue agents increased during FY 2005 because almost 1,000 revenue agents were hired this FY.

5. b. *Correct.* Requesting personal financial data by e-mail is not a method used by the IRS.
a. *Incorrect.* Return preparer fraud is not new and has been on the Dirty Dozen list of scams for some time.
c. *Incorrect.* Tax avoidance or evasion using offshore tax havens is not a new occurrence for the Dirty Dozen.
d. *Incorrect.* Only one of the three choices is a new addition to the warning list.

6. d. *Correct.* All three choices are actual scams that have been subject to court injunctions or prosecution.
a. *Incorrect.* This Internet-hawked scheme, called Tax Buster, claimed that customers could avoid income taxes through such a renunciation.
b. *Incorrect.* A Tennessee federal court barred the owner of a tax preparation business from future return preparation because she either made up or vastly inflated itemized deductions on her clients' returns.
c. *Incorrect.* An individual urged taxpayers to transfer assets to a corporation sole and claim it was a religious organization.

7. c. *Correct.* The IRS reported that 90 percent of settlement participants were high-income individuals.
a. *Incorrect.* Middle-income taxpayers were not likely participants in the scam or in the settlements initiative.
b. *Incorrect.* Corporate taxpayers composed just 10 percent of taxpayers electing to participate in Son of BOSS.
d. *Incorrect.* Trusts were not likely participants in the initiative.

8. b. *Correct.* The taxpayer receives a Code Sec. 6707A(e) penalty for failing to disclose the other three penalties to the SEC.
a. *Incorrect.* The IRS is not offering such an amnesty.
c. *Incorrect.* Failure to disclose a penalty must be indicated on the taxpayer's following-year Form 10-K.
d. *Incorrect.* One of the choices is the IRS requirement for the nondisclosures.

9. False. *Correct.* The actions taken against the firm and its former employees involved only government redress and provided no relief directly to taxpayers who used the firm's services.

True. *Incorrect.* The indictments and fine were government settlement actions distinct from whatever redress the IRS pursues for this case.

10. d. *Correct.* All three choices are practitioners' reactions to the key provisions of the revised version of Circular 230.

a. *Incorrect.* Ambiguous key terms are a feature practitioners have noted about the revision.

b. *Incorrect.* Penalties are harsh, including permanent disbarment and sanctions against an entire tax advisory firm.

c. *Incorrect.* Practitioners are hampered in giving responses to clients' follow-up questions.

TOP FEDERAL TAX ISSUES FOR 2006 CPE COURSE

Index

All references are to paragraph (¶) numbers.

D

Debt repayment in DRP ... 215.06

Deductions
allocating and apportioning
methods for ... 115.02
for business ... 325.02
decision whether to itemize ... 325.01
disallowed under 2004 Jobs Act ... 205.03
85 percent. *See* Dividends-received deduction
for individuals affected by AMT ... 325.03
for retirees, importance in deciding whether
to start designated Roth account of ... 415
sunsetting after 2005 ... 525.01–.03
2005 Energy Act business incentive ... 505.03

**Deemed distributions from
retirement plans ... 420.01**
traps incurred through loans
considered as ... 430–430.02

Deferred compensation ... 401–480

**Delays for interactions with IRS
by practitioners ... 620.09**

**Department of Justice (DOJ) enforcement
actions with IRS ... 705.05–.06, 710.02,
710.04, 735**

Depletion refigured for AMT ... 310.02

Depreciation recalculated for AMT ... 310.02

**Design and development activities
for tangible property ... 110.05**

**Designated entity (DE), payments to
U.S. shareholder by ... 210.03–.04**

Designated Roth accounts
advantages of ... 405.02
contributions of after-tax dollars to ... 405,
530.02
contributions of before-tax
dollars to ... 405.02
deciding whether to start ... 415
distributions from ... 410, 415, 420–420.02
employer matching contributions to, as
gross income ... 405.02
penalties and exemptions for ... 420.02,
425.01–.03
petition for abatement of
penalties for ... 420.02
separate accounting required for ... 405.01

**Disbarment or loss of license
by authority ... 620.09**

**Discharge of indebtedness without taxation
for Hurricane Katrina victims ... 515.07**

**Disclosure of information to taxpayer's
representative ... 630.02**

**Discriminant Index Function (DIF)
formulas for audit potential ... 705.03**

**Dividends as disallowed investments
for DRP ... 215.07**

Dividends-received deduction
base period amount
for ... 205.02, 210.04, 220
ceiling on amounts for ... 205.02, 210.05
created by 2004 Jobs Act ... 201
directly allocable expenses for ... 210.08
disallowance rule for ... 210.07–.08
foreign tax credit interaction with ... 210.07
guidance for ... 205.01–.03
qualifying payments for ... 210.01–.09
reporting requirements for ... 220–220.02
tax years for electing ... 210.01
taxable income limitation for ... 210.09

**Domestic reinvestment plan (DRP) for
repatriated dividends ... 215.01–.07**
of acquired corporation ... 215.04
approval of ... 215.01, 215.03
description of anticipated
investments in ... 215.02
members of consolidated group making
investments for ... 215.03
nonpermissible investments for ... 215.07
record requirements for ... 220–220.02
timing and designation of
investments of ... 215.05
transition rules for ... 215.02
types of permissible investments for ... 215.06

Domestic production gross receipts (DPGR)
allocation of ... 115.03
calculating ... 115–115.08
COGS traced to ... 115
in computing QPAI ... 105.01
deductions allocated and
apportioned to ... 115.02
defined (Code Sec. 199) ... 105.02, 110
proceeds of disposition of real property
included in ... 110.09

**Donated employee leave for Hurricane
Katrina victim assistance, employer
and employee benefits for ... 515.10**

**Due diligence requirements for
practitioners ... 620.01**

E

**Early distributions from
retirement plans ... 435**
for victims of Hurricane Katrina ... 515.04

Earned Income Tax Credit (EITC)
abuse of ... 635.02
for victims of Hurricane Katrina ... 515.02

**Economic Growth and Tax Relief
Reconciliation Act of 2001 (EGTRRA)**
provisions first taking effect in
006 of ... 405, 530–520.02

CPE Quizzer Instructions

The CPE Quizzer is divided into three modules. There is a processing fee for each Quizzer Module submitted for grading. Successful completion of Module 1 is recommended for **5 CPE Credits.*** Successful completion of Module 2 is recommended for **8 CPE Credits.*** Successful completion of Module 3 is recommended for **4 CPE Credits.*** You can complete and submit one Module at a time, or all Modules at once for a total of **17 CPE Credits.***

To obtain CPE credit, return your completed Answer Sheet for each Quizzer Module to **CCH Tax and Accounting, Continuing Education Department, 4025 W. Peterson Ave., Chicago, IL 60646**, or fax it to (773) 866-3084. Each quizzer answer sheet will be graded and a CPE Certificate of Completion awarded for achieving a grade of 70 percent or greater. The Quizzer Answer Sheets are located after the Quizzer questions for this Course.

Express Grading: Processing time for your answer sheet is generally 8-12 business days. If you are trying to meet a reporting deadline, our Express Grading Service is available for an additional $19 per Module. To use this service, please check the "Express Grading" box on your Answer Sheet, and provide your CCH account or credit card number and your fax number. CCH will fax your results and a Certificate of Completion (upon achieving a passing grade) to you by 5:00 p.m. the business day following our receipt of your Answer Sheet. **If you mail your answer sheet for express grading, please write "ATTN: CPE OVERNIGHT" on the envelope.** NOTE: CCH will not Federal Express Quizzer results under any circumstances.

NEW ONLINE GRADING gives you immediate 24/7 grading with instant results and no Express Grading Fee.

The **CCH Testing Center** website gives you and others in your firm easy, free access to CCH print courses and allows you to complete your CPE exams online for immediate results. Plus, the **My Courses** feature provides convenient storage for your CPE course certificates and completed exams.

Go to **www.cchtestingcenter.com** to complete your exam online.

---

* Recommended CPE credit is based on a 50-minute hour. Participants earning credits for states that require self-study to be based on a 100-minute hour will receive ½ the CPE credits for successful completion of this course. Because CPE requirements vary from state to state and among different licensing agencies, please contact your CPE governing body for information on your CPE requirements and the applicability of a particular course for your requirements.

Date of Completion: The date of completion on your certificate will be the date that you put on your answer sheet. However, you must submit your answer sheet to CCH for grading within two weeks of completing it.

Expiration Date: December 31, 2006

Evaluation: To help us provide you with the best possible products, please take a moment to fill out the course evaluation located at the back of this Course located at page 255 and return it with your Quizzer Answer Sheets.

CCH INCORPORATED is registered with the National Association of State Boards of Accountancy (NASBA) as a sponsor of continuing professional education on the National Registry of CPE Sponsors. State boards of accountancy have final authority on the acceptance of individual courses for CPE credit. Complaints regarding registered sponsors may be addressed to the National Registry of CPE Sponsors, 150 Fourth Avenue North, Suite 700, Nashville, TN 37219-2417. Web site: www.nasba.org.

CCH INCORPORATED is registered with the National Association of State Boards of Accountancy (NASBA) as a Quality Assurance Service (QAS) sponsor of continuing professional education. State boards of accountancy have final authority on the acceptance of individual courses for CPE credit. Complaints regarding registered sponsors may be addressed to NASBA, 150 Fourth Avenue North, Suite 700, Nashville, TN 37219-2417. Web site: www.nasba.org.

Recommended CPE:	5 hours for Module 1
	8 hours for Module 2
	4 hours for Module 3
	17 hours for all modules
Processing Fee:	$50.00 for Module 1
	$80.00 for Module 2
	$40.00 for Module 3
	$170.00 for all modules

One **complimentary copy** of this Course is provided with certain CCH Federal Tax publications. Additional copies of this course may be ordered for $25.00 each by calling 1-800-248-3248 (ask for product 0-0905-200).

Quizzer Questions: Module 1

Answer the True/False questions by marking a "T" or "F" on the Quizzer Answer Sheet. Answer Multiple Choice questions by indicating the appropriate letter on the Answer Sheet.

1. Gross receipts derived from which of the following would be considered as domestic production gross receipts (DPGRs)?

    a. Coffee mugs manufactured in Seattle
    b. Architectural services performed in Guam
    c. Construction performed in Japan
    d. Telephones manufactured in Russia

2. Which of the following would **not** qualify as qualifying production property (QPP)?

    a. A tractor
    b. A sound recording
    c. A commercial building
    d. An automobile

3. How is qualifying production activities income (QPAI) determined?

    a. Product line-by-product line
    b. Division-by-division
    c. Transaction-by-transaction
    d. Item-by-item

4. Which of the following does **not** count toward the wage limitation for the manufacturing deduction?

    a. Deferred compensation
    b. Unreported cash payments
    c. Designated Roth IRA contributions
    d. W-2 wages

5. Which of the following is **untrue** about the wage limitation?

 a. Only items actually reported on Form W-2 count toward the wage limitation.
 b. Taxpayers can find all items that count toward the wage limitation in one box on Form W-2.
 c. It is equal to 50 percent of W-2 wages actually paid and reported on Form W-2.
 d. It is equal to 60 percent of the W-2 wages actually paid and reported on Form W-2.

6. Which of the following is an example of manufacturing computer software?

 a. Offering video games online for a fee
 b. Providing wireless Internet access
 c. Producing a video game
 d. Providing international long-distance calls through a computer modem

7. Which of the following activities would **not** satisfy the "in whole or in part" requirement?

 a. Building computers in Texas using parts entirely made in the United States except for screws made in Taiwan
 b. Purchasing wood grown in Oregon for use in making baseball bats in Kentucky
 c. Exporting Japanese cars to California where environmentally friendly mufflers are placed on the cars
 d. Building cars in Michigan for export to Canada where the cars are sold after having windshield wipers installed

8. Gross receipts derived from engineering and architectural services rendered on which of the following would **not** qualify as DPGRs?

 a. A subdivision of single-family homes in Arizona
 b. A new vehicle
 c. High-rise condos in Chicago, Illinois
 d. A shopping mall that was never actually built

9. What is the annual gross receipts threshold for using the simplified deduction method?

    a. $25 million
    b. $20 million
    c. $15 million
    d. $10 million

10. In allocation of DPGRs, the safe harbor applying to taxpayers having less than five percent of total gross receipts from items other than DPGRs is that:

    a. They may allocate just half of nonqualifying receipts.
    b. They may treat all gross receipts as DPGRs.
    c. They may omit tracing COGS to DPGRs.
    d. They may allocate NOLs to DPGRs.

11. What is the effective tax rate under the one-year window for the dividends received deduction under the 2004 Jobs Act?

    a. 3.5 percent
    b. 5.25 percent
    c. 10 percent
    d. 12.25 percent

12. Congress enacted the special tax rate as part of the 2004 Jobs Act to:

    a. Bring the tax rate on dividends in line with treaty obligations
    b. Encourage corporations to invest foreign income in the United States
    c. Generate additional tax income
    d. Enable corporations to pay higher dividends to domestic investors

13. Which of the following are distributions that qualify as cash dividends for the special rate?

    a. E&P included as income under Code Sec. 951
    b. Previously taxed income
    c. Distributions described in Code Sec. 959(c)(3)
    d. All of the above qualify

14. The annual ceiling amount for repatriated earnings is:

    a. $250 million
    b. $500 million
    c. $750 million
    d. $1 billion

15. When affiliated corporations are treated as one employer under Code Sec. 52:

a. Each has a separate $500 million limit on repatriated dividends
b. They are limited to one maximum of $500 million
c. The $500 million limit is ignored
d. None of the above applies

16. Under Notice 2005-64, for the related-party debt provision, a bank's increase in debt is:

a. Not treated as debt
b. Treated as short-term debt
c. Treated as long-term debt
d. None of the above

17. Under Code Sec. 965, the 85-percent deductible portion of dividend payments:

a. Is subject to the gross-up rules
b. Is prohibited from applying the foreign tax credit
c. Is considered foreign taxes deemed paid under Code Secs. 902 and 960
d. None of the above is a result of Code Sec. 965

18. In the reinvestment of repatriated funds, which pronouncement provides the *essential* guidance to establish a DRP?

a. Code Sec. 78
b. Notice 2005-64
c. Notice 2005-38
d. Notice 2005-10

19. Which of the following is *not* an expense type directly allocable to deductible dividends under Notice 2005-64?

a. Fees and expenses paid for advice and document preparation concerning plans to repatriate earnings in the election year
b. Currency exchange and other fees for paying qualified dividends
c. Code Sec. 861 stewardship expenses related to qualifying dividends
d. All of the above are directly allocable

20. When would having separate dividend reinvestment plans be useful for U.S. shareholders?

    a. When the shareholders wish to decline the deduction of properly reinvested amounts

    b. When the amount of dividends from specified CFCs are less than the total dollar amount of investments proposed in the DRPs

    c. When one CFC is located in a low-tax country and another CFC is in a high-tax country

    d. All of the above are situations in which separate DRPs may be useful

21. Permissible financial stabilization uses of repatriated dividends include all of the following *except*:

    a. Funding of qualified plans for U.S. shareholders' funding obligations

    b. Discretionary contributions to a stock bonus plan

    c. Debt repayments that improve cash flow

    d. All of the above are permissible

22. All of the following are nonpermissible investments of repatriated dividends *except*:

    a. Purchases of Treasury bills and municipal bonds

    b. Stock redemptions and buybacks

    c. R&D projects conducted in the United States

    d. All of the above are nonpermissible

23. The election year for the temporary dividends-received deduction *cannot* be a short taxable year. **True or False?**

24. The dividends-received deduction is *not* available for dividend payments made by a foreign partnership. **True or False?**

25. Under Notice 2005-64, distributions of previously taxed income treated as cash dividends are *not* subject to the disallowance rule. **True or False?**

Quizzer Questions: Module 2

26. Which of the following itemized deductions is disallowed under AMT?

    a. Home equity interest for loans where proceeds did not improve the home

    b. State and local property and income taxes

    c. Employee business deductions

    d. All of the above

27. AMTI is:

    a. Always the same as the taxpayer's regular taxable income

    b. Always the same as the taxpayer's total income

    c. Equal to regular taxable income less tax preference items

    d. Equal to regular taxable income plus tax preference items

28. The AMT exemption for married taxpayers (with AMTI below $150,000) filing jointly for 2005 was:

    a. $58,000

    b. $45,000

    c. $40,250

    d. $150,000

29. The AMT exemption for single taxpayers with AMTI below $112,500 for 2005 was:

    a. $19,000

    b. $29,000

    c. $40,250

    d. $58,000

30. For an individual taxpayer anticipating being liable for AMT, which of the following will *not* help against phaseout?

    a. Foregoing the use of the AMT Foreign Tax Credit

    b. Making IRA or pension distributions

    c. Payoff of home equity loans

    d. Using intra-family transactions

31. ATNOLDs _____ the regular amount of regular tax a taxpayer may take.

    a. Lower
    b. Raise
    c. Neither raise nor lower
    d. Either raise or lower, depending on the type of taxpayer

32. Married taxpayers are more likely than single taxpayers to be liable for AMT for all of the following reasons **except:**

    a. Married couples are more likely to have dependents.
    b. The exemption under AMT is a smaller percentage of income than under regular tax.
    c. The income cap to qualify for exemption that married couples use is not twice that for singles.
    d. All of the above are reasons married taxpayers are more liable for AMT.

33. Congress is **not** considering which of the following AMT reforms?

    a. Amnesty for late-filing taxpayers subject to the AMT
    b. Indexing the AMT for inflation
    c. Allowing dependent exemptions under the AMT
    d. Allowing for deduction of state and local taxes under the AMT

34. Eliminating the AMT would cost the federal government an estimated _____ in lost revenues over the next 10 years.

    a. $600 million
    b. $600 billion
    c. $370 million
    d. $370 billion

35. Although estates and trusts are generally treated much like individuals for AMT, estates and trusts are more likely to be subject to AMT. **True or False?**

36. Features of designated Roth accounts that differentiate the new vehicle from non-Roth 401(k) and 403(b) accounts include all of the following *except:*

   a. Taxation of payroll deductions for the designated Roth accounts
   b. The authorizing provision will sunset in 2010
   c. Contribution limits for designated Roth accounts are higher than for nondesignated accounts
   d. All of the above are differences between designated 401(k) and 403(b) accounts and nondesignated types

37. One disadvantage for employers in offering designated Roth accounts is:

   a. Employers are required to contribute a higher percentage of contributions
   b. Establishing a designated Roth account plan is more complex
   c. The separate accounting requirement
   d. All of the above are disadvantages for employers

38. Participants having designated Roth accounts must do all of the following *except:*

   a. Take required minimum distributions starting at age 70½
   b. Pay 50 percent excise tax on amounts by which the RMD exceeds actual distributions
   c. Not take qualified distributions of contributions for at least five years after making them
   d. All of the above are required for designated Roth accounts

39. A major reason contributors to Roth IRAs are candidates for designated Roth accounts is:

   a. Designated Roth account contributors can withdraw amounts at an earlier age than from Roth IRAs.
   b. Designated Roth accounts have higher contribution limits.
   c. Employers may make tax-free contributions to the designated accounts.
   d. None of the above is a major reason to open a designated account.

40. Which type of retirement plan distribution is **not** subject to additional tax or penalty?

    a. Early distributions for participants retiring before age 55
    b. Deemed distributions following bankruptcy
    c. Distributions at or after the contributor's death
    d. All of the above carry tax liabilities or penalties

41. If a participant in a retirement plan makes a rollover by receiving funds from one plan and depositing them into another account within 60 days:

    a. The participant cannot make another rollover distribution within one year.
    b. A second rollover in the same year must be a trustee-to-trustee transfer.
    c. Any second transfer must be net of the RMD.
    d. None of the above applies.

42. When loans taken from qualified retirement plans become deemed distributions, they are usually:

    a. Subject to the 10 percent early distribution penalty
    b. Subject to withholding for income tax that must be repaid as well as the loan
    c. Permanently prohibited from being repaid to replenish the account
    d. All of the above are the consequences of deemed distributions

43. To extend the payment period and thus reduce the amount of the required minimum distributions of designated Roth IRAs, the participant may:

    a. Begin taking RMDs at age 75 instead of 70½
    b. Roll over the designated Roth IRA tax- and penalty-free into a regular Roth IRA
    c. Name a younger individual as the beneficiary
    d. All of the above may be chosen to extend the payment period and reduce the RMD

44. The penalty for failure to take the RMD from a designated Roth account is _____ percent of the difference between the RMD and the actual withdrawal.

   a. 10
   b. 25
   c. 30
   d. 50

45. All of the following are disadvantages of flexible spending accounts **except:**

   a. FSA funds cannot be used to reimburse health care expenses if the same expenses can be reimbursed from another source.
   b. Unused FSA contributions for the year are forfeited.
   c. Taxpayers cannot participate in other health plans concurrently.
   d. None of the above is a disadvantage.

46. All of the following are disadvantages of Archer MSAs **except:**

   a. They have a "use-it-or-lose-it" provision for forfeiting unused contributions annually.
   b. The taxpayer may hold no other insurance than a high-deductible health plan.
   c. MSAs will not be available to new participants after 2005.
   d. All of the above are disadvantages of Archer MSAs.

47. Advantages of health savings accounts include all of the following **except:**

   a. The majority of employers now offer the plans, which are portable as employees switch employers.
   b. Participants older than age 55 will be able to make additional contributions over the stated maximums.
   c. HSA distributions used for qualified medical expenses are not included in the participant's gross income.
   d. All of the above are advantages.

48. The major advantage of health reimbursement arrangements is that:

    a. Employers may deduct qualified contributions to HRAs and the distributions are not included in the employee's gross income.

    b. HRA funds can be distributed as compensation as long as key employees are not favored.

    c. HRA funds may be distributed as bonuses to highly compensated employees.

    d. None of the above is the major advantage.

49. When a participant borrows funds from a qualified retirement plan rather than withdrawing the funds, their receipt is not considered a distribution but must be repaid in order not to be treated as a deemed distribution. ***True or False?***

50. In 2005 the IRS revised the "use-it-or-lose-it" rule for FSA funds so employee participants now have a six-month period (through June 2006) to pay expenses with unused contributions for 2005. ***True or False?***

51. For the Residential Energy Conservation Property Credit, all of the following are included in the building envelope ***except:***

    a. Windows

    b. Roof

    c. Furnace

    d. Insulation

52. To qualify for the Residential Energy Property Expenditures Credit, an expenditure:

    a. May not be made for a mixed-use property

    b. May not be paid for in 2005

    c. May not be used for a cooperative housing unit or condominium

    d. Is considered made when the property is ready for use

53. Which of the following credits may be used for vacation home energy-efficiency improvements?

    a. Residential Energy Property Expenditures Credit, each subcredit included

    b. Residential Alternative Energy Expenditures Credit

    c. Residential Energy Conservation Property Credit only

    d. Residential Energy Property Expenditures Credit only

54. The advantage of the energy-efficient commercial buildings deduction is that:

    a. Businesses can take immediate deductions for the full cost of the expenditure rather than depreciating it.

    b. Businesses can take immediate deductions for half the cost of the expenditure rather than depreciating it.

    c. Businesses can accelerate depreciation to five years rather than 20.

    d. Businesses can deduct 10 percent of costs and depreciate the remaining expenditure over five years.

55. All of the following credits or deductions use the International Energy Conservation Code (IECC) standards for energy conservation **except:**

    a. Residential Energy Conservation Property Credit

    b. Energy-Efficient New Home Production Credit

    c. Energy-Efficient Commercial Buildings Deduction

    d. Residential Alternative Energy Expenditures Credit

56. The 2005 Highway Act extends existing transportation and fuel-related excise taxes through the year:

    a. 2011

    b. 2010

    c. 2009

    d. 2007

57. KETRA rules affecting the child credit and EITC of displaced residents of core and general disaster areas allow:

    a. Double the usual credit for 2005

    b. Extended carryovers of credits for the next five years

    c. Use of 2004 income to calculate the credit

    d. All of the above are allowed

58. What change did KETRA implement for casualty losses?

    a. It lifted the percentage threshold for nonbusiness casualty loss deductions and the $100 floor.

    b. It lowered the threshold percentage of AGI from 10 percent to 3 percent and lowered the floor to $50.

    c. It allowed taxpayers to itemize deductions up to the usual threshold for casualty losses.

    d. None of the above is the change implemented for casualty losses of Katrina victims.

59. What is the benefit to employers of hiring Katrina employees?

    a. The federal government will match the employers' pay rate for Katrina employees dollar-for-dollar through 2006.

    b. The Work Opportunity Tax Credit will be available to offset 40 percent of $6,000 of pay.

    c. The federal government will reimburse out-of-state employers for relocating Katrina employees.

    d. None of the above is the benefit.

60. What is the maximum employee retention credit for employers located in the core disaster area?

    a. $2,000

    b. $2,400

    c. $2,750

    d. $3,500

61. Which of the following is *not* a requirement to claim the special personal exemption for providing housing to Katrina victims?

    a. The displaced victims must have had their principal residence in a disaster area on August 28, 2005.

    b. The individuals taking in the victims must own the residence where the housing is provided.

    c. The housing must be provided rent-free in the taxpayer's principal residence.

    d. The minimum length of stay qualifying for the exemption is 60 days.

62. Which of the following features was *not* included in the superdischarge that was eliminated by the 2005 Bankruptcy Act?

    a. Tax debt from failure to file a return

    b. Tax debt from fraudulent returns

    c. Tax debt from misfiled returns

    d. All of the above liabilities were included in ending the superdischarge

63. The maximum amount in IRA funds that may be protected from inclusion in a bankruptcy estate is:

   a. $500,000
   b. $750,000
   c. $1 million
   d. $1.5 million

64. For either the Residential Energy Conservation Property Credit or the Residential Energy Property Expenditures Credit, the taxpayer calculates the correct percentage of the total cost of the qualified improvement or property up to the lifetime limit of $500. *True or False?*

65. Qualifying energy property costs for the Residential Energy Property Expenditures Credit do *not* include on-site assembly and installation of the property. *True or False?*

Quizzer Questions: Module 3

66. One reason for the overhaul of Circular 230 rules for covered opinions was:

   a. To curb promotion of tax shelters
   b. To supplement initiatives begun by the Sarbanes-Oxley regulations
   c. To further separate auditing services from tax services by accounting firms
   d. None of the above was a primary reason for the revision

67. All of the following are complaints about the revisions to Circular 230's tax shelter opinion rules *except:*

   a. Final regulations do not allow practitioners to give complete, accurate advice to clients.
   b. Various categories of opinions and requirements are too complex.
   c. The final regulations favor nonlicensed practitioners.
   d. The regulations for tax shelters are too vague.

68. Under Circular 230, the type of opinion concluding that one or more tax issues could be resolved in the taxpayer's favor is a _____ opinion.

   a. Marketed
   b. Reliance
   c. Covered
   d. None of the above

69. All of the following are varieties of excluded advice for covered opinions *except:*

   a. Advice concerning a principal purpose transaction
   b. Advice regarding the qualification of a qualified plan
   c. Written advice on a transaction prepared after the return is filed
   d. All of the above are excluded advice

70. Which type of opinion does **not** consider or provide a conclusion regarding noncovered issues?

   a. Bond opinion
   b. Preliminary advice
   c. Reliance opinion
   d. Limited scope opinion

71. A highly unreasonable omission or an extreme departure from the standards of ordinary care by a practitioner is known as:

   a. Lack of due diligence
   b. Reckless conduct
   c. Misconduct
   d. None of the above

72. Under proposed legislation, the _____ would appoint the director of the IRS Office of Professional Responsibility.

   a. Secretary of the Treasury Department
   b. Secretary of the Justice Department
   c. IRS Commissioner
   d. IRS National Taxpayer Advocate

73. A designee is **not** authorized to do any of the following for a taxpayer **except:**

   a. Request and receive information about the taxpayer's return
   b. Represent the taxpayer during an examination (but not during Appeals)
   c. Continue to represent the taxpayer indefinitely using "check the box" authority
   d. All of the above are authorizations available to designees

74. Traditionally, bond opinions were an exception to the definition of tax shelter for Circular 230. The final Circular 230 tax shelter regs remove that exception, and some practitioners believe the regs will disrupt the municipal bond markets. **True or False?**

75. Under proposed amendments to Section 10.22 of Circular 230, a practitioner would lose the presumption of due diligence if he or she relied on the work product of another, even if the practitioner used reasonable care in engaging, supervising, training, and evaluating that person. **True or False?**

76. What encourages compliance in reporting taxable income?

    a. Verification of employers' tax records
    b. Use of third-party reporting such as W-2s and withholding reports
    c. Internal audits of tax filings
    d. None of the above

77. IRS Commissioner Mark Everson especially wishes to boost audits of:

    a. Middle-income individuals
    b. C corporations
    c. Small businesses
    d. High-income individuals

78. Commissioner Deborah Nolan of the IRS's Large and Mid-Size Business Division noted development in her division of a model for identifying tax shelter abuses by:

    a. Pass-through entities
    b. High-income resident aliens
    c. Users of offshore tax havens
    d. Large C corporations

79. What tool has the IRS employed to pursue abusive trusts, "zero income" tax return filers, and abuse of the disabled access credit?

    a. Rewards for informants
    b. Lifestyle audits
    c. Civil injunctions
    d. All of the above

80. In exchange for conceding all of their claimed tax losses, all interest, and payment of nondisclosure penalty, participants in the Son of BOSS initiatives received from the IRS:

    a. Forgiveness of their tax liabilities up to $2 million
    b. Reduced penalties and deduction of out-of-pocket transaction costs
    c. Reduced criminal sentences
    d. Cancellation of the 40-percent penalty imposed on all tax abusers

81. Under the terms of the executive stock option settlement initiative, participants had to do all of the following **except:**

    a. Recognize compensation equal to the FMV of the stock when exercised minus the costs of exercising the option in year exercised
    b. Pay the employee's share of FICA tax on the recognized compensation income
    c. Gain up to the amount of deferred obligation that exceeds the amount recognized as compensation;
    d. All of the above

82. In an individual settlement during 2005, contingent liability shelter participant Hercules Inc.:

    a. Agreed to a 40 percent penalty for a gross valuation misstatement
    b. Agreed to a total of $36 million in taxes and penalties
    c. Succeeded in winning a judgment against the IRS position that contingent liability transactions are patently abusive
    d. Did none of the above

83. Which legislation includes provisions to create a Whistleblowers Office within the IRS and provide incentives for turning in promoters and unscrupulous practitioners?

    a. The 2004 Jobs Act
    b. USA Patriot Act
    c. The Tax Shelter and Tax Haven Reform Act of 2005
    d. Bankruptcy Abuse Prevention and Consumer Protection Act of 2005

84. Use of simultaneous civil and criminal litigation cases resulted in a 20 percent increase of criminal referrals and increased criminal prosecutions for tax offenders in 2004. **True or False?**

85. It is often difficult to distinguish a legitimate from an abusive tax shelter. **True or False?**

TOP FEDERAL TAX ISSUES FOR 2006 CPE COURSE   (0716-2)

Module 1: Answer Sheet

NAME _____

COMPANY NAME _____

STREET _____

CITY, STATE, & ZIP CODE _____

BUSINESS PHONE NUMBER _____

E-MAIL ADDRESS _____

DATE OF COMPLETION _____

CFP REGISTRANT ID _____

On the next page, please answer the Multiple Choice questions by indicating the appropriate letter next to the corresponding number. Please answer the True/False questions by marking "T" or "F" next to the corresponding number.

You will be charged a $50.00 processing fee for each submission of Module 1.

Please remove both pages of this Answer Sheet from this booklet and return it with your completed Evaluation Form to CCH at the address below. You may also fax your Answer Sheet to CCH at 773-866-3084.

You may also go to **www.cchtestingcenter.com** to complete your exam online.

METHOD OF PAYMENT:

☐ Check Enclosed   ☐ Visa   ☐ Master Card   ☐ AmEx

☐ Discover   ☐ CCH Account* _____

Card No. _____ Exp. Date _____

Signature _____

* Must provide CCH account number for this payment option

EXPRESS GRADING: Please fax my Course results to me by 5:00 p.m. the business day following your receipt of this Answer Sheet. By checking this box I authorize CCH to charge $19.00 for this service.

☐ Express Grading $19.00   Fax No. _____

SEND TO:

CCH Tax and Accounting
Continuing Education Department
4025 W. Peterson Ave.
Chicago, IL 60646-6085
1-800-248-3248

Module 1: Answer Sheet

Please answer the Multiple Choice questions by indicating the appropriate letter next to the corresponding number. Please answer the True/False questions by marking "T" or "F" next to the corresponding number.

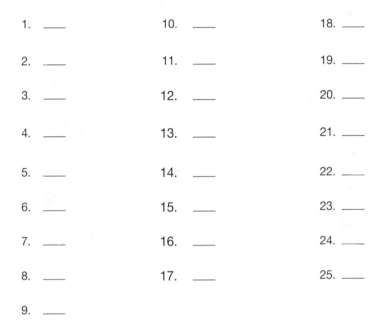

1. ⎯	10. ⎯	18. ⎯
2. ⎯	11. ⎯	19. ⎯
3. ⎯	12. ⎯	20. ⎯
4. ⎯	13. ⎯	21. ⎯
5. ⎯	14. ⎯	22. ⎯
6. ⎯	15. ⎯	23. ⎯
7. ⎯	16. ⎯	24. ⎯
8. ⎯	17. ⎯	25. ⎯
9. ⎯		

Please complete the Evaluation Form (located after the Module 3 Answer Sheet) and return it with this Quizzer Answer Sheet to CCH at the address on the previous page. Thank you.

TOP FEDERAL TAX ISSUES FOR 2006 CPE COURSE   (0717-2)

Module 2: Answer Sheet

NAME _____

COMPANY NAME _____

STREET _____

CITY, STATE, & ZIP CODE _____

BUSINESS PHONE NUMBER _____

E-MAIL ADDRESS _____

DATE OF COMPLETION _____

CFP REGISTRANT ID _____

On the next page, please answer the Multiple Choice questions by indicating the appropriate letter next to the corresponding number. Please answer the True/False questions by marking "T" or "F" next to the corresponding number.

You will be charged a $80.00 processing fee for each submission of Module 2.

Please remove both pages of this Answer Sheet from this booklet and return it with your completed Evaluation Form to CCH at the address below. You may also fax your Answer Sheet to CCH at 773-866-3084.

You may also go to **www.cchtestingcenter.com** to complete your exam online.

METHOD OF PAYMENT:

☐ Check Enclosed   ☐ Visa   ☐ Master Card   ☐ AmEx

☐ Discover   ☐ CCH Account* _____

Card No. _____ Exp. Date _____

Signature _____

* Must provide CCH account number for this payment option

EXPRESS GRADING: Please fax my Course results to me by 5:00 p.m. the business day following your receipt of this Answer Sheet. By checking this box I authorize CCH to charge $19.00 for this service.

☐ Express Grading $19.00   Fax No. _____

SEND TO:

CCH Tax and Accounting
Continuing Education Department
4025 W. Peterson Ave.
Chicago, IL 60646-6085
1-800-248-3248

Module 2: Answer Sheet

Please answer the Multiple Choice questions by indicating the appropriate letter next to the corresponding number. Please answer the True/False questions by marking "T" or "F" next to the corresponding number.

26. ____	40. ____	53. ____
27. ____	41. ____	54. ____
28. ____	42. ____	55. ____
29. ____	43. ____	56. ____
30. ____	44. ____	57. ____
31. ____	45. ____	58. ____
32. ____	46. ____	59. ____
33. ____	47. ____	60. ____
34. ____	48. ____	61. ____
35. ____	49. ____	62. ____
36. ____	50. ____	63. ____
37. ____	51. ____	64. ____
38. ____	52. ____	65. ____
39. ____		

Please complete the Evaluation Form (located after the Module 3 Answer Sheet) and return it with this Quizzer Answer Sheet to CCH at the address on the previous page. Thank you.

TOP FEDERAL TAX ISSUES FOR 2006 CPE COURSE   (0718-2)

Module 3: Answer Sheet

NAME _____

COMPANY NAME _____

STREET _____

CITY, STATE, & ZIP CODE _____

BUSINESS PHONE NUMBER _____

E-MAIL ADDRESS _____

DATE OF COMPLETION _____

CFP REGISTRANT ID _____

On the next page, please answer the Multiple Choice questions by indicating the appropriate letter next to the corresponding number. Please answer the True/False questions by marking "T" or "F" next to the corresponding number.

You will be charged a $40.00 processing fee for each submission of Module 3.

Please remove both pages of this Answer Sheet from this booklet and return it with your completed Evaluation Form to CCH at the address below. You may also fax your Answer Sheet to CCH at 773-866-3084.

You may also go to **www.cchtestingcenter.com** to complete your exam online.

METHOD OF PAYMENT:

☐ Check Enclosed   ☐ Visa   ☐ Master Card   ☐ AmEx

☐ Discover   ☐ CCH Account* _____

Card No. _____ Exp. Date _____

Signature _____

* Must provide CCH account number for this payment option

EXPRESS GRADING: Please fax my Course results to me by 5:00 p.m. the business day following your receipt of this Answer Sheet. By checking this box I authorize CCH to charge $19.00 for this service.

☐ Express Grading $19.00   Fax No. _____

SEND TO: **CCH** Tax and Accounting
Continuing Education Department
4025 W. Peterson Ave.
Chicago, IL 60646-6085
1-800-248-3248

TOP FEDERAL TAX ISSUES FOR 2006 CPE COURSE   (0718-2)

Module 3: Answer Sheet

Please answer the Multiple Choice questions by indicating the appropriate letter next to the corresponding number. Please answer the True/False questions by marking "T" or "F" next to the corresponding number.

66. ____	73. ____	80. ____
67. ____	74. ____	81. ____
68. ____	75. ____	82. ____
69. ____	76. ____	83. ____
70. ____	77. ____	84. ____
71. ____	78. ____	85. ____
72. ____	79. ____	

Please complete the Evaluation Form (located after the Module 3 Answer Sheet) and return it with this Quizzer Answer Sheet to CCH at the address on the previous page. Thank you.

TOP FEDERAL TAX ISSUES FOR 2006 CPE COURSE   (0905-2)

Evaluation Form

Please take a few moments to fill out and mail or fax this evaluation to CCH so that we can better provide you with the type of self-study programs you want and need. Thank you.

About This Program

1. Please circle the number that best reflects the extent of your agreement with the following statements:

	Strongly Agree				Strongly Disagree
a. The course objectives were met.	5	4	3	2	1
b. This course was comprehensive and organized.	5	4	3	2	1
c. The content was current and technically accurate.	5	4	3	2	1
d. This course was timely and relevant.	5	4	3	2	1
e. The prerequisite requirements were appropriate.	5	4	3	2	1
f. This course was a valuable learning experience.	5	4	3	2	1
g. The course completion time was appropriate.	5	4	3	2	1

2. This course was most valuable to me because of:

        _____ Continuing education credit   _____ Convenience of format
        _____ Relevance to my practice/   _____ Timeliness of subject matter
              employment   _____ Reputation of author
        _____ Price
        _____ Other (please specify)

        _____

3. How long did it take to complete this Course? (Please include the total time spent reading or studying reference materials, and completing CPE Quizzer).

        Module 1 _____   Module 2 _____   Module 3 _____

4. What do you consider to be the strong points of this course?

5. What improvements can we make to this Course?

TOP FEDERAL TAX ISSUES FOR 2006 CPE COURSE   (0905-2)

Evaluation Form *cont'd*

General Interests

1. Preferred method of self-study instruction:
   _____ Text   _____ Audio   _____ Computer-based/Multimedia   _____ Video

2. What specific topics would you like CCH to develop as self-study CPE programs?
   _____
   _____
   _____

3. Please list other topics of interest to you _____
   _____
   _____

About You

1. Your profession:

   _____ CPA   _____ Enrolled Agent
   _____ Attorney   _____ Tax Preparer
   _____ Financial Planner   _____ Other (please specify)
                                _____

2. Your employment:

   _____ Self-employed   _____ Public Accounting Firm
   _____ Service Industry   _____ Non-Service Industry
   _____ Banking/Finance   _____ Government
   _____ Education   _____ Other _____

3. Size of firm/corporation:

   _____ 1   _____ 2-5   _____ 6-10   _____ 11-20   _____ 21-50   _____ 51+

4. Your Name _____

   Firm/Company Name _____

   Address _____

   City, State, Zip Code _____

   E-mail Address _____

THANK YOU FOR TAKING THE TIME TO COMPLETE THIS SURVEY!

NOTES

NOTES